MY AUTOBIOGRAPHY

A FRAGMENT

Walker & Cockerell ph. sc.

F. Max Müller
Aged 4.

MY AUTOBIOGRAPHY

A FRAGMENT

WITH PORTRAITS

F. MAX MÜLLER

ASIAN EDUCATIONAL SERVICES
NEW DELHI ★ CHENNAI ★ 2009

ASIAN EDUCATIONAL SERVICES
* 6A SHAHPUR JAT, NEW DELHI - 110 049
Tel. : +91-11- 26491586, 26494059 Fax : 011- 26494946
email : aes@aes.ind.in

* 2/15, 2nd FLOOR, ANSARI ROAD,
DARYAGANJ, NEW DELHI - 1100 02
Tel : +91- 11- 23262044
email : aesdg@aes.ind.in

* 19, (NEW NO. 40), BALAJI NAGAR FIRST STREET,
ROYAPETTAH, CHENNAI - 600 014
Tel. : +91- 44 - 28133040 / 28131391 Fax : 044 - 28131391
email : asianeds@md3.vsnl.net.in

www.aes.ind.in

Printed and Hand-Bound in India

Price
First Published : New York, 1901.
First AES Reprint : New Delhi, 1993
Second AES Reprint : New Delhi, 2006.
Third AES Reprint : New Delhi, 2009.

ISBN: 81206008291
EAN : 978820608290

Published by Gautam Jetley
For ASIAN EDUCATIONAL SERVICES
6A, Shahpur Jat, New Delhi - 110 049.
Processed by AES Publications Pvt. Ltd., New Delhi-110049
Printed at Jaico Printers, New Delhi - 110002.

PREFACE

For some years past my father had, in the intervals of more serious work, occupied his leisure moments in jotting down reminiscences of his early life. In 1898 and 1899 he issued the two volumes of *Auld Lang Syne*, which contained recollections of his friends, but very little about his own life and career. In the Introductory Chapter to the Autobiography he explains fully the reasons which led him, at his advanced age, to undertake the task of writing his own Life, and he began, but alas! too late, to gather together the fragments that he had written at different times. But even during the last two years of his life, and after the first attack of the illness which finally proved fatal, he would not devote himself entirely to what he considered mere recreation, as can be seen from such a work as his *Six Systems of Indian Philosophy* published in May, 1889, and from the numerous articles which continued to appear up to the very time of his death.

During the last weeks of his life, when we all knew that the end could not be far off, the Autobiography was constantly in his thoughts, and his great desire was to leave as much as possible ready for publication. Even when he was lying in bed far too weak to sit up in a chair, he continued to work at the manuscript with me. I would read portions aloud to him, and he would suggest alterations and dictate additions. I see that we were actually at work on this up to the 19th of October, and on the 28th he was taken to his well-earned rest. One of the last letters that I read to him was a letter from Messrs. Longmans, his life-long publishers, urging the publication of the fragments of the Autobiography that he had then written.

My father's object in writing his Autobiography was twofold: firstly, to show what he considered to have been his mission in life, to lay bare the thread that connected all his labours; and secondly, to encourage young struggling scholars by letting them see how it had been possible for one of themselves, without fortune, a stranger in a strange land, to arrive at the position to which he attained, without ever sacrificing his independence, or abandoning the unprofitable and not very popular subjects to which he had determined to devote his life.

Unfortunately the last chapter takes us but little beyond the threshold of his career. There is enough, however, to enable us to see how from his earliest student days his leanings were philosophical and religious rather than classical; how the study of Herbart's philosophy encouraged him in the work in which he was engaged as a mere student, the Science of Language and Etymology; how his desire to know something special, that no other philosopher would know, led him to explore the virgin fields of Oriental literature and religions. With this motive he began the study of Arabic, Persian, and finally Sanskrit, devoting himself more especially to the latter under Brockhaus and Rückert, and subsequently under Burnouf, who persuaded him to undertake the colossal work of editing the Rig-veda.

The Autobiography breaks off before the end of the period during which he devoted himself exclusively to Sanskrit. It is idle to speculate what course his life's work might have taken, had he been elected to the Boden Professorship of Sanskrit; but he lived long enough to realize that his rejection for that chair in 1860, which was so hard to bear at the time, was really a blessing in disguise, as it enabled him to turn his attention to more general subjects, and devote himself to those philological, philosophical, religious and mythological studies, which found their expression in a series of works commencing with his *Lectures on the Science of Language*, 1861, and terminating with his *Contributions to the Science of Mythology*, 1897,—"the thread that connects the origin of thought and language with the origin of mythology and religion."

As to his advice to struggling scholars, the self-depreciation, which, as Professor Jowett said, is one of the greatest dangers of an autobiography, makes my father rather conceal the real causes of his success in life. He even goes so far as to say, "everything in my career came about most naturally, not by my own effort, but owing to those circumstances or to that environment, of which we have heard so much of late": or again, "it was really my friends who did everything for me and helped me over many a stile and many a ditch." No doubt in one sense this is true, but not in the sense in which it would have been true had he, when at the University, accepted the offer which he tells us a wealthy cousin made him, to adopt him and send him into the Austrian diplomatic service, and even to procure him a wife and a title into the bargain. The friends who helped him, men such as Humboldt, Burnouf, Bunsen, Stanley, Kingsley, Liddell, to mention only a few, were men whose very friendship was the surest proof of my father's merits. The real secret of his success lay not in his friends, but in himself;—in the knowledge that his success or failure in life depended entirely on his own efforts; in the fixity of purpose which made him refuse all offers that would lead him from the pathway that he had laid down for himself; and in the unflagging industry with which he strove to reach the goal of his ambition. "My very struggles," he writes, "were certainly a help to me."

When I came to examine the manuscript with

a view to sending it to press, I found that there was a good deal of work necessary before it could be published in book form. The fragments were in many cases incomplete; there was no division into chapters, no connexion between the various periods and episodes of his life; important incidents were omitted; while, owing to the intermittent way in which he had been writing, there were frequent repetitions. My father was always most critical of his own style, and would often, when correcting his proof-sheets, alter a whole page, because a word or a phrase displeased him, or because some new idea, some happier mode of expression, occurred to him; but in the case of his Autobiography, the only revision that he was able to give, was on his death-bed, while I read the manuscript aloud to him.

My father points out how rarely the sons of great musicians or great painters become distinguished in the same line themselves. "It seems," he says, "almost as if the artistic talent were exhausted by one generation or one individual"; and I fear that, in my case at all events, the same remark applies to literary talent. I have done my best to string the fragments together into one connected whole, only making such insertions, elisions and alterations as appeared strictly necessary. Any deficiency in literary style that may be noticeable in portions of the book should be ascribed to the inexperience of the editor.

I have thought it right to insert the last chapter,

which I call "A Confession," though I am not sure that my father intended it to be included in his Autobiography. It will, however, explain the attitude which he observed throughout his life, in keeping aloof, as far as possible, from the arena of academic contention at Oxford. He was never chosen a member of the Hebdomadal Council, he rarely attended meetings of Convocation or Congregation; he felt that other people, with more leisure at their disposal, could be of more use there; but he never refused to work for his University, when he felt that he was able to render good service, and he acted for years as a Curator of the Bodleian Library and of the Taylorian Institute, and as a Delegate of the Clarendon Press.

With reference to the illustrations, it may be of interest to readers to know that the portraits of my grandfather and grandmother are taken from pencil drawings by Adolf Hensel, the husband of Mendelssohn's sister Fanny, herself a great musician, who, as my father tells us in *Auld Lang Syne*, really composed several of the airs that Mendelssohn published as his *Songs without Words*. The last portrait of my father is from a photograph taken soon after his arrival in Oxford by his great friend Thomson, afterwards Archbishop of York.

Nothing now remains for me but to acknowledge the debt that I owe personally to this book. "Work," my father used often to say to me, "is the best healer of sorrow. In grief or disappointment, try hard work; it will not fail you." And certainly during these three sad months, I have proved the truth of this saying. He could not have left me a surer comfort or more welcome distraction than the duty of preparing for press these pages, the last fruits of that mind which remained active and fertile to the last.

W. G. MAX MÜLLER.

OXFORD, *January*, 1901.

CONTENTS

LIST OF PORTRAITS

MY AUTOBIOGRAPHY

CHAPTER I

INTRODUCTORY

After the publication of the second volume of my *Auld Lang Syne*, 1899, I had a good deal of correspondence, of public criticism, and of private communings also with myself, whether I should continue my biographical records in the form hitherto adopted, or give a more personal character to my recollections. Some of my friends were evidently dissatisfied. "The recollections of your friends and the account of the influence they exercised on you," they said, "are interesting, no doubt, as far as they go, but we want more. We want to know the springs, the aspirations, the struggles, the failures, and achievements of your life. We want to know how you yourself look at yourself and at your past life and its various incidents." What they really wanted was, in fact, an autobiography. "No one," as a friend of mine, not an Irishman, said, "could do that so well as yourself, and you will never escape a biographer." I confess that did not frighten me very much. I did not think the danger of a biography very imminent. Besides, I had already revised two biographies and several biographical notices even during my lifetime. No sensible man ought to care about posthumous praise or posthumous blame. Enough for the day is the evil thereof. Our contemporaries are our right judges, our peers have to give their votes in the great academies and learned societies, and if they on the whole are not dissatisfied with the little we have done, often under far greater difficulties than the world was aware of, why should we care for the distant future? Who was a greater giant in philosophy than Hegel? Who towered higher than Darwin in natural science? Yet in one of the best German reviews [1] the following words of a young German biologist [2] are quoted, and not without a certain approval: "Darwinism belongs now to history, like that other *curiosum* of our century, the Hegelian philosophy. Both are variations on the theme, How can a generation be led by the nose? and they are not calculated to raise our departing century in the eyes of later generations."

If I was afraid of anything, it was not so much the severity of future judges, as the extreme kindness and leniency which distinguish most biographies in our days. It is true, it would not be easy for those who have hereafter to report on our labours

[1] *Deutsche Rundschau*, Feb., 1900, p. 249.

[2] Driesch, *Biologisches Centralblatt*, 1896, p. 335.

to discover the red thread that runs through all of them from our first stammerings to our latest murmurings. It might be said that in my own case the thread that connects all my labours is very visible, namely, the thread that connects the origin of thought and languages with the origin of mythology and religion. Everything I have done was, no doubt, subordinate to these four great problems, but to lay bare the connecting links between what I have written and what I wanted to write and never found time to write, is by no means easy, not even for the author himself. Besides, what author has ever said the last word he wanted to say, and who has not had to close his eyes before he could write Finis to his work? There are many things still which I should like to say, but I am getting tired, and others will say them much better than I could, and will no doubt carry on the work where I had to leave it unfinished. We owe much to others, and we have to leave much to others. For throwing light on such points an autobiography is, no doubt, better adapted than any biography written by a stranger, if only we can at the same time completely forget that the man who is described is the same as the man who describes.

"Friends," as Professor Jowett said, "always think it necessary (except Boswell, that great genius) to tell lies about their deceased friend; they leave out all his faults lest the public should exaggerate them. But we want to know his faults,

—that is probably the most interesting part of him."

Jowett knew quite well, and he did not hesitate to say so, that to do much good in this world, you must be a very able and honest man, thinking of nothing else day and night; and he adds, "you must also be a considerable piece of a rogue, having many reticences and concealments; and I believe a good sort of roguery is never to say a word against anybody, however much they may deserve it."

Now Professor Jowett has certainly done some good work at Oxford, but if any one were to say that he also was a considerable piece of a rogue, what an outcry there would be among the sons of Balliol. Jowett thought that the only chance of a good biography was for a man to write memoirs of himself, and what a pity that he did not do so in his own case. His friends, however, who had to write his Life were wise, and he escaped what of late has happened to several eminent men. He escaped the testimonials for this, and testimonials for another life, such as they are often published in our days.

Testimonials are bad enough in this life, when we have to select one out of many candidates as best fitted for an office, and it is but natural that the electors will hardly ever look at them, but will try to get their information through some other channel. But what are called *post obit* testimonials really go beyond everything yet known in funeral panegyrics. Of course, as no one is asked for such testimonials except those who are known to have been friends of the departed, these testimonials hardly ever contain one word of blame. One feels ashamed to write such testimonials, but if you are asked, what can you do without giving offence? We are placed altogether in a false position. Let any one try to speak the truth and nothing but the truth, and he will find that it is almost impossible to put down anything that in the slightest way might seem to reflect on the departed. The mention of the most innocent failings in an obituary notice is sure to offend somebody, the widow or the children, or some dear friend. I thought that my Recollections had hitherto contained nothing that could possibly offend anybody, nothing that could not have been published during the lifetime of the man to whom it referred. But no; I had ever so many complaints, and I gladly left out, in later editions, names which in many cases were really of no consequence compared with what they said and did.

Surely every man has his faults and his little and often ridiculous weaknesses, and these weaknesses belong quite as much to a man's character as his strength; nay, with the suppression of the former the latter would often become almost unintelligible.

I like the biographies of such friends of mine as Dean Stanley, Charles Kingsley, and Baron Bunsen. But even these are deficient in those shadows which would but help to bring out all the more clearly the bright points in their character. We should remember the words of Dr. Wendell Holmes: "We all want to draw perfect ideals, and all the coin that comes from Nature's mint is more or less clipped, filed, 'sweated,' or bruised, and bent and worn, even if it was pure metal when stamped, which is more than we can claim, I suppose, for anything human." True, very true; and what would the departed himself say to such biographies as are now but too common,—most flattering pictures no doubt, but pictures without one spot or wrinkle? In Germany it was formerly not an uncommon thing for the author of a book to write a self-review (Selbst-Kritik), and these were generally far better than reviews written by friends or enemies. For who knows the strong and weak points of a book so well as the author? True; but a whole life is more difficult to review and to criticize than a single book. Nevertheless it must be admitted that an autobiography has many advantages, and it might be well if every man of note, nay, every man who has something to say for himself that he wishes posterity to know, should say it himself. This would in time form a wonderful archive for psychological study. Something of the kind has been done already at Berlin in preserving private correspondences. Of course it is difficult to keep such archives within reasonable limits, but here again I am not afraid of self-laudation so much as of self-depreciation.

Professor Jowett, who did not write his own biography, was quite right in saying that there is great danger of an autobiography being rather self-depreciatory; there is certainly something so nauseous in self-praise that most people would shrink far more from self-praise than from self-blame. There may be some kind of subtle self-admiration even in the fault-finding of an out-spoken autobiographer; but who can dive into those deepest depths of the human soul? To me it seems that if an honest man takes himself by the neck, and shakes himself, he can do it far better than anybody else, and the castigation, if well deserved, comes certainly with a far better grace from himself than if administered by others.

Few men, I believe, know their real goodness and greatness. Some of the most handsome women, so we are assured, pass through life without ever knowing from their looking-glass that they are handsome. And it is certainly true that men, from sad experience, know their weak points far better than their good points, which they look on as no more than natural.

The Autos, for instance, described by John Stuart Mill, has no cause to be grateful to the Autos that wrote his biography. Mill had been threatened by several future biographers, and he therefore wrote the short biographical account of himself almost in self-defence. But besides the truly miraculous, and, if related by anybody else, hardly credible achievements of his early boyhood and youth, his great achievements in later life, the influence which he exercised both by his writings and still more by his personal and public character, would have found a far more eloquent and truthful interpreter in a stranger than in Mill himself. I remember another case where a most distinguished author tried to escape the oil and the blessings, perhaps the opposite also, from the hands of his future biographers. Froude destroyed the whole of his correspondence, and he wished particularly that all letters written to him in the fullest confidence should be burnt,—and they were. I think it was a pity, for I know what valuable letters were destroyed in that *auto da fé;* and yet when he had done all this, he seems to have been seized with fear, and just before he returned to Oxford as Regius Professor of Modern History he began to write a sketch of his own life, which was found among his papers. Interesting it certainly was, but fortunately his best friends prevented its publication. It would have added nothing to what we know of him in his writings, and would never have put his real merits in their proper light. Besides, it came to an end with his youth and told us little of his real life.

I flattered myself that I had found the true way out of all these difficulties, by writing not exactly my own life, but recollections of my friends and acquaintances who had influenced me most, and guided me in my not always easy passage through life. As in describing the course of a river, we cannot do better than to describe the shores which hem in and divert the river and are reflected on its waves, I thought that by describing my environment, my friends, and fellow workers, I could best describe the course of my own life. I hoped also that in this way I myself could keep as much as possible in the background, and yet in describing the wooded or rocky shores with their herds, their cottages, and churches, describe their reflected image on the passing river.

But now I am asked to give a much fuller account of myself, not only of what I have seen, but also of what I have been, what were the objects or ideals of my life, how far I have succeeded in carrying them out, and, as I said, how often I have failed to accomplish what I had sketched out as my task in life. People wished to know how a boy, born and educated in a small and almost unknown town in the centre of Germany, should have come to England, should have been chosen there to edit the oldest book of the world, the Veda of the Brahmans, never published before, whether in India or in Europe, should have passed the best part of his life as a professor in the most famous and, as it was thought, the most exclusive University in England, and should actually have ended his days as a Member of Her Majesty's most honourable Privy Council. I confess myself it seems a very strange career, yet everything came about most naturally, not by my own effort, but owing again to those circumstances or to that environment of which we have heard so much of late.

Young, struggling men also have written to me, and asked me how I managed to keep my head above water in that keen struggle for life that is always going on in the whirlpool of the learned world of England. They knew, for I had never made any secret of it, how poor I was in worldly goods, and how, as I said at Glasgow, I had nothing to depend on after I left the University, but those fingers with which I still hold my pen and write so badly that I can hardly read my manuscript myself. When I arrived I had no family connections in England, nor any influential friends, "and yet," I was told, "in a foreign country, you managed to reach the top of your profession. Tell us how you did it; and how you preserved at the same time your independence and never forsook the not very popular subjects, such as language, mythology, religion, and philosophy, on which you continued to write to the very end of your life."

I generally said that most of these questions could best be answered from my books, but they replied that few people had time to read all I had written, and many would feel grateful for a thread to lead them through this labyrinth of books, essays, and pamphlets, which have issued from my workshop during the last fifty years.[1]

[1] As giving a clear and complete abstract of my writings I may now recommend M. Montcalm's *L'origine de la Pensée et de la Parole*, Paris, 1900.

All I could say was that each man must find his own way in life, but if there was any secret about my success, it was simply due to the fact that I had perfect faith, and went on never doubting even when everything looked grey and black about me. I felt convinced that what I cared for, and what I thought worthy of a whole life of hard work, must in the end be recognized by others also as of value, and as worthy of a certain support from the public. Had not Layard gained a hearing for Assyrian bulls? Did not Darwin induce the world to take an interest in Worms, and in the Fertilization of Orchids? And should the oldest book and the oldest thoughts of the Aryan world remain despised and neglected?

For many years I never thought of appointments or of getting on in the world in a pecuniary sense. My friends often laughed at me, and when I think of it now, I confess I must have seemed very Quixotic to many of those who tried for this and that, got lucrative appointments, married rich wives, became judges and bishops, ambassadors and ministers, and could hardly understand what I was driving at with my Sanskrit manuscripts, my proof-sheets and revises. Perhaps I did not know myself. Still I was not quite so foolish as they imagined. True, I declined several offers made to me which seemed very advantageous in a worldly sense, but would have separated me entirely from my favourite work.

When at last a professorship of Modern Literature was offered me at Oxford, I made up my mind, though it was not exactly what I should have liked, to give up half of my time to studies required by this professorship, keeping half of my time for the Veda and for Sanskrit in general. This was not so bad after all. People often laughed at me for being professor of the most modern languages, and giving so much of my time and labour to the most ancient language and literature in the world. Perhaps it was not quite right my giving up so much of my time to modern languages, a subject so remote from my work in life, but it was a concession which I could make with a good conscience, having always held that language was one and indivisible, and that there never had been a break between Sanskrit, Latin, and French, or Sanskrit, Gothic, and German. One of my first lectures at Oxford was "On the antiquity of modern languages," so that I gave full notice to the University as to how I meant to treat my subject, and on the whole the University seems to have been satisfied with my professorial work, so that when afterwards for very good reasons, whether financial, theological, or national, I, or rather my friends, failed to secure a majority in Convocation for a professorship of Sanskrit, the University actually founded for me a Professorship of Comparative Philology, an honour of which I had never dreamt, and to secure which I certainly had never taken any steps.

Here is all my secret. At first, as I said, it required faith, but it also required for many years a perfect indifference as to worldly success. And here again in my career as a Sanskrit scholar, mere circumstances were of great importance. They were circumstances which I was glad to accept, but which I could never have created myself. It was surely a mere accident that the Directors of the Old East India Company voted a large sum of money for printing the six large quartos of the Rig-veda of about a thousand pages each. It was at the time when the fate of the Company hung in the balance, and when Bunsen, the Prussian Minister, made himself *persona grata* by delivering a speech at one of the public dinners in the City, setting forth in eloquent words the undeniable merits of the Old Company and the wonderful work they had achieved. It was likewise a mere accident that I should have become known to Bunsen, and that he should have shown me so much kindness in my literary work. He had himself tried hard to go to India to discover the Rig-veda, nay, to find out whether there was still such a thing as the Veda in India. The same Bunsen, His Excellency Baron Bunsen, the Prussian Minister in London, on his own accord went afterwards to see the Chairman and the Directors of the East India Company, and explained to them what the Rig-veda was, and that it would be a real disgrace if such a work were published in Germany; and they agreed to vote a sum of money such as they had never voted before for any literary undertaking. Though after the mutiny nothing could save them, I had at least the satisfaction of dedicating the first volume of my edition of the Rig-veda to the Chairman and the Directors of the much abused East India Company,—much abused though splendidly defended also by no less a man than John Stuart Mill.

This is what I mean by friends and circumstances, and that is the environment which I wished to describe in my Recollections instead of always dwelling on what I meant to do myself and what I did myself. Small and large things work wonderfully together. It was the change threatening the government of India, and a mighty change it was, that gave me the chance of publishing the Veda, a very small matter as it may seem in the eyes of most people, and yet intended to bring about quite as mighty a change in our views of the ancient people of the world, particularly of their languages and religions. This, too—the development of language and religion—seems of importance to some people who do not care two straws for the East India Company, particularly if it helps us to learn what we really are ourselves, and how we came to be what we are.

In one sense biographies and autobiographies are certainly among the most valuable materials for the historian. Biography, as Heinrich Simon, not Henri Simon, said, is the best kind of history, and the life of one man, if laid open before us with all he thought and all he did, gives us a better insight into the history of his time than any general account of it can possibly do.

Now it is quite true that the life of a quiet scholar has little to do with history, except it may be the history of his own branch of study, which some people consider quite unimportant, while to others it seems all-important. This is as it ought to be, till the universal historian finds the right perspective, and assigns to each branch of study and activity its proper place in the panorama of the progress of mankind towards its ideals. Even a quiet scholar, if he keeps his eyes open, may now and then see something that is of importance to the historian. While I was living in small rooms at Leipzig, or lodging *au cinquième* in the Rue Royale at Paris, or copying manuscripts in a dark room of the old East India House in Leadenhall Street, I now and then caught glimpses of the mighty stream of history as it was rushing by. At Leipzig I saw much of Robert Blum who was afterwards *fusillé* at Vienna by Windischgrätz in defiance of all international law, for he was a member of the German Diet, then sitting at Frankfurt. From my windows at Paris I looked over the *Boulevard de la Madeleine*, and down on the right to the *Chambre des Députés*, and I saw from my windows the throne of Louis Philippe carried along by its four legs by four women on horseback, with Phrygian caps and red scarfs, and I saw the next morning from the same windows the stretchers carrying the dead and wounded from the Boulevards to a hospital at the back of my street. In my small study at the East India House I saw several of the Directors, Colonel Sykes and others, and heard them discussing the fate of the East India Company and of the vast empire of India too, and at the same time the private interests of those who hoped to be Members of the new India Council, and those who despaired of that distinction. I was the first to bring the news of the French Revolution in February to London, and presented a bullet that had smashed the windows of my room at Paris, to Bunsen, who took it in the evening to Lord Palmerston. After I had seen the Revolution in Paris and the flight of the King and the Duchesse d'Orléans, I was in time to see in London the Chartist Deputation to Parliament, and the assembled police in Trafalgar Square, when Louis Napoleon served as a Special Constable, and I heard the Duke of Wellington explain to Bunsen, that though no soldier was seen in the streets there was artillery hidden under the bridges, and ready to act if wanted. I could add more, but I must not anticipate, and after all, to me all these great events seemed but small compared with a new manuscript of the Veda sent from India, or a better reading of an obscure passage. *Diversos diversa iuvant*, and it is fortunate that it should be so.

All these things, I thought, should form part of

my Recollections, and my own little self should disappear as much as possible. Even the pronoun I should meet the reader but seldom, though in Recollections it was as impossible to leave it out altogether as it would be to take away the lens from a photographic camera. Now I believe I have always been most willing to yield to my friends, and I shall in this matter also yield to them so far that in the Recollections which follow there will be more of my inward and outward struggles; but I must on the whole adhere to my old plan. I could not, if I would, neglect the environment of my life, and the many friends that advised and helped me, and enabled me to achieve the little that I may have achieved in my own line of study.

If my friends had been different from what they were, should I not have become a different man myself, whether for good or for evil? And the same applies to our natural surroundings also. And here I must invoke the patience of my readers, if I try to explain in as few words as possible what I think about *environment*, and what about *heredity* or *atavism*.

I was a thorough Darwinian in ascribing the shaping of my career to environment, though I was always very averse to atavism, of which we have heard so much lately in most biographies. Even with respect to environment, however, I could not go quite so far as certain of our Darwinian friends, who maintain that everything is the result of environment, or translated into biographical language, that everybody is a creature of circumstances. No, I could not go so far as that. Environment may shape our course and may shape us, but there must be something that is shaped, and allows itself to be shaped. I was once seriously asked by one who considers himself a Darwinian whether I did not know that the Mammoth was driven by the extreme cold of the Pleiocene Period to grow a thick fur in his struggle for life. That he grew then a thicker fur, I knew, but that surely does not explain the whole of the Mammoth, with and without a thick fur, before and after the fur. It is really a pity to see for how many of these downright absurdities Darwin is made responsible by the Darwinians. He has clearly shown how in many cases the individual may be modified almost beyond recognition by environment, but the individual must always have been there first. Before we had a spaniel and a Newfoundland dog there must have been some kind of dog, neither so small as the spaniel nor so large as the Newfoundland, and no one would now doubt that these two belonged to the same species and presupposed some kind of a less modified canine creature. It is equally true that every individual man has been modified by his surroundings or environment, if not to the same extent as certain animals, yet very considerably, as in the case of Kaspar Hauser, the man with the iron mask, or the mutineers of the *Bounty* in the Pitcairn Islands.

But there must have been the man first, before he could be so modified. Now it was this very individual, my own self in fact, the spiritual self even more than the physical, that interested my critics, while I thought that the circumstances which moulded that self would be of far greater interest than the self itself. Of course all the modifications that men now undergo are nothing if compared to the early modifications which produced what we speak of as racial, linguistic, or even national peculiarities. That we are English or German, that we are white or black, nay, if you like, that we are human beings at all, all this has modified our self, or our germ-plasm, far more powerfully than anything that can happen to us as individuals now.

When my friends and readers assured me that an account of my early struggles in the battle of life would be useful to many a young, struggling man, all I could say was that here again it was really my friends who did everything for me, and helped me over many a stile, and many a ditch, nay, without whom I should never have done whatever I did for the Sciences of Language, of Mythology, and Religion, in fact for Anthropology in the widest sense of that word. My very struggles were certainly a help to me, even my opponents were most useful to me. The subjects on which I wrote had hardly been touched on in England, at least from the historical point of view which I took, and I had not only to overcome the indifference of the public, but to disarm as much as possible the prejudices often felt, and sometimes expressed also, against anything made in Germany! Now I confess I could never understand such a prejudice among men of science. Was I more right or more wrong because I was born in Germany? Is scientific truth the exclusive property of one nation, of Germany, or of England? If I say two and two make four in German, is that less true because it is said by a German? and if I say, no language without thought, no thought without language, has that anything to do with my native country? The prejudice against strangers and particularly against Germans is, no doubt, much stronger now than it was at the time when I first came to England. I had spent nearly two years in Paris, and there too there existed then so little of unfriendly feeling towards Germany, that one of the best reviews to which the rising scholars and best writers of Paris contributed was actually called *Revue Germanique*. Who would now venture to publish in Paris such a review and under such a title? If there existed such an anti-German feeling anywhere in England when I arrived here in the year 1846, one would suppose that it existed most strongly at Oxford. And so it did, no doubt, particularly among theologians. With them German meant much the same as unorthodox, and unorthodox was enough at that time to taboo a man at Oxford. In one of the sermons preached in these early days at St. Mary's, German theologians such as Strauss and Neander (*sic*) were spoken of as fit only to be drowned in the German Ocean, before they reached the shores of England. I do not add what followed: the story is too well known. I was chiefly amused by the juxtaposition of Strauss and Neander, whose most orthodox lectures on the history of the Christian Church I had attended at Berlin. Neander was certainly to us at Berlin the very pattern of orthodoxy, and people wondered at my attending his lectures. But they were good and honest lectures. He was quite a character, and I feel tempted to go a little out of my way in speaking of him. By birth a Jew, he became one of the most learned Christian divines. Ever so many stories were told of him, some true, some no doubt invented. I saw him often walking to and from the University to give his lectures in a large fur coat, with high black polished boots beneath, but showing occasionally as he walked along. It was told that he once sent for a doctor because he was lame. The doctor on examining his feet, saw that one boot was covered with mud, while the other was perfectly clean. The Professor had walked with one foot on the pavement, with the other in the gutter, and was far too much absorbed in his ideas to discover the true cause of his discomfort. He lived with his sister, who took complete care of him and saw to his wardrobe also. She knew that he wore one pair of trousers, and that on a certain day in the year the tailor brought him a new pair. Great was her amazement when one day, after her brother had gone to the University, she discovered his pair of trousers lying on a chair near his bed. She at once sent a servant to the Professor's lecture-room to inquire whether he had his trousers on. The hilarity of his class may be imagined. The fact was it was the very day on which the tailor was in the habit of bringing the new pair of trousers, which the Professor had put on, leaving his usual garment behind.

Many more stories of his absent-mindedness were *en vogue* about Dr. Neander, but that this man, a pillar of strength to the orthodox in Germany, who was looked up to as an infallible Pope, should have his name coupled with that of Strauss certainly gave one a little shock. Yet it was at Oxford that I pitched my tent, chiefly in order to superintend the printing of my Rig-veda at the University Press there, and never dreaming that a fellowship, still less a professorship in that ancient Tory University, would ever be offered to me.

For me to go to Oxford to get a fellowship or professorship would have seemed about as absurd as going to Rome to become a Cardinal or a Pope; and yet in time I was chosen a Fellow of All Souls, and the first married Fellow of the College, and even a professorship was offered to me when I least expected it. The fact is, I never thought of either, and no one was more surprised than myself when I was asked to act as deputy, and then as full Taylorian Professor; no one could have mistrusted his eyes more than I did, when one of the Fellows of All Soul's informed me by letter that it was the intention of the College to elect me one of its fellows. My ambition had never soared so high. I was thinking of returning to Leipzig as a *Privat-docent*, to rise afterwards to an extraordinary and, if all went well, to an ordinary professorship.

But after these two appointments at Oxford had secured to me what I thought a fair social and financial position in England, I did not feel justified in attempting to begin life again in Germany. I had not asked for a professorship or fellowship. They were offered me, and my ambition never went beyond securing what was necessary for my independence. In Germany I was supposed to have become quite wealthy; in England people knew how small my income really was, and wondered how I managed to live on it. They did not suppose that I had chiefly to depend on my pen in order to live as a professor is expected to live at Oxford. I could not see anything anomalous in a German holding a professorship in England. There were several cases of the same kind in Germany. Lassen (1800–1876), our great Sanskrit professor at Bonn, was a Norwegian by birth, and no one ever thought of his nationality. What had that to do with his knowledge of Sanskrit? Nor was I ever treated as an alien or as intruder at Oxford, at least not at that early time. As to myself, I had now obtained what seemed to me a small but sufficient income with perfect independence. The quiet life of a quiet student had been from my earliest days my ideal in life. Even at school at Dessau, when we boys talked of what we hoped to be, I remember how my ideal was that of a monk, undisturbed in his monastery, surrounded by books and by a few friends. The idea that I should ever rise to be a professor in a university, or that any career like that of my father, grandfather, and other members of my family would ever be open to me, never entered my mind then. It seemed to me almost disloyal to think of ever taking their places. Even when I saw that there were no longer any Protestant monks, no Benedictines, the place of an assistant in a large library, sitting in a quiet corner, was my highest ambition.

I do not see why it should have been so, for all my relations and friends occupied high places in the public service, but as I had no father to open my eyes, and to stimulate my ambition—he having died before I was four years old—my ideas of life and its possibilities were evidently taken from my young widowed mother, whose one desire was to be left alone, much as the world tempted her, then not yet thirty years old, to give up her mourning and to return to society. Thus it soon became my own philosophy of life, to be left alone, free to go my own way, or like Diogenes, to live in my own tub. Here we see what I call the influence of circumstances, of surroundings, or as others call it, of environment. This, however, is very different from atavism, as we shall see presently. Atavism also has been called a kind of environment, attacking us and influencing us from the past, and as it were, from behind, from the North in fact instead of the South, the East, and the West, and from all the points of the compass.

But atavism means really a very different thing, if indeed it means anything at all.

I must ease my conscience once for all on this point, and say what I feel about atavism and environment. Environment in the shape of friends, of locality, and other material circumstances, has certainly influenced my life very much, and I could never see why such a hybrid word as environment should be used instead of surroundings or circumstances. Creatures of circumstances would be far better understood than creatures of environment; but environment, I suppose, would sound more scientific. Atavism also is a new word, instead of family likeness, but unless carefully defined, the word is very apt to mislead us.

When it is said [1] that children often resemble their grandfathers or grandmothers more than their immediate parents, and that this propensity is termed atavism, this does not seem quite correct even etymologically, for atavus in Latin did not mean father or grandfather, but at first great-great

[1] *Oxford Dictionary*, s. v.; J. Rennie, *Science of Gardening*, p. 113.

great-grandfather, and then only ancestors; and what should be made quite clear is that this mysterious atavism should not be used by careful speakers, to express the supposed influence of parents or even grandparents, but that of more distant ancestors only, and possibly of a whole family.

Many biographers, such is the fashion now, begin their works with a long account not only of father and mother, but of grandparents and of ever so many ancestors, in order to show how these determined the outward and inward character of the man whose life has to be written. Who would deny that there is some truth, or at least some plausibility, in atavism, though no one has as yet succeeded in giving an intelligible account of it? It is supposed to affect the moral as well as the physical peculiarities of the offspring, and that here, too, physical and moral qualities often go together cannot be denied. A blind person, for instance, is generally cautious, but happy and quite at his ease in large societies. A deaf person is often suspicious and unhappy in society. In inheriting blindness, therefore, a man could well be said to have inherited cautiousness; in inheriting deafness, suspiciousness would seem to have come to him by inheritance.

But is blindness really inherited? Is the son of a father who has lost his eyesight blind, and necessarily blind? We must distinguish between atavistic and parental influences. Parental influences would mean the influence of qualities acquired by the parents, and directly bequeathed to their offspring; atavistic influences would refer to qualities inherited and transmitted, it may be, through several generations, and engrained in a whole family. In keeping these two classes separate, we should only be following Weismann's example, who denies altogether that acquired qualities are ever heritable. His examples are most interesting and most important, and many Darwinians have had to accept his amendment. Besides, we should always consider whether certain peculiarities are constant in a family or inconstant. If a father is a drunkard, surely it does not follow that his sons must be drunkards. Neither does it follow that all the children must be sober if the parents are sober. Of course, in ordinary conversation both parental and ancestral influences seem clear enough. But if a child is said to favour his mother, because like her he has blue eyes and fair hair, what becomes of the heritage from the father who may have brown eyes and dark hair? Whatever may happen to the children, there is always an excuse, only an excuse is not an explanation. If the daughter of a beautiful woman grows up very plain, the Frenchman was no doubt right when he remarked, *C'était alors le père qui n'était pas bien,* and if the son of a teetotaller should later in life become a drunkard, the conclusion would be even worse. In fact, this kind of atavistic or parental influence is a very pleasant subject for gossips, but from a scientific point of view, it is perfectly futile. If it is not the father, it is the mother; if it is not the grandmother, it is the grandfather; in fact, family influences can always be traced to some source or other, if the whole pedigree may be dug up and ransacked. But for that very reason they are of no scientific value whatever. They can neither be accounted for, nor can they be used to account for anything themselves. Even of twins, though very like each other in many respects, one may be phlegmatic, the other passionate. Some scientists, such as Weismann and others, have therefore denied, and I believe rightly, that any acquired characters, whether physical or mental, can ever be inherited by children from their parents. Whatever similarity there is, and there is plenty, is traced back by him to what he calls the germ-plasm, working on continuously in spite of all individual changes. If that germ-plasm is liable to certain peculiar modifications in the father or grandfather, it is liable to the same or similar modifications in the offspring, that is, if the father could become a drunkard, so could the son, only we must not think that the *post hoc* is here the same as the *propter hoc*. If we compare the germ-plasm to the molecules constituting the stem or branches of a vine, its grapes and leaves in their similarity and their variety would be comparable to the individuals belonging to the same family, and springing from the same family tree. But then the grape we see would not be what the grape of last year, or the grape immediately preceding it on the same branch, had made it, though there can be no doubt that the antecedent possibilities of the new grape were the same as those of the last. If one grape is blue, the next will be blue too, but no one would say that it was blue because the last grape was blue. The real cause would be that the molecules of the protoplasm have been so affected by long continued generation, that some of the peculiar qualities of the vine have become constant.

The child of a negro must always be a negro; his peculiarities are constant, though it may be quite true that the negro and other races are not different species, but only varieties rendered constant by immense periods of time. What the cause of these constant and inconstant peculiarities may be, not even Weismann has yet been able to explain satisfactorily.

The deafness of my mother and the prevalence of the misfortune in numerous members of her family acted on me as a kind of external influence, as something belonging to the environment of my life; it never frightened me as an atavistic evil. It justified me in being cautious and in being prepared for the worst, and so far it may be said to have helped in shaping or narrowing the course of my life. Fortunately, however, this tendency to deafness seems now to have exhausted itself. In my own generation there is one case only, and the next two generations, children and grandchildren of mine, show no signs of it. If, on the other hand, my son was congratulated when entering the diplomatic service, on being the son of his father, it is clear that the difference between inherited and acquired qualities, so strongly insisted on by Weismann, had not been fully appreciated by his friends. Besides, my own power of speaking foreign languages has always been very limited, and I have many times declined the compliment of being a second Mezzofanti.[1] I worked at languages as a musician studies the nature and capacities of musical instruments, though without attempting to perform on every one of them. There was no time left for acquiring a practical familiarity with languages, if I wanted to carry on my researches into the origin, the nature and history of language. My own study of languages could therefore have been of very little use to me, nor did my son himself perceive such an advantage in learning to converse in French, Spanish, Turkish, &c. The facts were wrong, and the theory of atavism perfectly unreasonable as applied to such a case.

If the theory of atavism were stretched so far, it would soon do away with free will altogether. That heredity has something to do with our moral character, no one would deny who knows the influence of our national, nay even of racial character. We are Aryan by heredity; we might be Negroes or Chinese, and share in their tendencies. Animals

[1] *Science of Language*, vol. i. p. 24 (1861).

also have their instincts. Only while animals, like serpents for instance, would never hesitate to follow their innate propensity, man, when he feels the power of what we may call inherited human instinct, feels also that he can fight against it, and preserve his freedom, even while wearing the chains of his slavery. This may have removed some of Dr. Wendell Holmes' scruples in writing his powerful story, *Elsie Venner*, and may likewise quiet the fears of his many critics.

I believe that language also—our own inherited language—exercises the most powerful influence on our reason and our will, far more powerful than we are aware of.

A Greek speaking Greek and a Roman speaking Latin would certainly have been very different beings from the Romance and French descendants of a Horace or a Cicero, and this simply on account of the language which they had to speak, whether Greek, Latin, French, or Spanish. We cannot tell whether the original differentiation of language, symbolized by the story of the Tower of Babel, took place before or after the racial differentiation of men. Anyhow it must have taken place in quite primordial times. Without speaking positively on this point, I certainly hold as strongly as ever that language makes the man, and that therefore for classificatory purposes also language is far more useful than colour of skin, hair, cranial or gnathic peculiarities. Whether it be true that with every new language we speak we become new men, certain it is that language prepares for us channels in which our thoughts have to run, unless they are so powerful as to break all dams and dykes, and to dig for themselves new beds.

For a long time people would not see that languages can be classified; and as languages always presuppose speakers of language, these speakers also can be classified accordingly. It is quite true that some of these Aryan speakers may in some cases have Negro blood and Negro features, as when a Negro becomes an English bishop. Conquered tribes also may in time have learnt to speak the language of their conquerors, but this too is exceptional, and if we call them Aryas, we do not commit ourselves to any opinion as to their blood, their bones, or their hair. These will never submit to the same classification as their speech, and why should they? Nor should it be forgotten that wherever a mixture of language takes place, mixed marriages also would most likely take place at the same time. But whatever confusion may have arisen in later times in language and in blood, no language could have arisen without speakers, and we mean by Aryas no more than speakers of Aryan languages, whatever their skulls or their hair may have been. An Octoroon, and even a Quadroon, may have blonde waving hair, but if he speaks English he would be classified as Aryan, if Berber as a Negro. But who is injured by such a classification? Let blood and skulls and hair and jaws be classified by all means, but let us speak no longer of Aryan skulls or Semitic blood. We might as well speak of a prognathic language.

While fully admitting, therefore, the influence which family, nationality, race, and language exercise on us, it should be clearly perceived that habits acquired by our parents are not heritable, that the sons of drunkards need not be drunkards, as little as the sons of sober people must be sober. But though biographers may agree to this in general they seem inclined to hold out very strongly for what are called *special talents in certain families*. This subject is decidedly amusing, but it admits of no scientific treatment, as far as I can see.

The grandfather of Felix Mendelssohn Bartholdy for instance, though not a composer, was evidently a man of genius, a philosopher of considerable intellectual capacity and moral strength. The father of the composer was a rich banker at Berlin, and he used to say: "When I was young I was the son of the great Mendelssohn, now that I am old, I am the father of the great Mendelssohn; then what am I?" Even a poor man to become a rich banker must be a kind of genius, and so far the son may be said to have come of a good stock. But the great musical talent that was developed in the third generation both in Felix and his sisters, failed entirely in his brother, who, to save his life, could never have sung "God save the Queen." In the little theatrical performances of the whole family for which Felix composed the music, and his sister Fanny (Hensel) some of the songs, the unmusical brother—was it not Paul?—had generally to be provided with some such part as that of a night watchman, and he managed to get through his song with as much credit as the *Nachtwächter* in the little town of Germany, where he sang or repeated, as I well remember, in his cracked voice:

> "Hört, ihr Herren, und lasst euch sagen,
> Die Glock' hat zwölf geschlagen;
> Wahret das Feuer und auch das Licht,
> Dass Keinem kein Schade geschicht."

> "Listen, gents, and let me tell,
> The clock struck twelve by its last knell;
> Watch o'er the fire and o'er the light
> That no one suffer any plight."

I have known in my life many musicians and their families, but I remember very few instances indeed, where the son of a distinguished musician was a great musician himself. If the children take to music at all they may become very fair musicians, but never anything extraordinary. The Bach family may be quoted against me, but music, before Sebastian Bach, was almost like a profession, and could be learned like any other handicraft.

Nor are the cases of painters being the sons of great painters, or of poets being the sons of great poets, more numerous. It seems almost as if the artistic talent was exhausted by one generation or one individual, so that we often see the sons of great men by no means great, and if they do anything in the same line as their fathers, we must remember that there was much to induce them to follow in their steps without admitting any atavistic influences.

For the present, I can only repeat the conclusion I arrived at after weighing all the arguments of my friends and critics, namely, to continue my Recollections much as I began them, to try to explain what made me what I am, to describe, in fact, my environment; though as my years advance, and my labours and plans grow wider and wider, I shall, no doubt, have to say a great deal more about myself than in the volumes of *Auld Lang Syne.* In fact, my Recollections will become more and more of an autobiography, and the I and the Autos will appear more frequently than I could have wished.

In an autobiography the painter is of course supposed to be the same as the sitter, but quite apart from the metaphysical difficulties of such a supposition, there is the physical difficulty when the writer is an old man, and the model is a young boy. Is the old man likely to be a fair judge of the young man, whether it be himself or some one else? As a rule, old men are very indulgent, while young men are apt to be stern and strict in their judgments. The very fact that they often invent excuses for themselves shows that they feel that they want excuses. The words of the Preacher, vii. 16: "Be not righteous over much; neither make thyself over wise: why shouldest thou destroy thyself? Be not over much wicked, neither be thou foolish: why shouldest thou die before thy time?" are evidently the words of an old man when judging of himself or of others. A young man would have spoken differently. He would have made no allowance; for anything like compassion for an erring friend is as yet unknown to him. In an autobiography written by an old man there is therefore a double danger, first the indulgence of the old man, and secondly the kindly feeling of the writer towards the object of his remarks.

All these difficulties stand before me like a mountain wall. And it seems better to confess at once that an old man writing his own life can never be quite just, however honest he tries to be. He may be too indulgent, but he may also be too strict and stern. To say, for instance, of a man that he has not kept his promise, would be a very serious charge if brought against anybody else. Yet my oldest friend in the world knows how many times he has made a promise to himself, and has not only not kept it but has actually found excuses why he did not keep it. The more sensitive our conscience becomes, the more blameworthy many an act of our life seems to be, and what to an ordinary conscience is no fault at all, becomes almost a sin under a fiercer light.

This changes the moral atmosphere of youth when painted by an old man, but the physical atmosphere also assumes necessarily a different hue. Whether we like it or not, distance will always lend enchantment to the view. If the azure hue is inseparable from distant mountains and from the distant sky, we need not wonder that it veils the distant paradise of youth. A man who keeps a diary from his earliest years, and who as an old man simply copies from its yellow pages, may give us a very accurate black and white image of what he saw as a boy, but as in old faded photographs, the life and light are gone out of them, while unassisted memory may often preserve tints of their former reality. There is life and light in such recollections, but I am willing to admit that memory can be very treacherous also. Thus in my own case I can vouch that whatever I relate is carefully and accurately transcribed from the tablets of my memory, as I see them now, but though I can claim truthfulness to myself and to my memory, I cannot pretend to photographic accuracy. I feel indeed for the historian who uses such materials unless he has learnt to make allowance for the dim sight of even the most truthful narrators.

I doubt whether any historian would accept a statement made thirty years after the event without independent confirmation. I could not give the date of the battle of Sadowa, though I well remember reading the full account of it in the *Times* from day to day. I can of course get at the date from historical books, and from that kind of artificial memory which arises by itself without any *memoria technica*. There is a favourite German game of cards called Sixty-six, and it was reported that when the French in 1870 shouted *À Berlin*, the then Crown-Prince who had won the battle of Sadowa, or Königgrätz, said: "Ah, they want another game of Sixty-six!" that is they want a battle like that of Sadowa. In this way I shall always remember the date of that decisive battle. But I could not give the date of the Crimean battles nor a trustworthy account of the successive stages of that war. I doubt whether even my old friend, Sir William H. Russell, could do that now without referring to his letters in the *Times*. After thirty years no one, I believe, could take an oath to the accuracy of any statement of what he saw or heard so many years ago.

All then that I can vouch for is that I read my memory as I should the leaves of an old MS. from which many letters, nay, whole words and lines have vanished, and where I am often driven to decipher and to guess, as in a palimpsest, what the original uncial writing may have been. I am the first to confess that there may be flaws in my memory, there may be before my eyes that magic azure which surrounds the distant past; but I can promise that there shall be no invention, no *Dichtung* instead of *Wahrheit*, but always, as far as in me lies, truth.

I know quite well that even a certain dislocation of facts is not always to be avoided in an old memory. I know it from sad experience. As the spires of a city—of Oxford for instance—arrange themselves differently as we pass the old place on the railway, so that now one and now the other stands in the centre and seems to rise above the heads of the rest, so it is with our friends and acquaintances. Some who seemed giants at one time assume smaller proportions as others come into view towering above them. The whole scenery changes from year to year. Who does not remember the trees in our garden that seemed like giants in our childhood, but when we see them again in our old age, they have shrunk, and not from old age only?

And must I make one more confession? It is well known that George the Fourth described the battle of Waterloo so often that at last he persuaded himself that he had been present, in fact that he had won that battle. I also remember Dr. Routh, the venerable president of Magdalen College, who died in his hundredth year, and who had so often repeated all the circumstances of the execution of Charles I, that when Macaulay expressed a wish to see him, he declined "because that young man has given quite a wrong account of the last moments of the king," which he then proceeded to relate, as if he had been an eye-witness throughout.

Are we not liable to the same hallucination, though, let us hope, in a more mitigated form?

Have we never told a story as if it were our own, not from any wish to deceive, but simply because it seemed shorter and easier to do so than to explain step by step how it reached us? And after doing that once or twice, is there not great danger of our being surprised at somebody else claiming the story as his own, or actually maintaining that it was he who told it to us?

Not very long ago I remember reading in a journal a story of the Duke of Wellington. His servant had been sent before to order dinner for him at an out-of-the-way hotel, and in order to impress the landlord with the dignity of his coming guest, he had recited a number of the Duke's titles, which were very numerous. The landlord, thinking that the Duke of Vittoria, the Prince of Waterloo, the Marquis of Torres Vedras, and all the rest, were friends invited to dine with the Duke of Wellington, ordered accordingly a very sumptuous banquet to the great dismay of the real Duke. This may or may not be a very old and a very true story; all I know is that much the same thing was told at Oxford of Dr. Bull, who was Canon of Christ Church, Canon of Exeter, Prebendary of York, Vicar of Staverton, and lastly, the Rev. Dr. Bull himself. Dinner was provided for each of these persons, and we are told that the reverend pluralist had to eat all the dishes on the table and pay for them. This also may have been no more than one of the many "Common-roomers" which abounded in Oxford when Common Rooms were more frequented than they are now. But what I happen to know as a fact is that Dean Stanley received no less than four invitations to a ball at Blenheim, addressed A. P. Stanley, Esq., the Rev. A. P. Stanley, Canon Stanley, Professor Stanley, all evidently copied from some books of reference.

I may perhaps claim one advantage in trying to describe what happened to myself in my passage through life. From the earliest days that I can recollect, I felt myself as a twofold being—as a subject and an object, as a spectator and as an actor. I suppose we all talk to ourselves, and say to our better and worse selves, O thou fool! or, Well done, my boy! Well this inward conversation began with me at a very early time, and left the impression that I was the coachman, but at the same time the horse too which he drove and sometimes whipped very cruelly. And this phase of thought, or rather this state of feeling, seems soon to have led me on to another view which likewise dates from a very early time, though it afterwards vanished. As a little boy, when I could not have the same toys which other boys possessed, I could fully enjoy what they enjoyed, as if they had been my own. There is a German phrase, "Ich freue mich in deiner Seele," which exactly expressed what I often felt. It was not the result of teaching, still less of reasoning—it was a sentiment given me and which certainty did not leave me till much later in life, when competition, rivalry, jealousy, and envy seemed to accentuate my own I as against all other I's or Thou's. I suppose we all remember how the sight of a wound of a fellow creature, nay even of a dog, gives us a sharp twitch in the same part of our own body. That bodily sympathy has never left me, I suffer from it even now as I did seventy years ago. And is there anybody who has not felt his eyes moisten at the sudden happiness of his friends? All this seems to me to account, to a certain extent at least, for that feeling of identity with so-called strangers, which came to me from my earliest days, and has returned again with renewed strength in my old age. The "know thyself," ascribed to Chilon and other sages of ancient Greece, gains a deeper meaning with every year, till at last the I which we looked upon as the most certain and undoubted fact, vanishes from our grasp to become the Self, free from the various accidents and limitations which make up the I, and therefore one with the Self that underlies all individual and therefore vanishing I's. What that common Self may be is a question to be reserved for later times, though I may say at once that the only true answer given to it seems to me that of the Upanishads and the Vedanta philosophy. Only we must take care not to mistake the moral Self, that finds fault with the active Self, for the Highest Self that knows no longer of good or evil deeds.

Long before I had worked and thought out this

problem as the fundamental truth of all philosophy, it presented itself to me as if by intuition, long before I could have fathomed it in its metaphysical meaning. I had just heard of the death of a dear little child, and was standing in our garden, looking at a rose-bush, covered in summer with hundreds of rose-buds and rose-flowers. While I was looking I broke off one small withered bud from the midst of a large cluster of roses, and after I had done so a question came to me, and I said to myself, What has happened? Is it only that one small bud is dead and gone, or have not all the other roses been touched by the breath of death that fell on it? Have they not all suffered from the death of their sister, for they all spring from the same stem, they all have their life from the same source? And if one rose suffers, must not all the others suffer with it? Then all the buds and flowers of the cluster seemed to me to become one, as it were a family of roses, and each single bud seemed but the repetition of the same thing, the manifestation of the same thought, namely the thought of the rose. But my eyes were carried still further, and the stem from which the bunch of roses sprang was lost with other stems in a branch, and it was that branch on which all the roses of the branchlets and stems depended, and without which they could not flower or exist. The single roses thus became identified with the branch from which they had sprung, and by which they lived. I wondered more and more, and after another look all the branches with all their branchlets became absorbed in the stem, and the stem was the tree, and the tree sprang from a seed, or as it is now called, the protoplasm; but beyond that seed there was nothing else that the eye could see or the mind could grasp. And while this vision floated before my eyes I thought of my little friend, and the home from which she had been broken off, and the same vision which had changed the rose-bush with all its flowers, and buds, and branchlets, and branches, into a stem and a tree, and at last into one invisible germ and seed, seemed now to change my little friend and her brothers and sisters, her parents too and all her family, into one being which, like an old oak tree, started from an invisible stem, or an invisible seed, or from an invisible thought, and that divine thought was man, as the other divine thought had been rose.

Perhaps I did not see it so fully then as I see it now, and I certainly did not reason about it. I simply felt that in the death of my little friend, something of myself had gone, though she was no relation, but only a stray human friend. We see many things as children which we cannot see as grown-up men and women, for, as Longfellow said, "the thoughts of youth are long long thoughts." Nay, I feel convinced that He who spoke the parable of the vine had seen the same vision when He said: "I am the vine, ye are the branches. Abide in Me, and I in you. As the branch cannot bear fruit of itself except it abide in the vine, no more can ye, except ye abide in Me." And it is on this vision, or this parable of the vine, that immediately afterwards follows the lesson, "Love one another, as I have loved you." In loving one another we are in truth loving the others as ourselves, as one with ourselves; and while we are loving Him who is the vine, we are loving the branches, ourselves —aye, even our own little selves.

Such vague visions or intuitions often remain with us for life, but while they seem to be the same, they vary as we vary ourselves. We imagine we saw their deepest meaning from the first, but, like a parable, they gain in meaning every time they come back to us.

CHAPTER II

CHILDHOOD AT DESSAU

In a small town such as Dessau was when I lived there as a child and as a boy, one lived as in an enchanted island. The horizon was very narrow, and nothing happened to disturb the peace of the little oasis. The Duchy was indeed a little oasis in the large desert of Central Germany. The landscape was beautiful: there were rivers small and large—the Mulde and the Elbe; there were magnificent oak forests; there were regiments of firs standing in regular columns like so many grenadiers; there were parks such as one sees in England only. The town, the capital of the Duchy of Anhalt-Dessau, had been cared for by successive rulers—men mostly far in advance of their time—who had read and travelled, and brought home the best they could find abroad. Their old castle, centuries old, overawed the town; it was by far the largest building, though there were several other smaller places in the town for members of the ducal family. All the public buildings, theatres, libraries, schools, and barracks, had been erected by the Dukes, as well as several private residences intended for some of the higher officials. The whole town was, in fact, the creation

MY FATHER

of the Dukes; the whole ground on which it stood had been originally their property, but it was mostly held as freehold by those who had built their own private houses on it. No one would have built a house on leasehold land, and several of the houses were of so substantial a character that one saw they had been intended to last for more than ninety-nine years. The same family often remained in their house for generations, and the different stories were occupied by three generations at the same time—by grandparents, parents, and children. In this small town I was born on December 6, 1823. My father, Wilhelm Müller, was Librarian of the Ducal Library, and one of the most popular poets in Germany. A national monument was erected to his memory at Dessau in the year 1891, nearly a hundred years after his birth.

What a blessing it would be if such a rule were followed with all great men, who seem so great at the time of their death, and who, a hundred years later, are almost forgotten, or at all events appreciated by a small number of admirers only. This Monument- and Society-mania is indeed becoming very objectionable, for if for some time there has been no room for tombs and statues in Westminster Abbey, there will soon be no room for them in the streets of London. The result is that many of the people who walk along the Thames Embankment, particularly foreigners, often ask, "Cur?" when looking at the human idols in bronze and marble put up there; while historians, remembering the really great men of England, would ask quite as often, "Cur non?" There is a curious race of people, who, as soon as a man of any note dies, are ready to found anything for him—a monument, a picture, a school, a prize, a society—to keep alive his memory. Of course these societies want presidents, members of council, committees, secretaries, &c., and at last, subscriptions also. Thus it has happened that the name of founder (*Gründer*) has assumed, particularly in Germany, a perfume by no means sweet. Those who are asked to subscribe to such testimonials know how disagreeable it is to decline to give at least their name, deeply as they feel that in giving it they are offending against all the rules of historical perspective. I should not say that my father was one of the great poets of Germany, though Heine, no mean critic, declared that he placed his lyric poetry next to that of Goethe. Besides, he was barely thirty-three when he died. He had been a favourite pupil of F. A. Wolf, and had proved his classical scholarship by his *Homerische Vorschule*, and other publications. His poems became popular in the true sense of the word, and there are some which the people in the street sing even now without being aware of the name of their author. Schubert's compositions also have contributed much to the wide popularity of his *Schöne Müllerin* and his *Winterreise*, so that though it might truly be said of him that he wanted no monument in bronze or stone, it seemed but natural that a small town like Dessau should wish to honour itself by honouring the memory of one of its sons. In the company of Mendelssohn, the philosopher, and of F. Schneider, the composer, a monument of my father in the principal street of his native town, and before the school in which he had been a pupil and a teacher, could hardly seem out of place. That the Greek Parliament voted the Pentelican marble for the poet of the *Griechenlieder*, as it had done for Lord Byron, was another inducement for his fellow citizens to do honour to their honoured poet. He died when I was hardly four years old, so that my recollection of him is very faint and vague, made up, I believe, to a great extent, of pictures, and things that my mother told me. I seem to remember him as a bright, sunny, and thoroughly joyful man, delighted with our little naughtinesses. One book I still possess which he bought for me and which was to be the first book of my library. It was a small volume of Horace, printed by Pickering in 1820. It has now almost vanished among the 12,000 big volumes that form my library, but I am delighted that I am still able, at seventy-six, to read it without spectacles. I think I remember my father taking my sister and me on his knees, and telling us the most delightful stories, that set us wondering and laughing and crying till we could laugh and cry no longer. He had been a fellow worker with the brothers Grimm, and the stories he told were mostly from their collection, though he knew how to embellish them with anything that could make a child cry and laugh.

People have little idea how great and how lasting an influence such popular stories about kings and queens, and princesses and knights, about ogres and witches, about men that have been changed into animals, and about animals that talk and behave like human beings, exercise on the imagination of young children. While we listened, a new world seemed to open before us, and anything like doubt as to the reality of these beings never existed. What was reality or unreality to young children of four and five? How few people know what real reality is, even after they have reached the age of fifty or sixty. For children, such names as reality and unreality do not exist, nor the ideas which they express. They listen to what their father tells them, and they cannot see any difference between what he tells them of Frederick Barbarossa, of Romulus and Remus suckled by a wolf, or of the dwarfs that guarded the coffin of Schneewittchen.

Some people, however, have thought that from an educational point of view, a belief in this imaginary world must be mischievous. I doubt it, and it would be easy to show that originally these stories and fables were really meant to inculcate right and good principles. Luther declared that he would not lose these wonderful stories of his tender childhood for any sum of money, and Camerarius (*Fabulae Aesopeae*, p. 406, Lipsiae, 1570) speaks of these German fables as filling the minds of the people, and particularly of children, with terror, hope, and religion. The oldest collections in which some of these Aesopean fables occur, the Pantschatantra and Hitopadesa in Sanskrit, were distinctly intended for the education of princes, and though they may make the young listeners inclined to be superstitious, such superstitiousness is not likely to last long. Children delight in *Märchen* as in a kind of pantomime, and when the curtain has fallen on that fairy world they often think of it as of a beautiful dream that has passed away. The stories are certainly more impressive than the proverbs and wise saws which many of them were meant to illustrate, without always saying, *haec fabula docet.* Even if some of these stories touch sometimes on what may not seem to us quite correct, it is done to make children laugh rather at the silliness than cry at the downright wickedness of some of the heroes. It is by no means uncommon, for instance, that a good-for-nothing fellow succeeds, while his virtuous companions fail. But there is either a reason for it, or the injustice provokes the indignation of children, long before they have learnt that in real life also virtue does not always receive its reward, while falsehood often prospers, at least for a time. There is no harm, I think, in a certain dreaminess in children. I remember that I have often laughed with all my heart at Rumpelstilzchen, and shed bitter tears at Brüderchen and Schwesterchen. I seemed to see brother and sister driven into the wood, the brother being changed into a deer, and the sister sleeping with her head on his warm fur, till at last the deer was killed by a huntsman, and the little sister had to travel on quite alone in the forest. Of course in the end she became a princess, and the brother a prince who married a queen, and all ended in great joy and jubilation in which we all joined. How good for children that they should for a time at least have lived in such a dreamland, in which truthfulness was as a rule rewarded, and falsehood punished in the end.

It was like a recollection of a Paradise, and such a recollection, even if it brought out the contrast between the dream-world and the real world, would often set children musing on what ought and what ought not to be. They did not long believe in Dornröschen and Schneewittchen, they learnt but too soon that Dornröschen and Schneewittchen belonged to another world. They may even have come to learn that Dornröschen (thorn-rose) and Schneewittchen (snow-white) were meant originally for the sleep or death of nature in her snow-white shroud, and the return of the sun; but woe to the boy who on first learning these stories should have declared that they were mere bosh, or, as Sir Walter Scott says, the detritus of nature-myths.

My father's father, whom I never knew, seems

not to have been distinguished in any way. He was, however, a useful tradesman and a respected citizen of Dessau, and, as I see, the founder of the first lending library in that small town. He married a second time, a rich widow, chiefly, as I was told, to enable him to give his son, my father, a liberal education. She grew to be very old, and I well remember her, to me, forbidding and terrifying appearance. She quite belonged to a past generation, and when I saw her again after having been in England, she asked me whether I had seen Napoleon who had been taken prisoner and sent to England, but had lately escaped and resumed his throne in Paris. She evidently mixed up the two Napoleons, and I did not contradict her. To me her conversation was interesting as showing how little the traditions of the people can be relied on, and how easily, by the side of real history, a popular history could grow up. After all, the poems of Charlemagne besieging Jerusalem owed their origin very likely to some similar confusion in the minds of old women. My sister and I were always terrified when we were sent to visit her, for with her dishevelled grey hair, her thin white face, and her piercing eyes, she was to us the old grandmother, or the witch of Grimm's stories; and the language she used was such that, if we repeated it at home, we were severely reprimanded. She knew very little about my father, but her memory about her first husband and about her own youth and childhood was very clear, though not always edifying. Her stories about ghosts, witches, ogres, nickers, and the whole of that race were certainly enough to frighten a child, and some of them clung to me for a very long time. On my mother's side my relations were more civilized, and they had but little social intercourse with my grandmother and her relatives. My mother's father was von Basedow, the President, that is Prime Minister of the Duchy of Anhalt-Dessau, a position in which he was succeeded by his eldest son, my uncle. He was the first man in the town; the Duke and he really ruled the Duchy exactly as they pleased. There was no check on them of any kind, and yet no one, as far as I know, ever complained of any tyranny. My grandfather's father again was the famous reformer of public education in Germany. He (1723–1790) had to brave the conservative and clerical parties throughout the country. His home at Hamburg was burnt in a riot, and it was then that he migrated to Dessau, to become the founder of the *Philanthropinum*, and at the same time the path-breaker for men such as Pestalozzi (1746–1827) and Froebel (1782–1852). Considering his lifelong struggles, he deserved a better monument at Dessau than he has found there. No doubt he was a passionate and violent man, and his outbreaks are still remembered at Dessau, while his beneficial activity has almost been forgotten. I was often told that I took after my mother's family, whatever that may mean, and this was certainly the case in outward appearance, though I hope not in temper. My great grandfather, the Pedagogue as he was called, was a friend of Goethe's, and is mentioned in his poems.

My childhood at home was often very sad. My mother, who was left a widow at twenty-eight with two children, my sister and myself, was heart-broken. The few years of her married life had been most bright and brilliant. My father was a rising poet, and such was his popularity that he was able to indulge his tastes as he liked, whether in travelling or in making his house a pleasant centre of social life. Contemporaries and friends of my father, particularly Baron Simolin, a very intimate friend, who spent the Christmas of 1825 in our house, have written of the bright gaiety, the whole-hearted enjoyment of life that reigned there, and have told how, though his income was to say the least of it small, Wilhelm Müller's home was the rallying-point for all the cultivated, scientific, and artistic society of Dessau, who felt attracted by the simple and unaffected yet truly genial disposition of the master of the house.

It would be interesting to know how much an author could make at that time by his pen. Publishers seem to have been far more liberal then than they are now. The circumstances were different. The number of writers was of course much smaller, and the sale of really popular books probably much larger. Anyhow, my father, whose salary was minute, seems to have been able to enjoy the few years of his married life in great comfort. The thought of saving money, however, seems never to have entered his poetical mind, and after his unexpected death, due to paralysis of the heart, it was found that hardly any provision had been made for his family. Even the life insurance, which is obligatory on every civil servant, and the pension granted by the Duke, gave my mother but a very small income, fabulously small, when one considers that she had to bring up two children on it. It has been a riddle to me ever since how she was able to do it.

However, it was done, and could only have been done in a small town like Dessau, where education was as good as it was cheap, and where very little was expected by society. We must also take into account the very low prices which then ruled at Dessau with regard to almost all the necessaries of life. I see from the old newspapers that beef sold at about threepence a pound (two groschen), mutton at about twopence. Wine was sold at seven to eight groschen a bottle, a better sort for twelve to fourteen groschen—a groschen being about a penny. People drank mostly beer, and this was sold under Government inspection at two to three groschen per quart. Fish was equally cheap, and such, at the beginning of the century, was the abundance of salmon caught in the Elbe, and even in the Mulde at Dessau, that it was stipulated as in Scotland, that servants should not have salmon more than twice or thrice in the week. The lowest price for salmon was then twopence halfpenny a pound. As a boy I can remember seeing the salmon in large numbers leap over a weir in the very town of Dessau, and though they had travelled for so many miles inland, the fish was very good, though not so good as Severn salmon. Game also was very cheap, and sold for not much more than mutton, nay, at certain times it was given away; it could not be exported. Corn was sold at three shillings per *Scheffel*, and by corn was chiefly meant rye. No one took wheaten bread, and the bread was therefore called brown bread and black bread. White bread was only taken with coffee, and peasants in the villages would not have touched it, because it was not supposed to make such strong bones as rye-bread. With such prices we can understand that a salary of £300 was considered sufficient for the highest officers of state.

My mother's relations, who were all high in the public service, my grandfather, as I said, being the Duke's chief minister, made life more easy and pleasant for us; but for many years my mother never went into society, and our society consisted of members of our own family only. All I remember of my mother at that time was that she took her two children day after day to the beautiful *Gottesacker* (God's Acre), where she stood for hours at our father's grave, and sobbed and cried. It was a beautiful and restful place, covered with old acacia trees. The inscription over the gateway was one of my earliest puzzles. *Tod ist nicht Tod, ist nur Veredlung menschlicher Natur* (Death is not death, 'tis but the ennobling of man's nature). On each side there stood a figure, representing the genius of sleep and the genius of death. All this was the work of the old Duke, Leopold Friedrich Franz, who tried to educate his people as he had educated himself, partly by travel, partly by intercourse with the best men he could attract to Dessau.

At home the atmosphere was certainly depressing to a boy. I heard and thought more about death than about life, though I knew little of course of what life or death meant. I had but few pleasures, and my chief happiness was to be with my mother. I shared her grief without understanding much about it. She was passionately devoted to her children, and I was passionately fond of her. What there was left of life to her, she gave to us, she lived for us only, and tried very hard not to deprive our childhood of all brightness. She was certainly most beautiful, and quite different from all other ladies at Dessau, not only in the eyes of her son, but as it seemed to me, of everybody. Then she had a most perfect voice, and when I first began music she helped and encouraged me in every possible way. We played *à quatre mains*, and soon she made me accompany her when she sang. As far as I can recollect, I was never so happy as when I could be with her. She read so much to us that I was quite satisfied, and saw perhaps less of my young

MY MOTHER

friends than I ought. When my mother said she wished to die, and to be with our father, I feel sure that my sister and I were only anxious that she should take us with her, for there were few golden chains that bound us as yet to this life. I see her now, sitting on a winter's evening near the warm stove, a candle on the table, and a book from which she read to us in her hands, while the spinning-wheel worked by the servant-maid in the corner went on humming all the time. She read Paul Gerhard's translation of St. Bernard's:

> " Salve caput cruentatum,
> Totum spinis coronatum,
> Conquassatum, vulneratum,
> Arundine verberatum,
> Facies sputis illita."

> " O Haupt voll Blut und Wunden,
> Voll Schmerz und voller Hohn!
> O Haupt zu Spott gebunden
> Mit einer Dornenkron,
> O Haupt sonst schön gezieret
> Mit höchster Ehr und Zier,
> Jetzt aber hoch schimpfiret:
> Gegrüsset seist du mir!"

Though the German translation does not come near the powerful majesty of the original, yet such was the effect produced on me that I saw the bleeding head before my eyes, and cried and cried until my mother had to comfort me by assuring me that the sufferer was now in Heaven and that it was only a song to be sung in church. How deeply such scenes seem engraved on the memory; how vividly they return when the rubbish of many years is swept away and all is again as it was then, and the *caput cruentatum* looks down on us once more, as it did then, with the human eyes full of divine love, so truly human that one could say with St. Bernard, "Tuum caput huc inclina, in meis pausa brachiis." But willingly as I listened to these readings at home, and full as my heart was of love to Christ, I suffered intensely when I was taken to church as a young boy. It was a very large church, and in winter bitterly cold. Even though I liked the singing, the long sermon was real torture to me. I could not understand a word of it, and being thinly clad my teeth would have chattered if I had not been told that it was wrong "to make a noise in church." Oh! what misery is inflicted on childhood by this enforced attendance at church. When a church can be warmed the suffering is less intense, but a huge whitewashed church that feels like an ice-cellar is about the worst torture that human ingenuity could have invented to make children hate the very name of church. These early impressions often remain for life, and the worst of it is that the idea remains in the minds of children, and of grown-up people too, that by going to church and repeating the same prayers over and over again, and listening to long and often dreary sermons, they are actually doing a service to God (*Gottesdienst*).

Why does no new prophet arise and say in the name of God, as David did in the name of Jehovah, "Sermons and long prayers 'thou didst not desire'"?

Many years later I had to discuss the same question with Keshub Chunder Sen, the Indian Reformer. He wanted to know what kind of service should be adopted by his new church, the Brahmo Somaj; his friends thought of sermons, singing, and processions with flags and flowers through the streets. "No," I said to him, "service of God should be service of men; if you want divine service, let it be a real service, such as God would approve of. Let other people go to church, to their mosques or their temples, but take you your own friends on certain days of the week to whatever you like to call your meeting-place, and after a short prayer or a few words of advice send some of them to the poorest streets in the city, others to the prisons, others to the hospitals. Let them pray with all who wish to pray, but let them speak words of true love and comfort also, and when they can, let them help them with their alms. That would be a real Divine Service and a divine Sunday for you, and you would all come home, it may be sadder, but certainly wiser and better men."

I am afraid he did not agree with me. He did not think that true religion was to visit the poor and the afflicted. That might do for a practical people like the English, but the Hindu wanted something else, he wanted some outward show and ceremony for the people, and at the same time some silent communion with God. Who can tell what different people understand by religion? and who can prescribe the spiritual food that is best for them? "Only," I said, "do not call it practical to encourage millions of people to waste hours and hours in mere repetition, and to spend millions and millions in supplying this cold comfort, when next door to the magnificent cathedral there are squalid streets, and squalid houses, and squalid beds to lie and die on."

The religious and devotional element is very strong in Germany, but the churches are mostly empty. A German keeps his religion for weekdays rather than for Sunday. When the German regiments marched, and when they made ready for battle, they did not sing ribald songs, they sang the songs of Luther and Paul Gerhard, which they knew by heart and which strengthened them to face death as it ought to be faced.

Fortunately, while enforced attendance at church was apt to produce the strongest aversion in the young heart against anything that was called religion, religious instruction both at home and at school too was excellent, and undid much of the mischief that had been done during cold winter days. True religious sentiments can be planted in the soul at home only, by a mother better even than by a father. The sense of a divine presence everywhere, *πάντα πλήρη θεῶν*, once planted in the heart of a child remains for life. Of course the child soon begins to argue, and says to his mother that God cannot be at the same time in two rooms. But only let a mother show to the child the rays of the sun in the sky, in the streets, and in every corner of the house, and it will begin to understand that nothing can be hid from the eyes of Him who is greater than the sun. And when a child doubts whether the voice of conscience can be the voice of God, and asks how he could hear that voice without seeing the speaker, ask him only whose voice it can be that tells him not to do what he himself wishes to do, and not to say what he could say without any fear of men; and his idea of God will be raised from that of a visible being like the sun, to the concept of a presence that never vanishes, that is not only without, in the sky, in the mountains, and in the storm, but nearer also within, in the sense of fear, in the sense of shame, and in the hope of pardon and love.

At school our religious teaching was chiefly historical and moral. There was no difficulty in finding proper teachers for that, and there were no attempts on the part of parents to interfere with religious instruction or to demand separate teaching for each sect. It is true that religious sects are not so numerous in Germany as they are in England. Somc, though by no means all, children of Roman Catholic and Jewish parents were allowed to be absent from religious lessons. But most parents knew that the history of the Jewish religion would be taught at school in so impartial and truly historical a spirit as never to offend Jewish children. Respect for historical truth, and an implanted sense of the reverence due to children, would keep any teacher from making the history of the Christian Church, whether before or after the Reformation, an excuse for offending one of the little ones committed to his care. If Jews or Roman Catholics wished for any special religious instruction it was given by their own priests or Rabbis, and was given without any interference on the part of the Government. But such was at my time the state of public feeling that I hardly knew at school who among my young friends were Roman Catholics, or Lutherans, or Reformed. I must admit, however, that the very name of Luther might have offended Roman Catholics. He was represented to us as a perfect saint, almost as inspired and infallible. His hymns sung in church seemed to us little different from the Psalms of David, and I well remember what a shock it gave me when at Oxford, much later in life, I heard Luther spoken of like any other mortal, nay, as a heretic, and a most dangerous heretic too. When I was a boy I remember that in some places the same building had to be used for Protestant and Roman Catholic services. All that, I am afraid, is now changed, and the old liberal and tolerant feeling then prevailing on all sides is now often stigmatized as indifference, and by other ugly names. It should really be called the golden age of Christianity, and this so-called indifference should be classed among the highest Christian virtues, and as the fullest realization of the spirit of Christ.

Thus we grew up from our earliest youth, being taught to look upon Christianity as an historical fact, on Christ and His disciples as historical characters, on the Old and New Testaments as real historical books. Though we did not understand as yet the deeper meaning of Christ and of His words, we had at least nothing to unlearn in later times, or to feel that our parents had ever told us what they themselves could not have held to be true. Our simple faith was not shaken by mere questions of criticism, or by the problem how any human being could take upon himself to declare any book to be revealed, unless he claimed for himself a more than human insight. The simplest rules of logic should make such a declaration impossible, whatever the sacred book may be to which it is applied. Granted that the Pope was infallible, how could the Cardinals know that he was, unless they claimed for themselves the same or even greater infallibility? It is far more easy to be inspired than to know some one else is or was inspired; the true inspiration is, and always has been, the spirit of truth within, and this is but another name for the spirit of God. It is truth that makes inspiration, not inspiration that makes truth. Whoever knows what truth is, knows also what inspiration is: not only *theopneustos*, blown into the soul by God, but the very voice of God, the real presence of God, the only presence in which we, as human beings, can ever perceive Him.

How often have I in later life tried to explain this to my friends in France and in England who endured mental agonies before they could arrive at the simple conclusion that revelation can never be objective, but must always be subjective. I may return to this question at a later period of my life, when I had to discuss with Renan, at Paris, with Froude, Kingsley, and Liddon, in England, and tried to show how entirely self-made some of their difficulties were. At present I have only to explain how it was that I had never to extricate myself from a net in which so many honest thinkers find themselves entangled without any fault of their own; as Samson, when he awoke, found himself bound with seven green withs and had to break them with all his might before he could hope to escape from the Philistines. The Philistines never bound me. During my early schooldays these difficulties did not exist, but I have often been grateful in after life that the seven locks of my head have never been woven with the web.

I remember a number of small events in my school-life at Dessau, but though they were full of interest to me, nay, full of meaning, and not without an influence on my later life, they would have no meaning and no interest for others, and may remain as if they had never been. The influence which music exercised on my mind, and, I believe, on my heart also, I have related in my *Musical Recollections*. The image of those passing years, though its general tone was melancholy, chiefly owing to my mother's melancholy, seemed to me at the time free from all unhappiness. My work at school and at home was not too heavy; I was fond of it, and very fond of books. Books were scarce then, and whoever possessed a new and valuable book was expected to lend it to his friends in the little town. If a man was known to possess, say, Goethe's works or Jean Paul's works, the consequence was that one went to him or to her to ask for the loan of them. And not only books, but paper and pens also were scarce. The first steel pens came in when I was still in the lower school, and bad as they were they were looked upon as real treasures by the schoolboys who possessed them. Paper was so dear that one had to be very sparing in its use. Every margin and cover was scribbled over before it was thrown away, and I felt often so hampered by the scarcity of paper that I gladly accepted a set of copybooks instead of any other present that I might have asked for on my birthday or at Christmas. I am sorry to say I have had to suffer all my life from the inefficiency of our writing master, or maybe from the fact that my thoughts were too quick for my pen. In other subjects I did well, but though I was among the first in each class,

I was by no means cleverer than other boys. In the lower school work was more like conversation or like hearing news from our teachers. The idea of effort did not yet exist. The drudgery began, however, when I entered the upper school, the gymnasium, and learnt the elements of Latin and Greek. Though our teachers were very conscientious, they tried to make our work no burden to us, and the constant change of places in each class kept up a lively rivalry among the boys, though I am not sure that it did not make me rather ambitious and at times conceited. Still, I had few enemies, and it seemed of much more consequence who could knock down another boy than who could gain a place above him. I feel sure I could have done a great deal more at school than I did, but it was partly my music and partly my incessant headaches that interfered with my school work.

I remember as a boy that certain streets were inhabited exclusively by Jewish families. A large number of Jews had been received at Dessau by a former Duke; but though he granted them leave to settle at Dessau when they were persecuted in other parts of Germany, he stipulated that they should only settle in certain streets. These streets were by no means the worst streets of the town; on the contrary they showed greater comfort and hardly any of the squalor which disgraced the Jewish quarters in other towns in Germany. As children we were brought up without any prejudice against the Jews, though we had, no doubt, a certain feeling that they were tolerated only, and were not quite on the same level with ourselves. We also felt the religious difficulty sometimes very strongly. Were not the Jews the murderers of Christ? and had they not said: "the blood be on us and on our children"? But as we were told that it was wrong to harbour feelings of revenge, we boys soon forgot and forgave, and played together as the best friends. I remember picking up a number of Jewish words which would not have been understood anywhere else. I was hardly aware that they were Jewish and used them like any other words. But I once gave great offence to my friend Professor Bernays, who was a Jew. He had uttered some quite incredible statement, and I exclaimed, "Sind Sie denn ganz maschukke?"—Hebrew for "mad." I meant no harm, but he was very much hurt.

I knew several Jewish families, and received much kindness from them as a boy. Many of these families were wealthy, but they never displayed their wealth, and in consequence excited no envy. All that is changed now. The children of the Jews who formerly lived in a very quiet style at Dessau, now occupy the best houses, indulge in most expensive tastes, and try in every way to outshine their non-Jewish neighbours. They buy themselves titles, and, when they can, stipulate for stars and orders as rewards for successful financial operations, carried out with the money of princely personages.

Hence the revulsion of feeling all over Germany, or what is called Anti-Semitism, which has assumed not only a social but a political significance. I doubt whether there is anything religious in it, as there was when we were boys. The Anti-Semitic hatred is the hatred of money-making, more particularly of that kind of money-making which requires no hard work, but only a large capital to begin with, and boldness and astuteness in speculating, that is in buying and selling at the right moment. The sinews of war for that kind of financial warfare were mostly supplied by the fathers and grandfathers of the present generation. Sometimes, no doubt, the capital was lost, and in those cases it must be said that the Jewish speculator disappears from the stage without a sigh or a cry. He begins again, and if he should have to do what his grandfather did, walk from house to house with a bag on his back, he does not whine.

One cannot blame the Jews or any other speculators for using their opportunities, but they must not complain either if they excite envy, and if that envy assumes in the end a dangerous character. The Jews, so far from suffering from disabilities, enjoy really certain privileges over their Christian competitors in Germany. They belong to a *regnum*, but also to a *regnum in regno.* They have, so to say, our Sunday and likewise their Sabbath. Jew will always help Jew against a Christian; and again who can blame them for that? All one can say is that they should not complain of their unpopularity, but take into account the risk they are running. No one hated the Jews such as they were in Dessau fifty years ago. They had their own schools and synagogues, and no one interfered with them when they built their bowers in the streets at the time of their Feast of Tabernacles, and lived, feasted, and slept in them to keep up the memory of their sojourning in the desert. They indulged in even more offensive practices, such as, for instance, putting three stones in the coffins to be thrown by the dead at the Virgin Mary, her husband, and their Son. No one suspected or accused them of kidnapping Christian children, or offering sacrifices with their blood. They were known too well for that. Conversions of Jews were not infrequent, and converted Jews were not persecuted by their former co-religionists as they are now. Even marriages between Christians and Jews were by no means uncommon, particularly when the young Jewesses were beautiful or rich, still better if they were both. Disgraceful as the Anti-Semitic riots have been in Germany and Russia, there can be no doubt that in this as in most cases both sides were to blame, and there is little prospect of peace being re-established till many more heads have been broken.

What helped very much to keep the peace in the small town of Dessau, as it did all over Germany, nay, all over the world, till about the year 1848, was the small number of newspapers. In my childhood and youth their number was very small. In Dessau I only knew of one, which was then called the *Wochenblatt*, afterwards the *Staatsanzeiger*. At that time newspapers were really read for the news which they contained, not for leading or misleading articles and all the rest. What a happy time it was when a newspaper consisted of a sheet, or half a sheet in quarto, with short paragraphs about actual events, which had often taken place weeks and months before. A battle might have been fought in Spain or Turkey, in India or China, and no one knew of it till some official information was vouchsafed by the respective Governments or by Jewish bankers. War-correspondents or regular reporters did not exist, and the old telegraphic dispatches were sent by wooden telegraphs fixed on high towers, which from a distance looked like gallows on which a criminal was hanging and gesticulating with arms and feet. Anybody who watched these signals could decipher them far more easily than a hieroglyphic inscription.

The peace of Europe, nay, of the whole world, was then in the keeping of sovereigns and their ministers, and Prince Metternich might certainly take some credit for having kept what he called the Thirty Years' Peace. Shall we ever, as long as there are newspapers, have peace again—peace between the great nations of the world, and peace at home between contending parties, and peace in our mornings at home which are now so ruthlessly broken in upon, nay, swallowed up by those paper-giants, most unwelcome yet irresistible callers, just when we want to settle down to a quiet day's work? It is no use protesting against the inevitable, nor can we quite agree with those who maintain that no newspaper carries the slightest weight or exercises the smallest influence on home or foreign politics. A very influential statesman and wise thinker used to say that we should never have had Christianity if newspapers had existed at the time of Augustus. When unsuccessful *littérateurs* or bankrupt bankers' clerks were the chief contributors to the newspapers, their influence might have been small; but when Bismarcks turned journalists, and Gortchakoffs prompted, newspapers could hardly be called *quantités négligeables.*

The horizon of Dessau was very narrow, but within its bounds there was a busy and happy life. Everybody did his work honestly and conscientiously. There were, of course, two classes, the educated and the uneducated. The educated consisted of the members of the Government service, the clergy, the schoolmasters, doctors, artists, and officers; the uneducated were the tradesmen, mechanics, and labourers. The trade was mostly in the hands of Jews, it had become almost a Jewish monopoly. When one of these tradesmen went bankrupt, there was a commotion over the whole town, and I remember being taken to see one of these bankrupt shops, expecting to find the whole house broken up and demolished, and being surprised to see the tradesman standing whole, and sound, and smiling, in his accustomed place. My etymological tastes must have developed very early, for I had asked why this poor Jew was called a bankrupt, and had been duly informed that it was because his bank had been broken, *banca rotta*, which of course I took in a literal sense, and expected to see all the furniture broken to pieces. The commercial relations of our Dessau tradesmen did not extend much beyond Leipzig, Berlin, possibly Hamburg and Cologne. If a burgher of Dessau travelled to these or to more distant parts the whole town knew of it and talked about it, whereas a journey to Paris or London was an event worthy to be mentioned and discussed in the newspapers. These old newspapers are full of curious information. We find that if a person wished to travel to Cologne or further, he advertised for a companion, and it was for the Burgomaster to make the necessary arrangements for him.

French was studied and spoken, particularly at Court, but English was a rare acquirement, still more Italian or Spanish. There was, however, a small inner circle where these languages were studied, chiefly in order to read the master-works of modern literature. And this was all the more creditable because there were no good teachers to be found at Dessau, and people had to learn what they wished to learn by themselves, with the help of a grammar and dictionary. We learnt French at school, but the result was deplorable. As in all public schools, the French master who had to teach the language at the Ducal Gymnasium could not keep order among the boys. He of course spoke French, but that was all. He did not know how to teach, and could not excite any interest in the boys, who insisted on pronouncing French as if it were German. The poor man's life was made a burden to him. His name was Noel, and he had all the pleasing manners of a Frenchman, but that served only to rouse the antagonism of the young barbarians. The result was that we learnt very little, and I was sent to an old Jew to learn French and a little English. That old Jew, called Levy Rubens, was a perfect gentleman. He probably had been a commercial traveller in his early days, though no one knew exactly where he came from or how he had learnt languages. He had taught my father and grandfather and he was delighted to teach the third generation. He certainly spoke French and English fluently, but with the strongest Jewish accent, and this was inherited by all his pupils at Dessau. I feel ashamed when I think of the tricks we played the old man—putting mice into his pockets, upsetting inkstands over his table, and placing crackers under his chairs. But he never lost his temper; he never would have dared to punish us as we deserved; but he went on with his lesson as if nothing had happened. He took his small pay, and was satisfied when his lessons were over and he could settle down to his long pipe and his books. He lived quite alone and died quite alone, a hardworking, honest, poor Jew, not exactly despised or persecuted, but not treated with the respect which he certainly deserved, and which he would have received if he had not been a Jew.

Our public school was as good as any in Germany. These small duchies generally followed the example of Prussia, and they carried out the instructions issued by the Ministry of Education at Berlin according to the very letter. Besides, several of the reigning dukes had taken a very warm and personal interest in popular education, and at the beginning of the century the eyes of the whole of Germany, nay, of Europe, were turned towards the educational experiments carried on by my great-grandfather, Basedow,[1] at the so-called Philanthropinum at Dessau under the patronage of the Duke and of several of the more enlightened sovereigns of Europe, such as the Empress Catherine of Russia, the King of Denmark, the Emperor Joseph of Austria, Prince Adam Czartoryski, &c. Even after Basedow's death the interest in education was kept alive in Dessau, and all was done that could be done in so small a town to keep the different schools—elementary, middle-class, and high schools—on the highest possible level of efficiency.

[1] Johann Bernhard Basedow, von seinem Urenkel, F. M. M. (Essays, Band IV).

Bathing was a very healthful recreation, though I very nearly came to grief from trusting to my seniors. They could swim and I could not yet. But while bathing with two of my friends in a part of the river which was safe, they swam along and asked me to follow them. Having complete confidence in them I jumped in from the shore, but very soon began to sink. My shouts brought my friends back, and they rescued me, not without some difficulty, from drowning.

In an English school the influence of the master is, of course, more constant, because one of the masters is always within call, while in Germany he is visible during school-hours only. If a master is fond of his pupils, and takes an interest in them individually, he can do them more good than parents at home, or the teacher at a day school. The boys at a German school are, no doubt, a very mixed crew, but that cannot be helped. This mixture of classes may be a drawback in some respects, but from an educational point of view the sons of very rich parents are by no means more valuable than the poor boys. Far from it. Many of the evils of schoolboy life come from the sons of the rich, while the sons of poor parents are generally well behaved. But for all that, there was a rough and rude tone among some of the boys at school, arising from defects in the education at home, and this sometimes embittered what ought to be the happiest time of life, particularly in the case of delicate boys. The son of a Minister has often to sit by the side of the son of a wealthy butcher, and the very fact that he is the son of a gentleman often exposes the more refined boy to the bullying of his muscular neighbour. I was fortunate at school. I could hold my own with the boys, and as to the masters, several of them had known my father or had been his pupils, and they took a personal interest in me.

I remember more particularly one young master who was very kind to me, and took me home for private lessons and for giving me some good advice. There was something sad and very attractive about him, and I found out afterwards that he knew that he was dying of consumption, and that besides that he was liable to be prosecuted for political liberalism, which at that time was almost like high treason. I believe he was actually condemned and sent to prison like many others, and he died soon after I had left Dessau. His name was Dr. Hönicke, and he was the first to try to impress on me that I ought to show myself worthy of my father, an idea which had never entered my mind before, nay, which at first I could hardly understand, but which, nevertheless, slumbered on in my mind till years afterwards it was called out and became a strong influence for the whole of my life. I still have some lines which he wrote for my album. They were the well-known lines from Horace, which, at the time, I had great difficulty in construing, but which have remained graven in my memory ever since:

"Fortes creantur fortibus et bonis,
Est in iuvencis est in equis patrum
Virtus nec imbellem feroces
Progenerant aquilae columbam.
Doctrina sed vim promovet insitam,
Rectique cultus pectora roborant;
Utcunque defecere mores,
Dedecorant bene nata culpae."

In my childhood I had to pass through the ordinary illnesses, but it was the faith in our doctor that always saved me. The doctor was to my mind the man who was called in to make me well again, and while my mother was agitated about her only son, I never dreamt of any danger. The very idea of death never came near me till my grandfather died (1835), but even then I was only about twelve years old, and though I had seen much of him, particularly during the years that my mother lived again in his house, yet he was too old to take much share in his grandchildren's amusements. He left a gap, no doubt, in our life, but that gap was filled again with new figures in the life of a boy of twelve. He was only sixty-one years old when he died, and yet my idea of him was always that of a very old man. Everything was done for him, his servant dressed him every morning, he was lifted into his carriage and out of it, and he certainly lived the life of an invalid, such as I should not consent to own to at seventy-six. He made no secret that he cared more for the son of his son who was the heir, and was to perpetuate the name of von Basedow, than for the son of his daughter. He was very fond of driving and of shooting, and he frequently took my cousin out shooting with him. When my cousin came home with a hare he had shot, I confess I was sometimes jealous, but I was soon cured of my wish to go with my grandfather into the forest. Once when I was with him in his little carriage, my grandfather, not being able to see well, had the misfortune to kill a doe which had come out with her two little ones. The misery of the mother and afterwards of her two young ones, was heart-rending, and from that day on I made up my mind never to go out shooting, and never to kill an animal. And I have kept my word, though I was much laughed at. It may be that later in life and after my grandfather's death I had little opportunity of shooting, but the cry of the doe and the whimpering of the young ones who tried to get suck from their dead mother have remained with me for life.

My grandfather, though he aged early, remained in harness as Prime Minister to the end of his life, and it was his great desire to benefit his country by new institutions. It was he who, at the time when people hardly knew yet what railroads meant, succeeded in getting the line from Berlin to Halle and Leipzig to pass by Dessau. He offered to build the bridge across the Elbe and to give the land and the wood for the sleepers gratis, and what seemed at the time a far too generous offer has proved a blessing to the duchy, making it as it were the centre of the great railway connecting Berlin, Leipzig, Magdeburg, the Elbe, Hanover, Bremen, nay, Cologne also, the Rhine, and Western Europe. He was in his way a good statesman, though we are too apt to measure a man's real greatness by the circumstances in which he moves.

As far back as I can remember I was a martyr to headaches. No doctor could help me, no one seemed to know the cause. It was a migraine, and though I watched it carefully I could not trace it to any fault of mine. The idea that it came from overwork was certainly untrue. It came and went, and if it was one day on the right side it was always the next time on the left, even though I was free from it sometimes for a week or a fortnight, or even longer. It was strange also that it seldom lasted beyond one day, and that I always felt particularly strong and well the day after I had been prostrate. For prostrate I was, and generally quite unable to do anything. I had to lie down and try to sleep. After a good sleep I was well, but when the pain had been very bad I found that sometimes the very skin of my forehead had peeled off. In this way I often lost two or three days in a week, and as my work had to be done somehow, it was often done anyhow, and I was scolded and punished, really without any fault of my own. After all remedies had failed which the doctor and nurses prescribed (and I well remember my grandmother using massage on my neck, which must have been about 1833 to 1835) I was handed over to Hahnemann, the founder of homeopathy. Hahnemann (born 1755) had been practising as doctor at Dessau as early as 1780—that is somewhat before my time—but had left it, and when in 1820 he had been prohibited by the Government from practising and lecturing at Leipzig, he took refuge once more in the neighbouring town of Coethen. From there he paid visits to Dessau as consulting physician, and after I had explained to him as well as I could all the symptoms of my chronic headache, he assured my mother that he would cure it at once. He was an imposing personality—a powerful man with a gigantic head and strong eyes and a most persuasive voice. I can quite understand that his personal influence would have gone far to effect a cure of many diseases. People forget too much how strong a curative power resides in the patient's faith in his doctor, in fact how much the mind can do in depressing and in reinvigorating the body. I shall never forget in later years consulting Sir Andrew Clarke, and telling him of ever so many, to my mind, most serious symptoms. I had lost sleep and appetite, and imagined myself in a very bad state indeed. He examined me and knocked me about for full three quarters of an hour, and instead of pronouncing my doom as I fully expected, he told me with a bright look and most convincing voice that he had examined many men who had worked their brains too much, but had never seen a man at my time of life so perfectly sound in every organ. I felt young and strong at once, and meeting my old friend Morier on my way home, we ate some dozens of oysters together and drank some pints of porter without the slightest bad effect. In fact I was cured without a pill or a drop of medicine.

And who does not know how, if one makes up one's mind at last to have a tooth pulled out, the pain seems to cease as soon as we pull the bell at the dentist's?

However, Hahnemann did not succeed with me. I swallowed a number of his silver and gold globules, but the migraine kept its regular course, right to left and left to right, and this went on till about the year 1860. Then my doctor, the late Mr. Symonds of Oxford, told me exactly what Hahnemann had told me—that he would cure me, if I would go on taking some medicine regularly for six months or a year. He told me that he and his brother had made a special study of headaches, and that there were ever so many kinds of headache, each requiring its own peculiar treatment. When I asked him to what category of headaches mine belonged, I was not a little abashed on being told that my headache was what they called the Alderman's headache. "Surely," I said, "I don't overeat, or overdrink." I had thought that mine was a mysterious nervous headache, arising from the brain. But no, it seemed to be due to turtle soup and port wine. However, the doctor, seeing my surprise, comforted me by telling me that it was the nerves of the head which affected the stomach, and thus produced indirectly the same disturbance in my digestion as an aldermanic diet. Whether this was true or was only meant as a *solatium* I do not know. But what I do know is, that by taking the medicine regularly for about half a year, the frequency and violence of my headaches were considerably reduced, while after about a year they vanished completely. I was a new being, and my working time was doubled.

One lesson may be learnt from this, namely, that the English system of doctoring is very imperfect. In England we wait till we are ill, then go to a doctor, describe our symptoms as well as we can, pay one guinea, or two, get our prescription, take drastic medicine for a month and expect to be well. My German doctor, when he saw the prescription of my English doctor, told me that he would not give it to a horse. If after a month we are not better we go again; he possibly changes our medicine, and we take it more or less regularly for another month. The doctor cannot watch the effect of his medicine, he is not sure even whether his prescriptions have been carefully followed; and he knows but too well that anything like a chronic complaint requires a chronic treatment. The important thing, however, was that my headaches yielded gradually to the continued use of medicine; it would hardly have produced the desired effect if I had taken it by fits and starts. All this seems to me quite natural; but though my English doctor cured me, and my German doctors did not, I still hold that the German system is better. Most families have their doctor in Germany, who calls from time to time to watch the health of the old and young members of the family, particularly when under medical treatment, and receives his stipulated annual payment, which secures him a safe income that can be raised, of course, by attendance on occasional patients. Perhaps the Chinese system is the best; they pay their doctor while they are well, and stop payment as long as they are ill. I know the unanswerable argument which is always thrown at my head whenever I suggest to my friends that there are some things which are possibly managed better in Germany than in England. If my remarks refer to the study and practice of medicine I am asked whether more men are killed in England than in Germany; if I refer to the study and practice of law I am assured that quite as many murderers are hanged in England as in Germany; and if I venture to hint that the study of theology might on certain points be improved at Oxford, I am told that quite as many souls are saved in England as in Germany, nay, a good many more. As I cannot ascertain the facts from trustworthy statistics, I have nothing to reply; all I feel is that most nations, like most individuals, are perfect in their own eyes, but that those are most perfect who are willing to admit that there is something to be learnt from their neighbours.

But to return to Hahnemann. He was very kind to me, and I looked up to him as a giant both in body and in mind. But he could not deliver me from my enemy, the ever recurrent migraine. The cures, however, both at Dessau and at Coethen, where he had been made a *Hofrath* by the reigning Duke, were very extraordinary. Hahnemann remained in Coethen till 1835, and in that year, when he was eighty, he married a young French lady, Melanie d'Hervilly, and was carried off by her to Paris, where he soon gained a large practice, and died in 1843, that is at the age of eighty-eight. Much of his success, I feel sure, was due to his presence and to the confidence which he inspired. How do I know that Sir Andrew Clarke, seeing that I was in low spirits about my health, did not think it right to encourage me, and by encouraging me did certainly make me feel confident about myself, and thus raised my vitality, my spirits, or whatever we like to call it? "Thy faith hath made thee whole" is a lesson which doctors ought not to neglect.

How little we know the effect of the environment in which we grow up. My old granny has drawn deeper furrows through my young soul than all my teachers and preachers put together. I am not going to add a chapter to that most unsatisfactory of all studies, child-psychology. It is an impossible subject. The victim—the child—cannot be interrogated till it is too late. The influences that work on the child's senses and mind cannot be determined; they are too many, and too intangible. The observers of babies, mostly young fathers proud of their first offspring, remind me always of a very learned friend of mine, who presented to the Royal Society most laborious pages containing his lifelong observations on certain deviations of the magnetic needle, and who had forgotten that in making these observations he always had a pair of steel spectacles on his nose. However, I have nothing to say against these observations, nor against their more or less successful interpretations. But the real harm begins when people imagine that in studying the ways of infants they can discover what man was like in his original condition, whether as a hairy or a hairless creature. To imagine that we can learn from the way in which children begin to use our old words, how the primitive language of mankind was formed, seems to me like imagining that children playing with counters would teach us how and for what purpose the first money was coined. There is no doubt a grain of truth in this infantile psychology, but it requires as many caveats as that which is called ethnological psychology, which makes us see in the savages of the present day the representation of the first ancestors of our race, and would teach us to discover in their superstitions the antecedents of the mythology and religion of the Aryan or Semitic races. The same philosophers who constantly fall back on heredity and atavism in order to explain what seems inexplicable in the beliefs and customs of the Brahmans, Greeks, or Romans, seem quite unconscious of the many centuries that must needs have passed over the heads of the Patagonians of the present day as well as of the Greeks at the time of Homer. They look upon the Patagonians as the *tabula rasa* of humanity, and they forget that even if we admitted that the ancestors of the Aryan race had once been more savage than the Patagonians, it would not follow that their savagery was identical with that of the people of Tierra del Fuego. Why should not the distance between Patagonian and Vedic Rishis have been at least as great as that between Vedic Rishis and Homeric bards? If there are ever so many kinds of civilized life, was there only one and the same savagery?

To take, for instance, the feeling of fear; is it likely that we shall find out whether it is innate in human nature or acquired and intensified in each generation, by shaking our fists in the face of a little baby, to see whether it will wink or shrink or shriek? Some children may be more fearless than others, but whether that fearlessness arises from ignorance or from stolidity is again by no means easy to determine. A burnt child fears the fire, an unburnt child might boldly grasp a glowing coal, but all this would not help us to determine whether fear is an innate or an acquired tendency or habit.

All I can say for myself is that my young life and even my later years were often rendered miserable by the foolish stories of one of my grandmothers, and that I had to make a strong effort of will before I could bring myself to walk across a churchyard in the dark. This shows how much our character is shaped by circumstances, even when we are least aware of it. I did not believe in ghosts and I was not a coward, but I felt through life a kind of shiver in dark passages and at the sound of mysterious noises, and the mere fact that I had to make an effort to overcome these feelings shows that something had found its way into my mental constitution that ought never to have been there, and that caused me, particularly in my younger days, many a moment of discomfort.

All such experiences constitute what may be called the background of our life. My first ideas of men and women, and of the world at large, that is of the unknown world, were formed within the narrow walls of Dessau, for Dessau was still surrounded by walls, and the gates of the city were closed every night, though the fears of a foreign enemy were but small. Of course the views of life prevailing at Dessau were very narrow, but they were wide enough for our purposes. Though we heard of large towns like Dresden or Berlin, and of large countries like France and Italy, my real world was Dessau and its neighbourhood. We had no interests outside the walls of our town or the frontiers of our duchy. If we heard of things that had happened at Leipzig or Berlin, in Paris or London, they had no more reality for us than what we had read about Abraham, or Romulus and Remus, or Alexander the Great. To us the pulse of the world seemed to beat in the *Haupt- und Residenzstadt* of Dessau, though we knew perfectly well how small it was in comparison with other towns.

And this, too, has left its impression on my thoughts all through life, if only by making everything that I saw in later life in such towns as Leipzig, Berlin, Paris, and London, appear quite overwhelmingly grand. Boys brought up in any of these large towns start with a different view of the world, and with a different measure for what they see in later life. I do not know that they are to be envied for that, for there is pleasure in admiration, pleasure even in being stunned by the first sight of the life in the streets of Paris or London. I certainly have been a great admirer all my life, and I ascribe this disposition to the small surroundings of my early years at Dessau.

And so it was with everything else. Having admired our Cavalier-Strasse, I could admire all the more the Boulevards in Paris, and Regent Street in London. Having enjoyed our small theatre, I stood aghast at the Grand Opera, and at Drury Lane. This power of admiration and enjoyment extended even to dinners and other domestic amusements. Having been brought up on very simple fare, I fully enjoyed the dinners which the Old East India Company gave, when we sat down about 400 people, and, as I was told, four pounds was paid for each guest. I mention this because I feel that not only has the Spartan diet of my early years given me a relish all through life for convivial entertainments, even if not quite at four pounds a head, but that the general self-denial which I had to exercise in my youth has made me feel a constant gratitude and sincere appreciation for the small comforts of my later years.

I remember the time when I woke with my breath frozen on my bedclothes into a thin sheet of ice. We were expected to wash and dress in an attic where the windows were so thickly frozen as to admit hardly any light in the morning, and where, when we tried to break the ice in the jug, there were only a few drops of water left at the bottom with which to wash. No wonder that the ablutions were expeditious. After they were performed we had our speedy breakfast, consisting of a cup of coffee and a *semmel* or roll, and then we rushed to school, often through the snow that had not yet been swept away from the pavement. We sat in school from eight to eleven or twelve, rushed home again, had our very simple dinner, and then back to school, from two to four. How we lived through it I sometimes wonder, for we were thinly clad and often wet with rain or snow; and yet we enjoyed our life as boys only can enjoy it, and had no time to be ill. One blessing this early roughing has left me for life—a power of enjoying many things which to most of my friends are matters of course or of no consequence. The background of my life at Dessau and at Leipzig may seem dark, but it has only served to make the later years of my life all the brighter and warmer.

The more I think about that distant, now very distant past, the more I feel how, without being aware of it, my whole character was formed by it. The unspoiled primitiveness of life at Dessau as it was when I was at school there till the age of twelve, would be extremely difficult to describe in all its details. Everybody seemed to know everybody and everything about everybody. Everybody knew that he was watched, and gossip, in the best sense of the word, ruled supreme in the little town. Gossip was, in fact, public opinion with all its good and all its bad features. Still the result was that no one could afford to lose caste, and that everybody behaved as well as he could. I really believe that the private life of the people of Dessau at the beginning of the century was blameless. The great evils of society did not exist, and if now and then there was a black sheep, his or her life became a burden to them. Everybody knew what had happened, and society being on the whole so blameless, was all the more merciless on the sinners, whether their sins were great or small. So from the very first my idea was that there were only two classes—one class quite perfect and pure as angels, the other black sheep, and altogether unspeakable. There was no transition, no intermediate links, no shading of light and dark. A man was either black or white, and this rigid rule applied not only to moral character, but intellectual excellence also was measured by the same standard. A work of art was either superlatively beautiful, or it was contemptible. A man of science was either a giant or a humbug. Some people spoke of Goethe as the greatest of all poets and philosophers the world had ever known; others called him a wicked man and an overvalued poet.[1]

It is dangerous, no doubt, to go through life with so imperfect a measure, and I have for a long time suffered from it, particularly in cases where I ought to have been able to make allowance for small failings. But as I had been brought up to approach people with a complete trust in their rectitude, and with an unlimited admiration of their genius, it took me many years before I learnt to make allowance for human weaknesses or temporary failures. I have lost many a charming companion and excellent friend in my journey through life, because I weighed them with my rusty Dessau balance. I had to learn by long experience that there may be a spot, nay, several spots on the soft skin of a peach,

[1] That this was not only the case at Dessau, may be seen by a number of contemporary reviews of Goethe's works republished some years ago and the exact title of which I cannot find.

and yet the whole fruit may be perfect. I acted very much like the merchant who tested a whole field of rice by the first handful of grains, and who, if he found one or two bad grains, would have nothing to do with the whole field. I had to learn what was, perhaps, the most difficult lesson of all, that a trusted friend could not always be trusted, and yet need not therefore be altogether a reprobate. What was most difficult for me to digest was an untruth: finding out that one who professed to be a friend had said and done most unfriendly things behind one's back. Still, in a long life one finds out that even that may not be a deadly sin, and that if we are so loth to forgive it, it is partly because the falsehood affected our own interests. Thus only can we explain how a man whom we know to have been guilty of falsehoods towards ourselves may be looked upon as perfectly honest, straightforward, and trustworthy, by a large number of his own friends. We see this over and over again with men occupying eminent positions in Church and State. We see how a prime minister or an archbishop is represented by men who know him as a liar and a hypocrite, while by others he is spoken of as a paragon of honour and honesty, and a true Christian. My narrow Dessau views became a little widened when I went to school at Leipzig; still more when I spent two years and a half at the University of Leipzig, and afterwards at Berlin. Still, during all this time I saw but little of what is called society, I only knew of people whom I loved and of people whom I disliked. There was no room as yet for indifferent people, whom one tolerates and is civil to without caring whether one sees them again or not. Of the simplest duties of society also I was completely ignorant. No one ever told me what to say and what to do, or what not to say and what not to do. What I felt I said, what I thought right I did. There was, in fact, in my small native town very little that could be called society. One lived in one's family and with one's intimate friends without any ceremony. It is a pity that children are not taught a few rules of life-wisdom by their seniors. I know that the Jews do not neglect that duty, and I remember being surprised at my young Jewish friends at Dessau coming out with some very wise saws which evidently had not been grown in their own hot-houses, but had been planted out full grown by their seniors. The only rules of worldly wisdom which I remember, came to me through proverbs and little verses which we had either to copy or to learn by heart, such as:

> "Wer einmal lügt, dem glaubt man nicht
> Und wenn er auch die Wahrheit spricht."

> "Morgenstunde hat Gold im Munde."

> "Kein Faden ist so fein gesponnen,
> Er kommt doch endlich an die Sonnen."

> "Jeder ist seines Glückes Schmied."

Some lines which hung over my bed I have carried with me all through life, and I still think they are very true and very terse:

> "Im Glück nicht jubeln und im Sturm nicht zagen,
> Das Unvermeidliche mit Würde tragen,
> Das Rechte thun, am Schönen sich erfreuen,
> Das Leben lieben und den Tod nicht scheuen,
> Und fest an Gott und bessere Zukunft glauben,
> Heisst leben, heisst dem Tod sein Bitteres rauben."

Still, all this formed a very small viaticum for a journey through life, and I often thought that a few more hints might have preserved me from the painful process of what was called rubbing off one's horns. Again and again I had to say to myself, "That would have done very well at home, but it was a mistake for all that." My social rawness and simplicity stuck to me for many years, just as the Dessau dialect remained with me for life; at least I was assured by my friends that though I had spoken French and English for so many years, they could always detect in my German that I came from Dessau or Leipzig.

CHAPTER III

SCHOOL-DAYS AT LEIPZIG

It was certainly a poor kind of armour in which I set out from Dessau. My mother, devoted as she was to me, had judged rightly that it was best for me to be with other boys and under the supervision of a man. I had been somewhat spoiled by her passionate love, and also by her passionate severity in correcting the ordinary naughtinesses of a boy. So having risen from form to form in the school at Dessau, I was sent, at the age of twelve, to Leipzig, to live in the house of Professor Carus and attend the famous Nicolai-Schule with his son, who was of the same age as myself and who likewise wanted a companion. It was thought that there would be a certain emulation between us, and so, no doubt, there was, though we always remained the best of friends. The house in which we lived stood in a garden and was really an orthopaedic institution for girls. There were about twenty or thirty of these young girls living in the house or spending the day there, and their joyous company was very pleasant. Of course the names and faces of my young friends have, with one or two exceptions, vanished from my memory, but I was surprised when a few years ago (1895) I was staying with Madame Salis-Schwabe at her delightful place on the Menai Straits, and discovered that we had known each other more than fifty years before in the house of Professor Carus at Leipzig. Though we had met from time to time, we never knew of our early meeting at Leipzig, till in comparing notes we discovered how we had spent a whole year in the same house and among the same friends. Hers has been a life full of work and entirely devoted to others. To the very end of her days she was spending her large income in founding schools on the system recommended by Froebel, not only in England, but in Italy. She died at Naples in 1896, while visiting a large school that had been founded by her with the assistance of the Italian Government. Her own house in Wales was full of treasures of art, and full of memorials of her many friends, such as Bunsen, Renan, Mole, Ary Scheffer, and many more. How far her charity went may be judged by her being willing to part with some of the most precious of Ary Scheffer's pictures, in order to keep her schools well endowed, and able to last after her death, which she felt to be imminent.

Public schools are nearly all day schools in Germany. The boys live at home, mostly in their own families, but they spend six hours every day at school, and it is a mistake to imagine that they are not attached to it, that they have no games together, and that they do not grow up manly or independent. Most schools have playgrounds, and in summer swimming is a favourite amusement for all the boys. There were two good public schools at Leipzig, the Nicolai School and the Thomas School. There was plenty of *esprit de corps* in them, and often when the boys met it showed itself not only in words but in blows, and the discussions over the merits of their schools were often continued in later life. I was very fortunate in being sent to the Nicolai School, under Dr. Nobbe as head master. He was at the same time Professor at the University of Leipzig, and is well known in England also as the editor of Cicero. He was very proud that his school counted Leibniz [1] among its former pupils. He was a classical scholar of the old school. During the last three years of our school life we had to write plenty of Latin and Greek verse, and were taught to speak Latin. The speaking of Latin came readily enough, but the verses never attained a very high level. Besides Nobbe we had Forbiger, well known by his books on ancient geography, and Palm, editor of the same Greek Dictionary which, in the hands of Dr. Liddell, has reached its highest perfection. Then there was Funkhänel, known beyond Germany by his edition of the Orations of Demosthenes, and his studies on Greek orators. We were indeed well off for masters, and most of them seemed to enjoy their

[1] His own spelling of his name.

work and to be fond of the boys. Our head master was very popular. He was a man of the old German type, powerfully built, with a large square head, very much like Luther, and, strange to say, when in 1839 a great Luther festival was celebrated all over Germany, he published a book in which he proved that he was a direct descendant of Luther.

The school was carried on very much on the old plan of teaching chiefly classics, but teaching them thoroughly. Modern languages, mathematics, and physical science had a poor chance, though they clamoured for recognition. Latin and Greek verse were considered far more important. In the two highest forms we had to speak Latin, and such as it was it seemed to us much easier than to speak French. Hebrew was also taught as an optional subject during the last four years, and the little I know of Hebrew dates chiefly from my school-days. Schoolboys soon find out what their masters think of the value of the different subjects taught at school, and they are apt to treat not only the subjects themselves but the teachers also according to that standard. Hence our modern language and our physical science masters had a hard time of it. They could not keep their classes in order, and it was by no means unusual for many of the boys simply to stay away from their lessons. The old mathematical master, before beginning his lesson, used to rub his spectacles, and after looking round the half empty classroom, mutter in a plaintive voice: "I see again many boys who are not here to-day." When the same old master began to lecture on physical science, he told the boys to bring a frog to be placed under a glass from which the air had been extracted by an air-pump. Of course every one of the twenty or thirty boys brought two or three frogs, and when the experiment was to be made all these frogs were hopping about the lecture-room, and the whole army of boys were hopping after them over chairs and tables to catch them. No wonder that during this tumult the master did not succeed with his experiment, and when at last the glass bowl was lifted up and we were asked to see the frog, great was the joy of all the boys when the frog hopped out and escaped from the hands of its executioner. Such was the wrath excited by these new-fangled lectures among the boys that they actually committed the vandalism of using one of the forms as a battering-ram against the enclosure in which the physical science apparatus was kept, and destroyed some of the precious instruments supplied by Government. Severe punishments followed, but they did not serve to make physical science more popular.

We certainly did very well in Greek and Latin, and read a number of classical texts, not only critically at school, but also cursorily at home, having to give a weekly account of what we had thus read by ourselves. I liked my classics, and yet I could not help feeling that there was a certain exaggeration in the way in which every one of them was spoken of by our teachers, nay, that as compared to German poets and prose writers they were somewhat overpraised. Still, it would have been very conceited not to admire what our masters admired, and as in duty bound we went into the usual raptures about Homer and Sophocles, about Horace and Cicero. Many things which in later life we learn to admire in the classics could hardly appeal to the taste of boys. The directness, the simplicity and originality of the ancient, as compared with modern writers, cannot be appreciated by them, and I well remember being struck with what we disrespectful boys called the cheekiness of Horace expecting immortality (*non omnis moriar*) for little poems which we were told were chiefly written after Greek patterns. We had to admit that there were fewer false quantities in his Latin verses than in our own, but in other respects we could not see that his odes were so infinitely superior to ours. His hope of immortality has certainly been fulfilled beyond what could have been his own expectations. With so little of ancient history known to him, his idea of the immortality of poetry must have been far more modest in his time than in our own. He may have known the past glories of the Persian Empire, but as to ancient literature, there was nothing for him to know, whether in Persia, in Babylonia, in Assyria, or even in Egypt, least of all in India. Literary fame existed for him in Greece only, and in the Roman Empire, and his own ambition could therefore hardly have extended beyond these limits. The exaggeration in the panegyrics passed on everything Greek or Latin dates from the classical scholars of the Middle Ages, who knew nothing that could be compared to the classics, and who were loud in praising what they possessed the monopoly of selling. Successive generations of scholars followed suit, so that even in our time it seemed high treason to compare Goethe with Horace, or Schiller with Sophocles. Of late, however, the danger is rather that the reaction should go too far and lead to a promiscuous depreciation even of such real giants as Lucretius or Plato. The fact is that we have learnt from them and imitated them, till in some cases the imitations have equalled or even excelled the originals, while now the taste for classical correctness has been wellnigh supplanted by an appetite for what is called realistic, original, and extravagant.

With all that has been said or written against making classical studies the most important element in a liberal education, or rather against retaining them in their time-honoured position, nothing has as yet been suggested to take their place. For after all, it is not simply in order to learn two languages that we devote so large a share of our time to the study of Greek and Latin; it is in order to learn to understand the old world on which our modern world is founded; it is in order to think the old thoughts, which are the feeders of our own intellectual life, that we become in our youth the pupils of Greeks and Romans. In order to know what we are, we have to learn how we have come to be what we are. Our very languages form an unbroken chain between us and Cicero and Aristotle, and in order to use many of our words intelligently, we must know the soil from which they sprang, and the atmosphere in which they grew up and developed.

I enjoyed my work at school very much, and I seem to have passed rapidly from class to class. I frequently received prizes both in money and in books, but I see a warning attached to some of them that I ought not to be conceited, which probably meant no more than that I should not show when I was pleased with my successes. At least I do not know what I could have been conceited about. What I feel about my learning at school is that it was entirely passive. I acquired knowledge such as it was presented to me. I did not doubt whatever my teachers taught me, I did not, as far as I can recollect, work up any subject by myself. I find only one paper of mine of that early time, and, curiously enough, it was on mythology; but it contains no inkling of comparative mythology, but simply a chronological arrangement of the sources from which we draw our knowledge of Greek mythology. I see also from some old papers, that I began to write poetry, and that twice or thrice I was chosen at great festivities to recite poems written by myself. In the year 1839 three hundred years had passed since Luther preached at Leipzig in the Church of St. Nicolai, and the tercentenary of this event was celebrated all over Germany. My poem was selected for recitation at a large meeting of the friends of our school and the notables of the town, and I had to recite it, not without fear and trembling. I was then but sixteen years of age.

In the next year, 1840, Leipzig celebrated the invention of printing in 1440. It was on this occasion that Mendelssohn wrote his famous *Hymn of Praise.* I formed part of the chorus, and I well remember the magnificent effect which the music produced in the Church of St. Thomas. Again a poem of mine was selected, and I had to recite it at a large gathering in the Nicolai-Schule on July 18, 1840.

On December 23 another celebration took place at our school, at which I had to recite a Latin poem of mine, *In Schillerum.* Lastly, there was my valedictory poem when I left the school in 1841, and a Latin poem "Ad Nobbium," our head master.

I have found among my mother's treasures the far too often flattering testimonial addressed to her by Professor Nobbe on that occasion, which ends thus: "I rejoice at seeing him leave this school with testimonials of moral excellence not often found in one of his years—and possessed of knowledge in more than one point, first-rate, and of intellectual capacities excellent throughout. May his young mind develop more and more, may the fruits of his labours hereafter be a comfort to his mother for the sorrows and cares of the past."

It was rather hard on me that I had to pass my examination for admission to the University (*Abiturienten-Examen*) not at my own school, but at Zerbst in Anhalt. This was necessary in order to enable me to obtain a scholarship from the Anhalt Government. The schools in Anhalt were modelled after the Prussian schools, and laid far more stress on mathematics, physical science, and modern languages than the schools in Saxony. I had therefore to get up in a very short time several quite new subjects, and did not do so well in them as in Greek and Latin. However, I passed with a first class, and obtained my scholarship, small as it was. It was only the other day that I received a letter from a gentleman who was at school at Zerbst when I came there for my examination. He reminds me that among my examiners there were such men as Dr. Ritter, the two Sentenis, and Professor Werner, and he says that he watched me when I came upstairs and entered the locked room to do my paper work. My friend's career in life had been that of Director of a Life Insurance Company, probably a more lucrative career than what mine has been.

During my stay at Leipzig, first in the house of Professor Carus, and afterwards as a student at the University, my chief enjoyment was certainly

Walker & Cockerell ph. sc.

F. Max Müller
Aged 14.

music. I had plenty of it, perhaps too much, but I pity the man who has not known the charm of it. At that time Leipzig was really the centre of music in Germany. Felix Mendelssohn was there, and most of the distinguished artists and composers of the day came there to spend some time with him and to assist at the famous Gewandhaus Concerts. I find among my letters a few descriptions of concerts and other musical entertainments, which even at present may be of some interest. I was asked to be present at some concerts where quartettes and other pieces were performed by Mendelssohn, Hiller, Kaliwoda, David, and Eckart. Liszt also made his triumphant entry into Germany at Leipzig, and everybody was full of expectation and excitement. His concert had been advertised long before his arrival. It was to consist of an Overture of Weber's; a Cavatina from *Robert le Diable*, sung by Madame Schlegel; a Concerto of Weber's, to be played by Liszt, the same which I had shortly before heard played by Madame Pleyel; Beethoven's Overture to *Prometheus;* Fantasia on *La Juive;* Schubert's *Ave Maria* and *Serenade*, as arranged by Liszt. I was the more delighted because I had myself played some of these pieces. But suddenly there appeared a placard stating that Liszt, on hearing that tickets were sold at one thaler (three shillings), had declared he would play a few pieces only and without an orchestra. In spite of that disappointment, the whole house was full, the staircase crowded from top to bottom, and when we had pushed our way through, we found that about 300 places had been retained for one and a half thalers (four shillings and sixpence), while tickets at the box-office were sold for two thalers (six shillings). Nevertheless, I managed to get a very good place, by simply not seeing a number of ladies who were pushing behind me. When Liszt appeared there was a terrible hissing—he looked as if petrified, glanced like a demon at the public, but nevertheless began to play the Scherzo and Finale of the Pastoral Symphony. Then there burst out a perfect thunder of applause, and all seemed pacified, while Madame Schmidt sang a song accompanied by a certain Mr. Kermann. As soon as that was over, a new storm of hisses arose, which was meant for this Mr. Kermann, who was a pupil, but at the same time the man of business of Liszt. He and three other men had made all arrangements, and Liszt knew nothing about them, as he cared very little for the money, which went chiefly to his managers. A Fantasia by Liszt followed, and lastly a *Galop Chromatique*—but the public would not go away, and at length Liszt was induced to play *Une grande Valse.* It was no doubt a new experience; but I could not go into ecstasies like others, for after all it was merely mechanical, though no doubt in the highest perfection. The day after Liszt advertised that his original Programme would be played, but at six o'clock Professor Carus, with whom I lived, was called to see Liszt, who was said to be ill; the fact being he had only sold fifty tickets at the raised prices. Many strangers who had come to Leipzig to hear him went away, anything but pleased with the new musical genius. At one concert, where he appeared in Magyar costume, the ladies offered him a golden laurel wreath and sword. He had just published his arrangement of *Adelaida*, which he promised to play in one of the concerts.

Another very musical family at Leipzig was that of Professor Fröge. He was a rich man, and had married a famous singer, Fräulein Schlegel. One evening the *Sonnambula* was performed in their house, which had been changed into a theatre. She acted the Sonnambula, and her singing as well as her acting was most finished and delightful. Mendelssohn was much in their house, and made her sing his songs as soon as they were written and before they were published. They were great friends, the bond of their friendship being music. He actually died when playing while she was singing. People talked as they always will talk about what they cannot understand, but they evidently did not know either Mendelssohn or Madame Fröge.

The house of Professor Carus was always open to musical geniuses, and many an evening men like Hiller, Mendelssohn, David, Eckart, &c., came there to play, while Madame Carus sang, and sang most charmingly. I too was asked sometimes to play at these evening parties. I see that Ernst gave a concert at Leipzig, and no doubt his execution was admirable. Still, I could not understand what David meant when he declared that after hearing Ernst he would throw his own instrument into the fire.

Mendelssohn, who was delighted with Liszt—and no one could judge him better than he—gave a soirée in honour of him. About 400 people were invited—I among the rest, being one of the tenors who sang in the Oratorio that Hiller was then rehearsing for the first performance. I think it was the *Destruction of Babylon.* There was a complete orchestra at Mendelssohn's party, and we heard a symphony of Schubert (posthumous), Mendelssohn's psalm "As the hart pants," and his overture *Meeresstille und glückliche Fahrt.* After that there was supper for all the guests, and then followed a chorus from his *St. Paul*, and a triple concerto of Bach, played on three pianofortes by Mendelssohn, Liszt, and Hiller. It was a difficult piece—difficult to play and difficult to follow. Lastly, Liszt played his new fantasia on *Lucia di Lammermoor*, and his arrangement of the *Erlkönig.* All was really perfect; and hearing so much music, I became more and more absorbed in it. I even gave some concerts with Grabau, a great violoncellist, at Merseburg, and at a Count Arnim's, a very rich nobleman near Merseburg, who had invited Liszt for one evening and paid him 100 ducats. This seemed at that time a very large sum, almost senseless. As a ducat was about nine shillings, it was after all only £45, which would not seem excessive at present for an artist such as Liszt.

I also heard Thalberg at Leipzig. They all came to see Mendelssohn, and I believe did their best to please him. At that time my idea of devoting myself altogether to the study of music became very strong; and as Professor Carus married again, I proposed to leave Leipzig, and to enter the musical school of Schneider at Dessau. But nothing came of that, and I think on the whole it was as well.

While at school at Leipzig I had but little opportunity of travelling, for my mother was always anxious to have me home during the holidays, and I was equally anxious to be with her and to see my relations at Dessau. Generally I went in a wretched carriage from Leipzig to Dessau. It was only seven German miles (about thirty-five English miles), but it took a whole day to get there; and during part of the journey, when we had to cross the deep and desert-like sands, walking on foot was much more expeditious than sitting inside the carriage. But then we paid only one thaler for the whole journey, and sometimes, in order to save that, I walked on foot the whole way. That also took me a whole day; but when I tried it the first time, being then quite young and rather delicate in health, I had to give in about an hour before I came to Dessau, my legs refusing to go further, and my muscles being cramped and stiff from exertion, I had to sit down by the road. During one vacation I remember exploring the valley of the Mulde with some other boys. We travelled for about a fortnight from village to village, and lived in the simplest way. A more ambitious journey I took in 1841 with a friend of mine, Baron von Hagedorn. He was a curious and somewhat mysterious character. He had been brought up by a great-aunt of mine, to whom he was entrusted as a baby. No one knew his parents, but they must have been rich, for he possessed a large fortune. He had a country place near Munich, and he spent the greater part of the year in travelling about, and amusing himself. He had been brought up with my mother and other members of our family, and he took a very kind interest in me. I see from my letters that in 1841 he took me from Dessau to Coethen, Brunswick, and Magdeburg. At Brunswick we saw the picture gallery, the churches, and the tomb of Schill, one of the German volunteers in the War of Independence against France. We also explored Hildesheim, saw the rose-tree planted, as we were told, by Charlemagne; then proceeded to Göttingen, and saw its famous library. We passed through Minden, where the Fulda and Werra join, and arrived late at Cassel. From Cassel we explored Wilhelmshöhe, the beautiful park where thirty years later Napoleon III was kept as a prisoner.

Hagedorn, with all his love of mystery and occasional exaggeration, was certainly a good friend to me. He often gave me good advice, and was more of a father to me than a mere friend. He was a man of the world; and he forgot that I never meant to be a man of the world, and therefore his advice was not always what I wanted. He was also a great friend of my cousin who was married to a Prince of Dessau, and they had agreed among themselves that I should go to the Oriental Academy at Vienna, learn Oriental languages, and then enter the diplomatic service. As there were no children from the Prince's marriage, I was to be adopted by him, and, as if the princely fortune was not enough to tempt me, I was told that even a wife had been chosen for me, and that I should have a new name and title, after being adopted by the Prince. To other young men this might have seemed irresistible. I at once said no. It seemed to interfere with my freedom, with my studies, with my ideal of a career in life; in fact, though everything was presented to me by my cousin as on a silver tray, I shook my head and remained true to my first love, Sanskrit and all the rest. Hagedorn could not understand this; he thought a brilliant life preferable to the quiet life of a professor. Not so I. He little knew where true happiness was to be found, and he was often in a very melancholy mood. He did not live long, but I shall never forget how much I owed him. When I went to Paris, he allowed me to live in his rooms. They were, it is true, *au cinquième*, but they were in the best quarter of Paris, in the Rue Royale St. Honoré, opposite the Madeleine, and very prettily furnished. This kept me from living in dusty lodgings in the Quartier Latin, and the five flights of stairs may have strengthened my lungs. I well remember what it was when at the foot of the staircase I saw that I had forgotten my handkerchief and had to toil up again. But in those days one did not know what it meant to be tired. Whether my friends grumbled, I cannot tell, but I myself pitied some of them who were old and gouty when they arrived at my door out of breath.

CHAPTER IV

UNIVERSITY

In order to enable me to go to the University, my mother and sister moved to Leipzig and kept house for me during all the time I was there—that is, for two years and a half. In spite of the *res angusta domi*, I enjoyed my student-life thoroughly, while my home was made very agreeable by my mother and sister. My mother was full of resource, and she was wise enough not to interfere with my freedom. My sister, who was about two years older than myself, was most kind-hearted and devoted both to me and to our mother. There was nothing selfish in her, and we three lived together in perfect love, peace, and harmony. My sister enjoyed what little there was of society, whereas I kept sternly aloof from it. She was much admired, and soon became engaged to a young doctor, Dr. A. Krug, the son of the famous professor of philosophy at Leipzig, whose works, particularly his *Dictionary of Philosophy*, hold a distinguished place in the history of German philosophy. He was a thorough patriot, and so public spirited that he thought it right to leave a considerable sum of money to the University, without making sufficient provision for his children. However, the young married couple lived happily at Chemnitz, and my sister was proud in the possession of her children. It was the sudden death of several of these children that broke her heart and ruined her health; she died very young. Standing by the grave of her children, she said to me shortly before her death, "Half of me is dead already, and lies buried there; the other half will soon follow."

Of society, in the ordinary sense of the word, I saw hardly anything. I am afraid I was rather a bear, and declined even to invest in evening dress. I joined a student club which formed part of the *Burschenschaft*, but which in order to escape prosecution adopted the title of *Gemeinschaft*. I went there in the evening to drink beer and smoke, and I made some delightful acquaintances and friendships. What fine characters were there, often behind a very rough exterior! My dearest friend was Prowe, of Thorn in East Prussia—so honest, so true, so straightforward, so over-conscientious in the smallest things. He was a classical scholar, and later on entered the Prussian educational service. As a master at the principal school at Thorn his time was fully occupied, and of course he was cut off there from the enlivening influences of literary society. Still he kept up his interest in higher questions, and published some extremely valuable books on Copernicus, a native of Thorn, for which he received the thanks of astronomers and historians, and flattering testimonials from learned societies. We met but seldom later in life, and my own life in England was so busy and full that even our correspondence was not regular. But I met him once more at Ems with a charming wife, and decidedly happy in his own sphere of activity. These early friendships form the distant landscape of life on which we like to dwell when the present ceases to absorb all our thoughts. Our memory dwells on them as a golden horizon, and there remains a constant yearning which makes us feel the incompleteness of this life. After all, the number of our true friends is small; and yet how few even of that small number remain with us for life. There are other faces and other names that rise from beyond the clouds which more and more divide us from our early years.

There were some wild spirits among us who fretted at the narrow-minded policy which went by the name of the Metternich system. Repression was the panacea which Metternich recommended to all the governments of Germany, large and small. No doubt the system of keeping things quiet secured to Germany and to Europe at large a thirty years' peace, but it could not prevent the accumulation of inflammable material which, after several threatenings, burst forth at last in the conflagration of 1848. Among my friends I remember several who were ready for the wildest schemes in order to have Germany united, respected abroad, and under constitutional government at home. Splendid fellows they were, but they either ended their days within the walls of a prison, or had to throw up everything and migrate to America. What has become of them? Some have risen to the surface in America, others have yielded to the inevitable and become peaceful citizens at home; nay, I am grieved to say, have even accepted service under Government to spy on their former friends and fellow-dreamers. But not a few saw the whole of their life wrecked either in prison or in poverty, though they had done no wrong, and in many cases were the finest characters it has been my good fortune to know. They were before their time, the fruit was not ripe as it was in 1871, but Germany certainly lost some of her best sons in those miserable years; and if my father escaped this political persecution, it was probably due to the influence of the reigning Duke and the Duchess, a Princess of Prussia, who knew that he was not a dangerous man, and not likely to blow up the German Diet.

I myself got a taste of prison life for the offence of wearing the ribbon of a club which the police regarded with disfavour. I cannot say that either the disgrace or the discomfort of my two days' durance vile weighed much with me, as my friends were allowed free access to me, and came and drank beer and smoked cigars in my cell—of course at my expense—but what I dreaded was the loss of my stipendium or scholarship, which alone enabled me to continue my studies at Leipzig, and which, as a rule, was forfeited for political offences. On my release from prison I went to the Rector of the University and explained to him the circumstances of the case—how I had been arrested simply for membership of a suspected club. I assured him that I was innocent of any political propaganda, and that the loss of my stipendium would entail my leaving the University. Much to my relief, the old gentleman replied: "I have heard nothing about this; and if I do, how am I to know that it refers to you, there are many Müllers in the University?" Fortunately the distinctive prefix Max had not yet been added to my name.

I must confess that I and my boon companions were sometimes guilty of practices which in more modern days, and certainly at Oxford or Cambridge, would be far more likely to bring the culprits into collision with the authorities than mere membership of societies in which comparatively harmless political talk was indulged in.

Duelling was then, as it is now, a favourite pastime among the students; and though not by nature a brawler, I find that in my student days at Leipzig I fought three duels, of two of which I carry the marks to the present day.

I remember that on one occasion before the introduction of cabs we hired all the sedan-chairs in Leipzig, with their yellow-coated porters, and went in procession through the streets, much to the astonishment of the good citizens, and annoyance also, as they were unable to hire any means of conveyance till a peremptory stop was put to our fun. Not content with this exploit, when the first cabs were introduced into Leipzig, thirty or forty being put on the street at first, I and my friends secured the use of all of them for the day, and proceeded out into the country. The inhabitants who were eagerly looking forward to a drive in one of the new conveyances were naturally annoyed at finding themselves forestalled, and the result was that a stop was put to such freaks in future by the issue of a police regulation that nobody was allowed to hire more than two cabs at a time.

Very innocent amusements, if perhaps foolish, but very happy days all the same; and it must be remembered that we had just emerged from the strict discipline of a German school into the unrestricted liberty of German university life.

It is in every respect a great jump from a German school to a German university. At school a boy even in the highest form, has little choice. All his lessons are laid down for him; he has to learn what he is told, whether he likes it or not. Few only venture on books outside the prescribed curriculum. There is an examination at the end of every half-year, and a boy must pass it well in order to get into a higher form. Boys at a public school (gymnasium), if they cannot pass their examination at the proper time, are advised to go to another school, and to prepare for a career in which classical languages are of less importance.

I must say at once that when I matriculated at Leipzig, in the summer of 1841, I was still very young and very immature. I had determined to study philology, chiefly Greek and Latin, but the fare spread out by the professors was much too tempting. I read Greek and Latin without difficulty; I often read classical authors without ever attempting to translate them; I also wrote and spoke Latin easily. Some of the professors lectured in Latin, and at our academic societies Latin was always spoken. I soon became a member of the classical seminary under Gottfried Hermann, and of the Latin Society under Professor Haupt. Admission to these seminaries and societies was obtained by submitting essays, and it was no doubt a distinction to belong to them. It was also useful, for not only had we to write essays and discuss them with the other members, generally teachers, and with the professor, but we could also get some useful advice from the professor for our private studies. In that respect the German universities do very little for the students, unless one has the good fortune to belong to one of these societies. The young men are let loose, and they can choose whatever lectures they want. I still have my *Collegien-Buch*, in which every professor has to attest what lectures one has attended. The number of lectures on various subjects which I attended is quite amazing, and

I should have attended still more if the honorarium had not frightened me away. Every professor lectured *publice* and *privatim*, and for the more important courses, four lectures a week, he charged ten shillings, for more special courses less or nothing. This seems little, but it was often too much for me; and if one added these honoraria to the salary of a popular professor, his income was considerable, and was more than the income of most public servants. I have known professors who had four or five hundred auditors. This gave them £250 twice a year, and that, added to their salary, was considered a good income at that time. All this has been much changed. Salaries have been raised, and likewise the honoraria, so that I well remember the case of Professor von Savigny, who, when he was chosen Minister of Justice at Berlin, declared that he would gladly accept if only his salary was raised to what his income had been as Professor of Law. Of course, professors of Arabic or Sanskrit were badly off, and *Privatdocenten* (tutors) fared still worse, but the *professores ordinarii*, particularly if they lectured on an obligatory subject and were likewise examiners, were very well off. In fact, it struck me sometimes as very unworthy of them to keep a *famulus*, a student who had to tell every one who wished to hear a distinguished professor once or twice, that he would not allow him to come a third time.

One great drawback of the professorial system is

certainly the small measure of personal advice that a student may get from the professors. Unless he is known to them personally, or has gained admission to their societies or seminaries, the young student or freshman is quite bewildered by the rich fare in the shape of lectures that is placed before him. Some students, no doubt, particularly in their early terms, solve this difficulty by attending none at all, and there is no force to make them do so, except the examinations looming in the distance. But there are many young men most anxious to learn, only they do not know where to begin. I open my old *Collegien-Buch* and I find that in the first term or Semester I attended the following lectures, and I may say I attended them regularly, took careful notes, and read such books as were recommended by the professors. I find

1. The first book of Thucydides .	Gottfried Hermann.
2. On Scenic Antiquities . .	The same.
3. On Propertius . . .	P. M. Haupt.
4. History of German Literature	The same.
5. The Ranae of Aristophanes .	Stallbaum.
6. Disputatorium (in Latin) .	Nobbe.
7. Aesthetics	Weisse.
8. Anthropology	Lotze.
9. Systems of Harmonic Composition	Fink.
10. Hebrew Grammar . . .	Fürst.
11. Demosthenes	Westermann.
12. Psychology	Heinroth.

This was enough for the summer half-year. Except Greek and Latin, the other subjects were entirely new to me, and what I wanted was to get an idea of what I should like to study. It may be interesting to add the other Semesters as far as I have them in my *Collegien-Buch*.

13. Aeschyli Persae	Hermann.
14. On Criticism	The same.
15. German Grammar . . .	Haupt.
16. Walther von der Vogelweide .	The same.
17. Tacitus, Agricola, and De Oratoribus	The same.
18. On Hegel	Weisse.
19. Disputatorium (Latin) . .	Nobbe.
20. Modern History . . .	Wachsmuth.
21. Sanskrit Grammar . .	Brockhaus.
22. Latin Society	Haupt.

Then follows the summer term of 1842.

23. Pindar	Hermann.
24. Nibelungen	Haupt.
25. Nala	Brockhaus.
26. History of Oriental Literature	The same.
27. Arabic Grammar . . .	Fleischer.
28. Latin Society	Haupt.
29. Plauti Trinumus . . .	Becker.

Winter term, 1842.

30. Prabodha Chandrodaya .	Brockhaus.
31. History of Indian Literature .	The same.
32. Aristophanes' Vespae . .	Hermann.
33. Plauti Rudens . . .	The same.
34. Greek Syntax	The same.
35. Juvenal	Becker.
36. Metaphysics and Logic .	Weisse.
37. Philosophy of History .	The same.

38.	Greek and Latin Seminary .	Hermann & Klotze.
39.	Latin Society	Haupt.
40.	Philosophical Society . .	Weisse.
41.	Philosophical Society . .	Drobisch.

Summer term, 1843.

42.	Greek and Latin Seminary .	Hermann & Klotze.
43.	Philosophical Society . .	Drobisch.
44.	Philosophical Society . .	Weisse.
45.	Soma-deva	Brockhaus.
46.	Hitopadesa	The same.
47.	History of Greeks and Romans	Wachsmuth.
48.	History of Civilization . .	The same.
49.	History after the Fifteenth Century	Flathe.
50.	History of Ancient Philosophy	Niedner.

Winter term, 1843–4.

51.	Rig-veda . . .	Brockhaus.
52.	Elementa Persica . . .	Fleischer.
53.	Greek and Latin Seminary .	Hermann & Klotze.

Here my *Collegien-Buch* breaks off, the fact being that I was preparing to go to Berlin to hear the lectures of Bopp and Schelling.

It will be clear from the above list that I certainly attempted too much. I ought either to have devoted all my time to classical studies exclusively, or carried on my philosophical studies more systematically. I confess that, delighted as I was with Gottfried Hermann and Haupt as my guides and teachers in classics, I found little that could rouse my enthusiasm for Greek and Latin literature, and I always required a dose of that to make me work hard. Everything seemed to me to have been done, and there was no virgin soil left to the plough, no ruins on which to try one's own spade. Hermann and Haupt gave me work to do, but it was all in the critical line—the genealogical relation of various MSS., or, again, the peculiarities of certain poets, long before I had fully grasped their general character. What Latin vowels could or could not form elision in Horace, Propertius, or Ovid, was a subject that cost me much labour, and yet left very small results as far as I was personally concerned. One clever conjecture, or one indication to show that one MS. was dependent on the other, was rewarded with a Doctissime or Excellentissime, but a paper on Aeschylus and his view of a divine government of the world received but a nodding approval.

They certainly taught their pupils what accuracy meant; they gave us the new idea that MSS. are not everything, unless their real value has been discovered first by finding the place which they occupy in the pedigree of the MSS. of every author. They also taught us that there are mistakes in MSS. which are inevitable, and may safely be left to conjectural emendation; that MSS. of modern date may be and often are more valuable than more ancient MSS., for the simple reason that they were copied from a still more ancient MS., and that often a badly written and hardly legible MS. proves more helpful than others written by a calligraphist, because it is the work of a scholar who copied for himself and not for the market. All these things we learnt and learnt by practical experience under Hermann and Haupt, but what we failed to acquire was a large knowledge of Greek and Latin literature, of the character of each author and of the spirit which pervaded their works. I ought to have read in Latin, Cicero, Tacitus, and Lucretius; in Greek, Herodotus, Thucydides, Plato, and Aristotle; but as I read only portions of them, my knowledge of the men themselves and their objects in life remained very fragmentary. For instance, my real acquaintance with Plato and Aristotle was confined to a few dialogues of the former and some of the logical works of the latter. The rest I learnt from such works as Ritter and Preller's *Historia Philosophiae Graecae et Romanae ex fontium locis contexta*, and from the very useful lectures of Niedner on the history of ancient philosophy. However, I thought I had to do what my professors told me, and shaped my reading so that they should approve of my work.

This must not be understood as in any way disparaging my teachers. Such an idea never entered my head at the time. People have no idea in England what kind of worship is paid by German students to their professors. To find fault with them or to doubt their *ipse dixit* never entered our minds. What they said of other classical scholars from whom they differed, as Hermann did from Otfried Müller, or Haupt from Orelli, was gospel, and remained engraved on our memory for a long time. Once when attending Hermann's lectures, another student who was sitting at the same table with me made disrespectful remarks about old Hermann. I asked him to be quiet, and when he went on with his foolish remarks, I could only stop him by calling him out. As soon as the challenge was accepted he had of course to be quiet, and a few days after we fought our duel without much damage to either of us. I only mention this because it shows what respect and admiration we felt for our professor, also because it exemplifies the usefulness of duelling in a German university, where after a challenge not another word can be said or violence be threatened even by the rudest undergraduate. A duel for a Greek conjecture may seem very absurd, but in duels of this kind all that is wanted is really a certain knowledge of fencing, care being taken that nothing serious shall happen. And yet, though that is so, the feeling of a possible danger is there, and keeps up a certain etiquette and a certain proper behaviour among men taken from all strata of society. Nor can I quite deny that when I went in the morning to a beautiful wood in the neighbourhood of Leipzig, certain misgivings were difficult to suppress. I saw myself severely wounded, possibly killed, by my antagonist, and carried to a house where my mother and sister were looking for me.

This went off when I met the large assembly of students, beautifully attired in their club uniforms, the beer barrels pushed up on one side, the surgeon and his instruments waiting on the other. There were ever so many, thirty or forty couples I think, waiting to fight their duels that morning. Some fenced extremely well, and it was a pleasure to look on; and when one's own turn came, all one thought of was how to stand one's ground boldly, and how to fence well. Some of the combatants came on horseback or in carriages, and there was a small river close by to enable us to escape if the police should have heard of our meeting. For popular as these duels are, they are forbidden and punished, and the severest punishment seemed always to be the loss of our uniforms, our arms, our flags, and our barrels of beer. However, we escaped all interference this time, and enjoyed our breakfast in the forest thoroughly, nothing happening to disturb the hilarity of the morning.

Not being satisfied with what seemed to me a mere chewing of the cud in Greek and Latin, I betook myself to systematic philosophy, and even during the first terms read more of that than of Plato and Aristotle. I belonged to the philosophical societies of Weisse, of Drobisch, and of Lotze, a membership in each of which societies entailed a considerable amount of reading and writing.

At Leipzig, Professor Drobisch represented the school of Herbart, which prided itself on its clearness and logical accuracy, but was naturally less attractive to the young spirits at the University who had heard of Hegel's Idea and looked to the dialectic process as the solution of all difficulties. I wished to know what it all meant, for I was not satisfied with mere words. There is hardly a word that has so many meanings as Idea, and I doubt whether any of the raw recruits, just escaped from school, and unacquainted with the history of philosophy, could have had any idea of what Hegel's Idea was meant for. Yet they talked about it very eloquently and very positively over their glasses of beer; and anybody who came from Berlin and could speak mysteriously or rapturously about the Idea and its evolution by the dialectic process, was listened to with silent wonder by the young Saxons, who had been brought up on Kant and Krug. The Hegelian fever was still very high at that time. It is true Hegel himself was dead (1831), and though he was supposed to have declared on his deathbed that he left only one true disciple, and that that disciple had misunderstood him, to be a Hegelian was considered a *sine qua non*, not only among philosophers, but quite as much among theologians, men of science, lawyers, artists, in fact, in every branch of human knowledge, at least in Prussia. If Christianity in its Protestant form was the state-religion of the kingdom, Hegelianism was its state-philosophy. Beginning with the Minister of Instruction down to the village schoolmaster, everybody claimed to be a Hegelian, and this was supposed to be the best road to advancement. Though Altenstein, who was then at the head of the Ministry of Instruction, began to waver in his allegiance to Hegel, even he could not resist the rush of public and of official opinion. It was he who, when a new professor of philosophy was recommended to him either by Hegel himself or by some of his followers, is reported to have said: "Gentlemen, I have read some of the young man's books, and I cannot understand a word of them. However, you are the best judges, only allow me to say that you remind me a little of the French officer who told his tailor to make his breeches as tight as possible, and dismissed him with the words: 'Enfin, si je peux y entrer, je ne les prendrai pas.' This seems to me very much what you say of your young philosopher. If I can understand his books, I am not to take him." This Hegelian fever was very much like what we have passed through ourselves at the time of the Darwinian fever; Darwin's natural evolution was looked upon very much like Hegel's dialectic process, as the general solvent of all difficulties. The most egregious nonsense was passed under that name, as it was under the name of evolution. Hegel knew very well what he meant, so did Darwin. But the empty enthusiasm of his followers became so wild that Darwin himself, the most humble of all men, became quite ashamed of it. The master, of course, was not responsible for the folly of his so-called disciples, but the result was inevitable. After the bow had been stretched to the utmost, a reaction followed, and in the case of Hegelianism, a complete collapse. Even at Berlin the popularity of Hegelianism came suddenly to an end, and after a time no truly scientific man liked to be called a Hegelian. These sudden collapses in Germany are very instructive. As long as a German professor is at the head of affairs and can do something for his pupils, his pupils are very loud in their encomiums, both in public and in private. They not only exalt him, but help to belittle all who differ from him. So it was with Hegel, so it was at a later time with Bopp, and Curtius, and other professors, particularly if they had the ear of the Minister of Education. But soon after the death of these men, particularly if another influential star was rising, the change of tone was most sudden and most surprising; even the sale of their books dwindled down, and they were referred to only as landmarks, showing the rapid advance made by living celebrities. Perhaps all this cannot be helped, as long as human nature is what it is, but it is nevertheless painful to observe.

I had the good fortune of becoming acquainted with Hegelianism through Professor Christian Weisse at Leipzig, who, though he was considered a Hegelian, was a very sober Hegelian, a critic quite as much as an admirer of Hegel. He had a very small audience, because his manner of lecturing was certainly most trying and tantalizing. But by being brought into personal contact with him one was able to get help from him wherever he could give it. Though Weisse was convinced of the truth of Hegel's Dialectic Method, he often differed from him in its application. This Dialectic Method consisted in showing how thought is constantly and irresistibly driven from an affirmative to a negative position, then reconciles the two opposites, and from that point starts afresh, repeating once more the same process. Pure being, for instance, from which Hegel's ideal evolution starts, was shown to be the same as empty being, that is to say, nothing, and both were presented as identical, and in their identity giving us the new concept of Becoming (*Werden*), which is being and not-being at the same time. All this may appear to the lay reader rather obscure, but could not well be passed over.

So far Weisse followed the great thinker, and I possess still, in his own writing, the picture of a ladder on which the intellect is represented as climbing higher and higher from the lowest concept to the highest—a kind of Jacob's ladder on which the categories, like angels of God, ascend and descend from heaven to earth. We must remember that the true Hegelian regarded the Ideas as the thoughts of God. Hegel looked upon this evolution of thought as at the same time the evolution of Being, the Idea being the only thing that could be said to be truly real. In order to understand this, we must remember that the historical key to Hegel's Idea was really the Neo-Platonic or Alexandrian Logos. But of this Logos we ignorant undergraduates, sitting at the feet of Prof. Weisse, knew absolutely nothing, and even if the Idea was sometimes placed before us as the Absolute, the Infinite, or the Divine, it was to us, at least to most of us, myself included, *vox et praeterea nihil.* We watched the wonderful evolutions and convolutions of the Idea in its Dialectic development, but of the Idea itself or himself we had no idea whatever. It was all darkness, a vast abyss, and we sat patiently and wrote down what we could catch and comprehend of the Professor's explanations, but the Idea itself we never could lay hold of. It would not have been so difficult if the Professor had spoken out more boldly. But whenever he came to the relation of the Idea to what we mean by God, there was always even with him, who was a very honest man, a certain theological hesitation. Hegel himself seems to shrink occasionally from the consequence that the Idea really stands in the place of God, and that it is in the self-conscious spirit of humanity that the ideal God becomes first conscious of himself. Still, that is the last word of Hegel's philosophy, though others maintain that the Idea with Hegel was the thought of God, and that human thought was but a repetition of that divine thought. With Hegel there is first the evolution of the Idea in the pure ether of logic from the simplest to the highest category. Then follows Hegel's Philosophy of Nature, that is, the evolution of the Idea in nature, the Idea having by the usual dialectic process negatived itself and entered into its opposite (*Anderssein*), passing through a new process of space and time, and ending in the self-conscious human soul. Thus nature and spirit were represented as dominated by the Idea in its logical development. Nature was one manifestation of the Idea, History the other, and it became the task of the philosopher to discover its traces both in the progress of nature and in the historical progress of thought.

And here it was where the strongest protests began to be heard. Physical Science revolted, and Historical Research soon joined the rebellion. Professor Weisse also, in spite of his great admiration for Hegel, protested in his Lectures against this idealization of history, and showed how often Hegel, if he could not find the traces he was looking for in the historical development of the Idea, was misled by his imperfect knowledge of facts, and discovered what was not there, but what he felt convinced ought to have been there. Nowhere has this become so evident as in Hegel's *Philosophy of Religion*. The conception was grand of seeing in the historical development of religion a repetition of the Dialectic Progress of the Idea. But facts are stubborn things, and do not yield even to the supreme command of the Idea. Besides, if the historical facts of religion were really such as the Dialectic Process of the Idea required, these facts are no longer what they were before 1831, and what would become then of the Idea which, as he wrote in his preface to his *Metaphysics*, could not possibly be changed to please the new facts? It was this part of Weisse's lectures, it was the protest of the historical conscience against the demands of the Idea, that interested me most. I see as clearly the formal truth as the material untruth of Hegel's philosophy. The thorough excellence of its method and the desperate baldness of its results, strike me with equal force. Though I did not yet know what kind of thing or person the Idea was really meant for, I knew myself enough of ancient Greek philosophy and of Oriental religions to venture to criticize Hegel's representation and disposition of the facts themselves. I could not accept the answer of my more determined Hegelian friends, *Tant pis pour les faits*, but felt more and more the old antagonism between what ought to be and what is, between the reasonableness of the Idea, and the unreasonableness of facts. I found a strong supporter in a young Privat-Docent who at that time began his brilliant career at Leipzig, Dr. Lotze. He had made a special study of mathematics and physical science, and felt the same disagreement between facts and theories in Hegel's *Philosophy of Nature* which had struck me so much in reading his *Philosophy of Religion*. I joined his philosophical society, and I lately found among my old papers several essays which I had written for our meetings. They amused me very much, but I should be sorry to see them published now. It is curious that after many years I, as a Delegate of the University Press at Oxford, was instrumental in getting the first English translation of Lotze's *Metaphysics* published in England; and it is still more curious that Mark Pattison, the late Rector of Lincoln, should have opposed it with might and main as a useless book which would never pay its expenses. I stood up for my old teacher, and I am glad to say to the honour of English philosophers, that the translation passed through several editions, and helped not a little to establish Lotze's position in England and America. He died in 1881.

It is extraordinary how the young minds in German universities survive the storms and fogs through which they have to pass in their academic career. I confess I myself felt quite bewildered for a time, and began to despair altogether of my reasoning powers. Why should I not be able to understand, I asked myself, what other people seemed to understand without any effort? We speak the same language, why should we not be able to think the same thought? I took refuge for a time in history—the history of language, of religion, and of philosophy. There was a very learned professor at Leipzig, Dr. Niedner, who lectured on the History of Greek Philosophy, and whose *Manual for the History of Philosophy* has been of use to me through the whole of my life. Socrates said of

Heraclitus: "What I have understood of his book is excellent, and I suppose therefore that even what I have not understood is so too; but one must be a Delian swimmer not to be drowned in it." I tried for a long time to follow this advice with regard to Hegel and Weisse, and though disheartened did not despair. I understood some of it, why should not the rest follow in time? Thus, I never gave up the study of philosophy at Leipzig and afterwards at Berlin, and my first contributions to philosophical journals date from that early time, when I was a student in the University of Leipzig. My very earliest, though very unsuccessful, struggles to find an entrance into the mysteries of philosophy date even from my school-days.

I remember some years before, when I was quite young, perhaps no more than fifteen years of age, listening with bated breath to some professors at Leipzig who were talking very excitedly about philosophy in my presence. I had no idea what was meant by philosophy, still less could I follow when they began to discuss Kant's *Kritik der reinen Vernunft*. One of my friends, whom I looked up to as a great authority, confessed that he had read the book again and again, but could not understand the whole of it. My curiosity was much excited, and once, while he was taking a walk with me, I asked him very timidly what Kant's book was about, and how a man could write a book that other men could not understand. He tried to explain what Kant's book was about, but it was all perfect darkness before my eyes; I was trying to lay hold of a word here and there, but it all floated before my mind like mist, without a single ray of light, without any way out of all that maze of words. But when at last he said he would lend me the book, I fell on it and pored over it hour after hour. The result was the same. My little brain could not take in the simplest ideas of the first chapters—that space and time were nothing by themselves; that we ourselves gave the form of space and time to what was given us by the senses. But though defeated I would not give in; I tried again and again, but of course it was all in vain. The words were here and I could construe them, but there was nothing in my mind which the words could have laid hold on. It was like rain on hard soil, it all ran off, or remained standing in puddles and muddles on my poor brain.

At last I gave it up in despair, but I had fully made up my mind that as soon as I went to the University I would find out what philosophy really was, and what Kant meant by saying that space and time were forms of our sensuous intuition. I see that, accordingly, in the summer of 1841, I attended lectures on Aesthetics by Professor Weisse, on Anthropology by Lotze, and on Psychology by Professor Heinroth, and I slowly learnt to distinguish between what was going on within me, and what I had been led to imagine existed outside me, or at least quite independent of me. But before I had got a firm grasp of Kant, of his forms of intuition, and the categories of the understanding, I was thrown into Hegelianism. This, too, was at first entire darkness, but I was not disheartened. I attended Professor Weisse's lectures on Hegel in the winter of 1841–2, and again in the winter of 1842–3 I attended his lectures on Logic and Metaphysics, and on the Philosophy of History. He took an interest in me, and I felt most strongly attracted by him. Soon after I joined his Philosophical Society, and likewise that of Professor Drobisch. In these societies every member, when his turn came, had to write an essay and defend it against the professor and the other members of the society. All this was very helpful, but it was not till I had heard a course of lectures on the History of Philosophy, by Professor Niedner, that my interest in Philosophy became strong and healthy. While Weisse was a leading Hegelian philosopher, and Drobisch represented the opposite philosophy of Herbart, Niedner was purely historical, and this appealed most to my taste. Still, my philosophical studies remained very disjointed. At last I was admitted to Lotze's Philosophical Society also, and here we chiefly read and discussed Kant's *Kritik.* Lotze was then quite a young man, undecided as yet himself between physical science and pure philosophy.

Weisse was certainly the most stirring lecturer, but his delivery was fearful. He did not read his lectures, as many professors did, but would deliver them *extempore*. He had no command of language, and there was a pause after almost every sentence. He was really thinking out the problem while he was lecturing; he was constantly repeating his sentences, and any new thought that crossed his mind would carry him miles away from his subject. It happened sometimes in these rhapsodies that he contradicted himself, but when I walked home with him after his lecture to a village near Leipzig where he lived, he would readily explain how it happened, how he meant something quite different from what he had said, or what I had understood. In fact he would give the whole lecture over again, only much more freely and more intelligibly. I was fully convinced at that time that Hegel's philosophy was the final solution of all problems; I only hesitated about his philosophy of history as applied to the history of religion. I could not bring myself to admit that the history of religion, nor even the history of philosophy as we know it from Thales to Kant, was really running side by side with his Logic, showing how the leading concepts of the human mind, as elaborated in the Logic, had found successive expression in the history and development of the schools of philosophy as known to us. Weisse was strong both in his analysis of concepts and in his knowledge of history, and though he taught Hegel as a faithful interpreter, he always warned us against trusting too much in the parallelism between Logic and History. Study the writings of the good philosophers, he would say, and then see whether they will or will not fit into the Procrustean bed of Hegel's Logic. And this was the best lesson he could have given to young men. How well founded and necessary the warning was I found out myself, the more I studied the religion and philosophies of the East, and then compared what I saw in the original documents with the account given by Hegel in his *Philosophy of Religion.* It is quite true that Hegel at the time when he wrote, could not have gained a direct or accurate knowledge of the principal religions of the East. But what I could not help seeing was that what Hegel represented as the necessity in the growth of religious thought, was far away from the real growth, as I had watched it in some of the sacred books of these religions. This shook my belief in the correctness of Hegel's fundamental principles more than anything else.

At that time Herbart's philosophy, as taught by Drobisch at Leipzig, came to me as a most useful antidote. The chief object of that philosophy is, as is well known, the analysing and clearing, so to speak, of our concepts. This was exactly what I wanted, only that occupied as I was with the problems of language, I at once translated the object of his philosophy into a definition of words. Henceforth the object of my own philosophical occupations was the accurate definition of every word. All words, such as reason, pure reason, mind, thought, were carefully taken to pieces and traced back, if possible, to their first birth, and then through their further developments. My interest in this analytical process soon took an historical, that is etymological, character in so far as I tried to find out why any words should now mean exactly what, according to our definition, they ought to mean. For instance, in examining such words as *Vernunft* or *Verstand*, a little historical retrospect showed that their distinction as reason and understanding was quite modern, and chiefly due to a scientific definition given and maintained by the Kantian school of philosophy. Of course every generation has a right to define its philosophical terms, but from an historical point of view Kant might have used with equal right *Vernunft* for *Verstand*, and *Verstand* for *Vernunft*. Etymologically or historically both words have much the same meaning. *Vernunft*, from *Vernehmen*, meant originally no more than perception, while *Verstand* meant likewise perception, but soon came to imply a kind of understanding, even a kind of technical knowledge, though from a purely etymological stand-point it had nothing that fitted it more for carrying the meaning, which is now assigned to it in German in distinction to *Vernunft*, than understanding had as distinguished from reason. It requires, of course, a very minute historical research to trace the steps by which such words as reason and understanding diverge in different directions, in the language of the people and in philosophical parlance. This teaches us a very important distinction, namely that between the popular development of the meaning of a word, and its meaning as defined and asserted by a philosopher or by a poet in the plenitude of his power. Etymological definition is very useful for the first stages in the history of a word. It is useful to know, for instance, that *deus*, God, meant originally bright, bright whether applied to sky, sun, moon, stars, dawn, morning, dayspring, spring of the year, and many other bright objects in nature, that it thus assumed a meaning common to them all, splendid, or heavenly, beneficent, powerful, so that when in the Veda already we find a number of heavenly bodies, or of terrestrial bodies, or even of periods of time called Devas, this word has assumed a more general, more comprehensive, and more exalted meaning. It did not yet mean what the Greeks called θεοί or gods, but it meant something common to all these θεοί, and thus could naturally rise to express what the Greeks wanted to express by that word. There was as yet no necessity for defining deva or θεός, when applied to what was meant by gods, but of course the most opposite meanings had clustered round it. While a philosophical Greek would maintain that θεός meant what was one and never many, a poetical Greek or an ordinary Greek would hold that it meant what was by nature many. But while in such a case philosophical analysis and historical genealogy would support each other, there are ever so many cases where etymological analysis is as hopeless as logical analysis. Who is to define *romantic*, in such expressions as romantic literature. Etymologically we know that romantic goes back finally to Rome, but the mass of incongruous meanings that have been thrown at random into the caldron of that word, is so great that no definition could be contrived to comprehend them all. And how should we define *Gothic* or *Romanic* architecture, remembering that as no Goths had anything to do with pointed arches, neither were any Romans responsible for the flat roofs of the German churches of the Saxon emperors.

Enough to show what I meant when I said that Professor Drobisch, in his Lectures on Herbart, gave one great encouragement in the special work in which I was already engaged as a mere student, the Science of Language and Etymology. If Herbart declared philosophy to consist in a thorough examination (*Bearbeitung*) of concepts, or conceptual knowledge, my answer was, Only let it be historical, nay, in the beginning, etymological; I was not so foolish as to imagine that a word as used at present, meant what it meant etymologically. *Deus* no longer meant brilliant, but it should be the object of the true historian of language to prove how *Deus*, having meant originally brilliant, came to mean what it means now.

For a time I thought of becoming a philosopher, and that sounded so grand that the idea of preparing for a mere schoolmaster, teaching Greek and Latin, seemed to me more and more too narrow a sphere. Soon, however, while dreaming of a chair of philosophy at a German University, I began to feel that I must know something special, something that no other philosopher knew, and that induced me to learn Sanskrit, Arabic, and Persian. I had only heard what we call in German the chiming, not the striking of the bells of Indian philosophy; I had read Frederick Schlegel's explanatory book *Über die Sprache und Weisheit der Indier* (1808), and looked into Windischmann's *Die Philosophie im Fortgange der Weltgeschichte* (1827–1834). These books are hardly opened now—they are antiquated, and more than antiquated; they are full of mistakes as to facts, and mistakes as to the conclusions drawn from them. But they had ushered new ideas into the world of thought, and they left on many, as they did on me, that feeling which the digger who prospects for minerals is said to have, that there must be gold beneath the surface, if people would only dig. That feeling was very vague as yet, and might have been entirely deceptive, nor did I see my way to go beyond the point reached by these two dreamers or explorers. The thought remained in the rubbish-chamber of my mind, and though forgotten at the time, broke forth ag when there was an opportunity. It was a fortuna coincidence that at that very time, in the winter of 1841, a new professorship was founded at Leipzig and given to Professor Brockhaus. Uncertain as I was about the course I had to follow in my studies, I determined to see what there was to be learnt in Sanskrit. There was a charm in the unknown, and, I must confess, a charm also in studying something which my friends and fellow students did not know. I called on Professor Brockhaus, and found that there were only two other students to attend his lectures, one Spiegel, who already knew the elements of Sanskrit, and who is still alive in Erlangen,[1] as a famous professor of Sanskrit and Zend, though no longer lecturing, and another, Klengel; both several years my seniors, but both extremely amiable to their younger fellow student. Klengel was a scholar, a philosopher, and a musician, and though after a term or two he had to give up his study of Sanskrit, he was very useful to me by his good advice. He encouraged me and praised me for my progress in Sanskrit, which was no doubt more rapid than his own, and he confirmed me in my conviction that something might be made of Sanskrit by the philologist and by the philosopher. It should not be forgotten that at that time there was a strong prejudice against Sanskrit among classical scholars. The number of men who stood up for it, though it included names such as W. von Humboldt, F. and A. W. von Schlegel, was still very small. Even

[1] **Herr Geheimrath von Spiegel now lives at Munich.**

Herder's and Goethe's prophetic words produced little effect. It is said that when the Government had been persuaded, chiefly by the two Humboldts, to found a chair of Sanskrit at the University of Würzburg, and had nominated Bopp as its first occupant, the philological faculty of the University protested against such a desecration, and the appointment fell through. It is true, no doubt, that in their first enthusiasm the students of Sanskrit had uttered many exaggerated opinions. Sanskrit was represented as the mother of all languages, instead of being the elder sister of the Aryan family. The beginning of all language, of all thought, of all religion was traced back to India, and when Greek scholars were told that Zeus existed in the Veda under the name of Dyaus, there was a great flutter in the dovecots of classical scholarship. Many of these enthusiastic utterances had afterwards to be toned down. How we did enjoy those enthusiastic days, which even in their exaggerated hopes were not without some use. Problems such as the beginning of language, of thought, of mythology and religion, were started with youthful hope that the Veda would solve them all, as if the Vedic Rishis had been present at the first outburst of roots, of concepts, nay, that like Pelops and other descendants of Zeus, those Vedic poets had enjoyed daily intercourse with the gods, and had been present at the mutilation of Ouranos, or at the over-eating of Kronos. We may be ashamed to-day of some of the dreams of the early spring of man's sojourn on earth, but they were enchanting dreams, and all our thoughts of man's nature and destiny on earth were tinged with the colours of a morning that threw light over the grey darkness which preceded it. It was delightful to see that Dyaus meant originally the bright sky, something actually seen, but something that had to become something unseen. All knowledge, whether individual or possessed by mankind at large, must have begun with what the senses can perceive, before it could rise to signify something unperceived by the senses. Only after the blue aether had been perceived and named, was it possible to conceive and speak of the sky as active, as an agent, as a god. Dyaus or Zeus might thus be called the most sublime, he who resides in the aether, *αἰθέρι ναίων ὑψίζυγος*, the heavenly one, or *οὐράνιος ὕπατος* and *ὕψιστος*, the highest, and at last *Iupiter Optimus Maximus*, a name applied even to the true God. When Zeus had once become like the sky, all seeing or omniscient (*ἐπόψιος*), would he not naturally be supposed to see, not only the good, but the evil deeds of men also, nay, their very thoughts, whether pure or criminal? And if so, would he not be the avenger of evil, the watcher of oaths (*ὅρκιος*), the protector of the helpless (*ἱκέσιος*)? Yet, if conceived, as for a long time all the gods were conceived and could only be conceived, namely, as human in their shape, should we not necessarily get that strange amalgamation of a human being doing superhuman work—hurling the thunderbolt, shouting in thunder, hidden by dark clouds, and smiling in the serene blue of the sky with its brilliant scintillations? All this and much more became perfectly intelligible, the step from the visible to the invisible, from the perceived to the conceived, from nature to nature's gods, and from nature's god to a more sublime unseen and spiritual power. All this seemed to pass before our very eyes in the Veda, and then to be reflected in Homer and Pindar.

Some details of this restored picture of the world of gods and men in early times, nay, in the very spring of time, may have to be altered, but the picture, the eidyllion remained, and nothing could curb the adventurous spirit and keep it from pushing forward and trying to do what seemed to others almost impossible, namely, to watch the growth of the human mind as reflected in the petrifactions of language. Language itself spoke to us with a different voice, and a formerly unsuspected meaning.

We knew, for instance, that *ewig* meant eternal, but whence eternal. Nothing eternal was ever seen, and it seemed to the philosopher that eternal could be expressed by a negation only, by a negation of what was temporary. But we now learnt that *ewig* was derived in word and therefore in thought from the Gothic *aiwar*, time. *Ewigkeit* was therefore originally time, and " for all time " came naturally to mean " for all eternity." Eternity also came from *aeternus*, that is *aeviternus*, for time, i. e. for all time, and thus for eternity, while *aevum* meant life, lifetime, age. But now came the question, if *aevum* shows the growth of this word, and its origin, and how it arrives in the end at the very opposite pole, life and time coming to mean eternity, could we not by the same process discover the origin and growth of such short Greek words as *ἀεί* and *αἰεί*? It seems almost impossible, yet remembering that *aevum* meant originally life, we find in Vedic Sanskrit *eva*, course, way, life, the same as *aevum*, while the Sanskrit *âyush*, likewise derived from *i*, to go, forms its locative *âyushi*. *Âyushi*, or originally *âyasi*, would mean "in life, in time," and turned into Greek would regularly become then *αἰεί*, lifelong, or ever. It was not difficult to find fault with this and other etymologies, and to ask for an explanation of *αἰέν* and *αἰές*, as derived from the same word *âyus*. It is curious that people will not see that etymologies, and particularly the gradual development in the form and meaning of words, can hardly ever be a matter of mathematical certainty.

Historical, nay, even individual, influences come in which prevent the science of language from becoming purely mechanical. Pott, and Curtius, and others stood up against Bopp and Grimm, maintaining that there could be nothing irregular in language, particularly in phonetic changes. If this means no more than that under the same circumstances the same changes will always take place, it would be of course a mere truism. The question is only whether we can ever know all the circumstances, and whether there are not some of these circumstances which cause what we are apt to call irregularities. When Bopp said that Sanskrit *d* corresponds to a Greek δ, but often also to a Greek θ, I doubt whether this is often the case. All I say is, if *deva* corresponds to θεός, we must try to find the reason or the circumstances which caused so unusual a correspondence. If no more is meant than that there must be a reason for all that seems irregular, no one would gainsay that, neither Bopp nor Grimm, and no one ever doubted that as a principle. But to establish these reasons is the very difficulty with which the Science of Language has to deal.

There is no word that has not an etymology, only if we consider the distance of time that separates us from the historical facts we are trying to account for, we should sometimes be satisfied with probabilities and not always stipulate for absolute certainty. Many of Bopp's, Grimm's, and Pott's etymologies have had to be surrendered, and yet our suzerainty over that distant country which they conquered, over the Aryan home, remains. If there is an etymology containing something irregular, and for which no reason has as yet been found, we must wait till some better etymology can be suggested, or a reason be found for that apparent irregularity. If the etymological meaning of *duhitar*, daughter, as milkmaid, is doubted, let us have a better explanation, not a worse; but the general picture of the early family among the Aryans "somewhere in Asia" is not thereby destroyed. The father, Sk. *pitar*, remains the protector or nourisher, though the *i* for *a* in *pater* and πατήρ is irregular. The mother, *mâtar*, remains the bearer of children, though *mâ* is no longer used in that sense in any of the Aryan languages. *Pati* is the lord, the strong one—therefore the husband; *vadhû*, the yoke-fellow, or the wife as brought home, possibly as carried off by force. *Vis* or *vesa* is the home, οἶκος or *vicus*, what was entered for shelter. *Svasura*, ἑκυρός, *Socer*, the father-in-law, is the old man of the *svas*, the *famuli*, or the family, or the clients, though the first *s* is irregular, and can be defended only on the ground of mistaken analogy. *Bhrâtar*, *frater*, brother, was the supporter; *svastar*, *soror*, sister, the comforter, &c.

What do a few objections signify? The whole picture remains, as if we could look into the *vesa*, the οἶκος the *veih*, the home, the village of the ancient Aryans, and watch them, the *svas*, the people, in their mutual relations. Even compound words, such as *vis-pati*, lord of a family or a village, have been preserved to the present day in the Lithuanian *Veszpats*, lord, whether King or God. It is enough for us to see that the relationship between husband and wife, between parents and children, between brothers and sisters, nay, even between children-in-law and parents-in-law, had been recognized and sanctified by names. That there are, and always will be, doubts and slight differences of opinion on these prehistoric thoughts and words, is easily understood. We were pleased for a long time to see in *vidua*, widow, the Sanskrit *vidua*, i. e. without a man or a husband. We now derive *vi-dhavâ*, widow, from *vidh*, to be separated, to be without (cf. *vido* in *divido*, and Sk. *vidh*), but the picture of the Aryan family remains much the same.

When these and similar antiquities were for the first time brought to light by Bopp, Grimm, and Pott, what wonder that we young men should have jumped at them, and shouted with delight, more even than the diggers who dug up Babylonian palaces or Egyptian temples! No one did more for these antiquarian finds and restorations than A. Kuhn, a simple schoolmaster, but afterwards a most distinguished member of the Berlin Academy. How often did I sit with him in his study as he worked, surrounded by his Greek, Latin, and Sanskrit books. In later times also, when I had made some discoveries myself as to the mythological names or beings identical in Vedic and Greek writings, how pleasant was it to see him rub his hands or shake his head. Long before I had published my identifications they were submitted to him, and he communicated to me his own guesses as I communicated mine to him. Kuhn would never appropriate what belonged to anybody else, and even in cases where we agreed, he would always make it clear that we had both arrived independently at the same result.

It is in the nature of things that every new generation of scholars should perfect their tools, and with these discover flaws in the work left by their predecessors. Still, what is the refined chiselling of later scholars compared with the rough-hewn stones of men like Bopp or Grimm? If the Cyclopean stones of the Pelasgians are not like the finished works of art by Phidias, what would the Parthenon be without the walls ascribed to the Cyclops? It is the same in all sciences, and we must try to be just, both to the genius of those who created, and to the diligence of those who polished and refined.

For all this, however, I met with but small sympathy and encouragement at Leipzig; nay, I had to be very careful in uttering what were supposed to be heretical or unscholarlike opinions in the seminary of Gottfried Hermann, or in the Latin society of Haupt. The latter particularly, though he knew very well how much light had been spread on the growth of language by the researches of Bopp, Grimm, and Pott, and though Grimm was his intimate friend of whom he always spoke with real veneration, could not bear his own pupils dabbling in this subject. And of course at that time my knowledge of comparative philology was a mere dabbling. If he could discover a false quantity in any etymology, great was his delight, and his sarcasm truly withering, particularly as it was poured out in very classical Latin. Gottfried Hermann was a different character. He saw there was a new light and he would not turn his back to it. He knew how lightly his antagonist, Otfried Müller, valued Sanskrit in his mythological essays, and he set to work, and in one of his last academical programs actually gave the paradigms of Sanskrit verbs as compared with those of Greek. He saw that the coincidences between the two could not be casual, and if they were so overwhelming in the mere termination of verbs, what might we not expect in words and names, even in mythological names? He by no means discouraged me, nay, he was sorry to lose me, when in my third year I went to Berlin. He showed me great kindness on several occasions, and when the time came to take my degree of M.A. and Ph.D., he, as Dean of the Faculty, invited me to return to Leipzig, offering me an exhibition to cover the expenses of the Degree.

My wish to go to Berlin arose partly from a desire to hear Bopp, but yet more from a desire to make the acquaintance of Schelling. My inclination towards philosophy had become stronger and stronger; I had my own ideas about the mythological as a necessary form of ancient philosophy, and when I saw that the old philosopher had advertised his lectures or lecture on mythology, I could not

F. MAX MULLER

Aged Twenty

resist, and went to Berlin in 1844. I must say at once that Professor Bopp, though he was extremely kind to me, was at that time, if not old—he was only fifty-three—very infirm. In his lectures he simply read his *Comparative Grammar* with a magnifying glass, and added very little that was new. He lent me some manuscripts which he had copied in Latin in his younger days, but I could not get much help from him when I came to really difficult passages. This, I confess, puzzled me at the time, for I looked on every professor as omniscient. The time comes, however, when we learn that even at fifty-three a man may have forgotten certain things, nay, may have let many books and new discoveries even in his own subject pass by, because he has plenty to do with his own particular studies. We remember the old story of the professor who, when charged by a young and rather impertinent student with not knowing this or that, replied: "Sir, I have forgotten more than you ever knew." And so it is indeed. Human nature and human memory are very strong during youth and manhood, but even at fifty there is with many people a certain decline of mental vigour that tells chiefly on the memory. Things are not exactly forgotten, but they do not turn up at the right time. They just leave a certain knowledge of where the missing information can be found; they leave also a kind of feeling that the ground is not quite safe and that we must no longer trust entirely to our memory. In one respect this feeling is very useful, for instead of writing down anything, trusting to our memory as we used to do, we feel it necessary to verify many things which formerly were perfectly clear and certain in our memory without such reference to books.

I remember being struck with the same thing in the case of Professor Wilson, the well-known Oxford Professor of Sanskrit. He was kind enough to read with me, and I certainly was often puzzled, not only by what he knew, but also by what he had forgotten. I feel now that I misjudged him, and that his open declaration, "I don't know, let us look it up," really did him great honour. I still have in my possession a portion of Pânini's Vedic grammar translated by him. I put by the side of it my own translation, and he openly acknowledged that mine, with the passages taken from the Veda, was right. There was no humbug about Wilson. He never posed as a scholar; nay, I remember his saying to me more than once, "You see, I am not a scholar, I am a gentleman who likes Sanskrit, and that is all." He certainly did like Sanskrit, and he knew it better than many a professor, but in his own way. He had enjoyed the assistance of really learned Pandits, and he never forgot to record their services. But he had himself cleared the ground—he had really done original work. In fact, he had done nothing but original work, and then he was abused for not having always found at the first trial what others discovered when standing on his shoulders. Again, he was found fault with for not having had a classical education. His education was, I believe, medical, but when once in the Indian Civil Service, he made himself useful in many ways, educational and otherwise. When he left India he was Master of the Mint. Such a man might not know Greek and Latin like F. A. von Schlegel, or any other professor, but he knew his own subject, and it is simply absurd if classical scholars imagine that anybody can carry on his Greek and Latin and at the same time make himself a perfect scholar in Sanskrit. Such a feeling is natural among small schoolmasters, but it is dying out at last among real scholars. I have known very good Sanskrit scholars who knew no Greek at all, and very little Latin. And I have also known Greek scholars who knew no Sanskrit and yet attempted comparisons between the two. When Lepsius was made a Member of the Berlin Academy, Lachmann, who ought to have known better, used to say of him: "He knows many things which nobody knows, but he also is ignorant of many things which everybody knows." Such remarks never speak well for the man who makes them.

Another disadvantage from which the aged scholar suffers is that he is blamed for not having known in his youth what has been discovered in his old age, and is still violently assailed for opinions he may have uttered fifty years ago. When quite a young man I wrote, at Baron Bunsen's request, a long letter on the Turanian Languages. It was published in 1854, but it still continues to be criticized as if it had been published last year. Of course, considering the rapid advance of linguistic studies, a great part of that letter became antiquated long ago; but at the time of its first appearance it contained nearly all that could then be known on these allophylian, that is, non-Aryan and non-Semitic languages; and I may, perhaps, quote the opinion of Professor Pott, no mean authority at that time, who, after severely criticizing my letter, declared that it belonged to the most important publications that had appeared on linguistic subjects for many years. And yet, though I have again and again protested that I could not possibly have known in 1854 what has been discovered since as to a number of these Turanian languages, everybody who writes on any of them seems to be most anxious to show that in 1894 he knows more than I did in 1854. No astronomer is blamed for not having known the planet Neptune before its discovery in 1846, or for having been wrong in accounting for the irregularities of Saturn. But let that pass; I only share the fate of others who have lived too long.

After all, all our knowledge, whatever show we may make of it, is very imperfect, and the more we know the better we learn how little it is that we do know, and how much of unexplored country there is beyond the country which we have explored. We must judge a man by what he has done—by his own original work. There are many scholars, and very useful they are in their own way, but if their books are examined, one easily finds the stores from which they borrowed their materials. They may add some notes of their own and even some corrections, particularly corrections of the authors from whom they have borrowed most; but at the end where is the fresh ore that they have raised; where is the gold they have extracted and coined? There are cases where the original worker is quite forgotten, whereas the retailers flourish. Well, facts are facts, whether known or not known, and the triumphal chariot of truth has to be dragged along by many hands and many shoulders.

CHAPTER V

PARIS

My stay in Paris from March, 1845, to June, 1846, was a very useful intermezzo. It opened my mind and showed me a new world; showed me, in fact, that there was a world besides Germany, though even of Germany and German society I had seen as yet very little. I had been working away at school and university, but with the exception of my short stay in Berlin, I had little experience of men and manners outside the small sphere of Dessau and Leipzig.

I had been at Berlin some nine months when, in December, 1844, my old friend Baron Hagedorn came to see me, and invited me to spend some time with him in Paris. He had his own apartments there, and promised to look after me. At the same time my cousin, Baroness Stolzenberg, whom I have mentioned before as wishing me to enter the Austrian diplomatic service, offered to send me to England at her expense as a teacher. I hesitated for some days between these two offers. I knew that my own patrimony had been nearly spent at Leipzig and Berlin, and the time had come for me to begin to support myself; and how was I to do that in Paris? On the other hand, I had long felt that for continuing my Sanskrit studies a stay in Paris, and later perhaps in London also, was indispensable. I had also to consider the feelings of my mother, whose whole heart was absorbed in her only son. However, Sanskrit, and my love of an independent life won the day, and I decided to accept Hagedorn's proposal. My mind once made up, I wanted to be off at once, but Hagedorn could not fix the exact time when he would be free to leave, and told me to keep myself in readiness to start whenever he found himself free to go. I accordingly went to stay with my mother and my married sister at Chemnitz, and indulged in idleness and the unwonted dissipations of parties, dances, and long skating expeditions. At last, feeling I could not afford to wait any longer, I went off to Dessau to see Hagedorn, and found to my great disappointment that he was detained by important legal business in connection with his property near Munich, and could not yet fix a date for his departure. So it was settled that I was to go on to Paris without him, and instal myself in his apartment, 25, Rue Royale St. Honoré.

I got my passport wherein I was carefully described with all my particular marks, and started off on my foreign travels. At first all went well. I stopped a few days at Bonn, and again at Brussels, where I had my first experience of hearing a foreign language spoken round me, and found that my French was sadly deficient. But from Brussels on, my experiences were anything but agreeable. The journey to Paris took twenty-four hours, and we travelled day and night without any stop for meals. Most of the passengers were well provided with food and wine, but had it not been for the kindness of some old ladies, my fellow-travellers, I should really have starved. When we crossed the frontier the luggage of all passengers was carefully examined. But the *douanier*, in trying to open my portmanteau, broke the lock, and then began a fearful cursing and swearing. I was perfectly helpless. I could hardly understand what the French *douaniers* said, still less make them understand what I had to say. They had done the damage, but would do nothing to remedy it. The train would not wait, and I should certainly have been left behind if the other travellers had not taken my part, and I was allowed to go on to Paris. I looked a mere boy, very harmless, not at all the clever smuggler the officials took me to be. If they had forced the portmanteau open they would have found nothing but the most essential wearing apparel and a few books and papers all in Sanskrit.

But my miseries were not yet over, on the contrary, they became much worse. On my arrival in Paris I got a *fiacre* and told the man to drive to 25, Rue St. Honoré; *Royale* I considered of no importance; but, alas! at the right number of the Rue St. Honoré, the *concierge* stared at me, telling me that no Baron Hagedorn lived there. Try

Faubourg St. Honoré, they said, but here the same thing happened. And all this was on a rainy afternoon, I being tired out with travelling and fasting, and perfectly overwhelmed by the immensity of Paris. I knew nobody at Paris, having trusted for all such things to Baron Hagedorn, in fact I was *au désespoir*. Then as I was driving along the Boulevard des Italiens, looking out of window, I saw a familiar figure—a little hunchback whom I had known at Dessau, where he studied music under Schneider. It was M. Gathy, a man well known by his musical writings, particularly his *Dictionary of Music*. I shrieked Gathy! Gathy! and he was as much surprised when he recognized the little boy from Dessau, as I was when in this vast Paris I discovered at last a face which I knew. I jumped out of my carriage, told Gathy all that had happened to me, being all the time between complete despair and perfect delight. He knew Hagedorn and his rooms very well. It was the Rue Royale St. Honoré. The *concierge* was quite prepared for my arrival, and took us both to the rooms which were *au cinquième*, but large and extremely well furnished. I was so tired that I lay down on the sofa, and called out in my best French, *Donnez-moi quelque chose à manger et à boire*. This was not so easily done as said, but at last, after toiling up and down five flights of stairs, he brought me what I wanted; I restored myself in the true sense of the word, and then began to discuss the most necessary matters with M. Gathy. He was the most charming of men, half German, half French, full of *esprit*, and, what was more important to me, full of real kindness and love. As soon as I saw him I felt I was safe, and so I was, though I had still some battles to fight. First of all, I had taken but little money with me, looking upon Hagedorn as my banker. Fortunately I remembered the name of one of his friends, about whom Hagedorn had often spoken to me and who was in Rothschild's Bank. I went there to find that he was away, but another gentleman there told me that I could have as much as I liked till Hagedorn or his friend came back. So I was lucky, unlucky as I had been before.

The next step I had to consider was what I should do for my breakfast, luncheon, and dinner. Breakfast I could have at home, but for the other meals I had to go out and get what I wanted wherever I could. It was not always what I wanted, for it had to be cheap, and even a dinner *à deux francs* in the Palais Royal seemed to me extravagant. I became more knowing by-and-by, and discovered smaller and simpler restaurants, where Frenchmen dined and had arranged for a less showy but more wholesome diet.

The impression that my first experience of life in one of the great capitals of the world made on me is still fresh in my memory. My principal amusement at first was to go on voyages of discovery through the town. The beauty of the city itself, and the rush and crowd in the streets delighted me, and I remember specially a few days after my arrival, when I went to watch "le tout Paris" going out to the races at Longchamps, that I was so struck by the difference between these streets full of equipages of all sorts, ladies in resplendent dresses, and well-groomed gentlemen, and the quiet streets that I had been accustomed to in Dessau and Leipzig, that I could hardly keep myself from laughing out loud. However, when the novelty wore off there was another contrast that struck me, and made me more inclined to cry this time than to laugh, and that was, that while at home I knew almost every face I passed, here in these crowds I was a stranger and knew no one, and I suffered cruelly from the solitude at first.

I began my work, however, at once, and on the third day after my arrival I was at the Bibliothèque Royale armed with a letter of introduction from Humboldt, and the very next day was already at work collating the MSS. of the *Kathaka Upanishad.* I had also to devote some hours daily to the study of French; for, much as I grudged these hours, I fully realized that in order to get full advantage from my stay in Paris, I must first master French.

Next came the great question, how to make the acquaintance of Burnouf. I did not know the world. I did not know whether I should write to him first, in what language, and to what address. I knew Burnouf from his books, and I felt a desperate respect for him. After a time Gathy discovered his address for me, and I summoned up courage to call on him. My French was very poor as yet, but I walked in and found a dear old gentleman in his *robe de chambre*, surrounded by his books and his children—four little daughters who were evidently helping him in collecting and alphabetically arranging a number of slips on which he had jotted down whatever had struck him as important in his reading during the day. He received me with great civility, such as I had not been accustomed to before. He spoke of some little book which I had published, and inquired warmly after my teachers in Germany, such as Brockhaus, Bopp, and Lassen. He told me I might attend his lectures in the Collège de France, and he would always be most happy to give me advice and help.

I at once felt perfect trust in the man, and was really *aux cieux* to have found such an adviser. He was, indeed, a fine specimen of the real French savant. He was small, and his face was decidedly German, with the *tête carrée* which one sees so often in Germany, only lighted up by a constant sparkle, which is distinctively French. I must have seemed very stupid to him when I tried to explain to him what I really wanted to do in Paris. He told me himself afterwards that he could not make me out at first. I wanted to study the Veda, but I had told him at the same time that I thought the Vedic hymns very stupid, and that I cared chiefly for their philosophy, that is, the Upanishads. This was really not true, but it came up first in conversation, and I thought it would show Burnouf that my interest in the Veda was not simply philological, but philosophical also. No doubt at first I chiefly copied the Upanishads and their commentaries, but Burnouf was not pleased. "We know what is in the Upanishads," he used to say, "but we want the hymns and their native comments." I soon came to understand what he meant; I carefully attended his lectures, which were on the hymns of the Rig-veda and opened an entirely new world to my mind. We had the first book of the Rig-veda as published by Rosen, and Burnouf's explanations were certainly delightful. He spoke freely and conversationally in his lectures, and one could almost assist at the elaboration of his thoughts. His audience was certainly small; there was nothing like Renan's eloquence and wit. But Burnouf had ever so many new facts to communicate to us. He explained to us his own researches, he showed us new MSS. which he had received from India, in fact he did all he could to make us fellow workers. Often did he tell us to look up some passage in the Veda, to compare and copy the commentaries, and to let him have the result of our researches at the next lecture. All this was very inspiriting, particularly as Burnouf, upon examining our work, was very generous in his approval, and quite ready, if we had failed, to point out to us new sources that should be examined. He never asserted his own authority, and if ever we had found out something which he had not known before, he was delighted to let us have the full credit for it. After all, it was a new and unknown country, that had to be explored and mapped out, and even a novice might sometimes find a grain of gold.

His select class contained some good men. There were Barthélemy St. Hilaire, the famous translator of Aristotle, and for a time Minister of Foreign Affairs in France, the Abbé Bardelli, R. Roth, Th. Goldstücker, and a few more.

Barthélemy St. Hilaire was a personal friend of Burnouf, and came to the Collège de France not so much to learn Sanskrit as to hear Burnouf's lucid exposition of ancient Indian religion and philosophy. Bardelli was a regular Italian Abbé, studying Sanskrit at Paris, but chiefly interested in Coptic. He was, like St. Hilaire, much my senior, but we became great friends, and he once confided to me what had certainly puzzled me—his reasons for becoming an ecclesiastic. He had been deeply in love with a young lady; his love was returned, but he was too poor to marry, and she was persuaded and almost forced to marry a rich man. Dear old Abbé, always taking snuff while he told me his agonies, and then finishing up by saying that he became a priest so as to put an end for ever to his passion. Who would have suspected such a background to his jovial face? I don't know how it was that people, much my seniors, so often confided to me their secret sufferings. I may have to mention some other cases, and I feel that after my friends are gone, and so many years have passed over their graves, there is no indiscretion in speaking of their confidences. It may possibly teach us to remember how much often lies buried under a grave bright with flowers. I saw Bardelli's own grave many years later in the famous cemetery at Pisa. R. Roth and Th. Goldstücker were both strenuous Sanskrit scholars. Both owed much to Burnouf, Roth even more than Goldstücker, though the latter has perhaps more frequently spoken of what he owed to Burnouf. Roth was my senior by several years, and engaged in much the same work as myself. But we never got on well together. It is curious from what small things and slight impressions our likes and dislikes are often formed. I have heard men give as a reason for disliking some one, that he had forgotten to pay half a cab-fare. So in Roth's case, I never got over a most ordinary experience. He and two other young students and myself, having to celebrate some festal occasion, had ordered a good luncheon at a restaurant. To me with my limited means this was a great extravagance, but I could not refuse to join. Roth, to my great surprise and, I may add, being very fond of oysters, annoyance, took a very unfair share of that delicacy, and whenever I met him in after life, whether in person or in writing, this incident would always crop up in my mind; and when later on he offered to join me in editing the Rig-veda, I declined, perhaps influenced by that early impression which I could not get rid of. I blame myself for so foolish a prejudice, but it shows what creatures of circumstance we are.

With Goldstücker I was far more intimate. He was some years older than myself and quite independent as far as money went. He knew how small my means were, and would gladly have lent me money. But through the whole of my life I never borrowed from my friends, or in fact from anybody, though I was forced sometimes when very hard up for ready money, and when I knew that money was due to me but had not arrived when I expected it, to apply to some friend for a temporary advance. I will try and recall the lines in which I once applied to Gathy for such a loan.

Versuch' ich's wohl, mein herzgeliebter Gathy,
Mit schmeichelndem Sonnet Sie anzupumpen ?
Ich bitte nicht um schwere Goldesklumpen,
Ich bitte nur um etliche Ducati.
Auch zahl' ich wieder ultimo Monati.
Auf Wiedersehn bei Morel und Frascati
Und Nachsicht für den Brief, den allzu plumpen !
Zwar reiche Nabobs sind die braven Inder,
Doch arme Teufel die Indianisten !
Reich sind hienieden schon die Heiden-Kinder,
Doch selig werden nur die armen Christen !
Reimsucher bin ich, doch kein Reimefinder,
Und *sans critique* sind all die Sanscritisten.

This kind of negotiating a loan I have to confess to, but the idea of borrowing money, without knowing when I could repay it, never entered my mind. Relations who could have helped me I had none, and nothing remained to me but to work for others. Indeed my want of money soon began to cause me very serious anxiety in Paris. Little as I spent, my funds became lower and lower. I did not, like many other scholars, receive help from my Government. I had mapped out my course for myself, and instead of taking to teaching on leaving the University, had settled to come to Paris and continue my Sanskrit studies, and it was in my own hands whether I should swim or sink. It was, indeed, a hard struggle, far harder than those who have known me in later life would believe. All I could do to earn a little money was to copy and collate MSS. for other people. I might indeed have given private lessons, but I have always had a strong objection to that form of drudgery, and would rather sit up a whole night copying than give an hour to my pupils. My plan was as follows: to sit up the whole of one night, to take about three hours' rest the next night, but without undressing, and then to take a good night's rest the third night, and start over again. It was a hard fight, and cannot have been very good for me physically, but I do not regret it now.

Often did I go without my dinner, being quite satisfied with boiled eggs and bread and butter, which I could have at home without toiling down and toiling up five flights of stairs that led to my room. Sometimes I went with some of my young friends *hors de la barrière*, that is, outside Paris, outside the barrier where the *octroi* has to be paid on meat, wine, &c. Here the food was certainly better for the price I could afford to pay, but the society was sometimes peculiar. I remember once seeing a strange lady sitting not very far from me, who was the well-known Louve of Eugène Sue's *Mystères de Paris*. One of my companions on these expeditions was Karl de Schloezer, who was then studying Arabic in Paris. He was always cheerful and amusing, and a delightful companion. He knew much more of the world than I did, and often surprised me by his diplomatic wisdom. "Let us stand up for each other," he said one day; "you say all the good you can of me, I saying all the good I can of you." I became very fierce at the time, charging him with hypocrisy and I do not know what. He, however, took it all in good part, and we remained friends all the time he was at Paris, and indeed to the day of his death. He was very fond of music, but I was, perhaps, the better performer on the pianoforte. He had invited me, a violin, and violoncello, to play some of Mozart's and Beethoven's Sonatas. Alas! when we found that he murdered his part, I sat down and played the whole evening, leaving him to listen, not, I fear, in the best of moods. He took his revenge, however; and the next time he asked me and the two other musicians to his room, we found indeed everything ready for us to play, but our host was nowhere to be found. He maintained that he had been called away; I am certain, however, that the little trick was played on purpose.

He afterwards entered the Prussian diplomatic service and was the protégé of the Princess of Prussia, afterwards the Empress of Germany. That was enough to make Bismarck dislike him, and when Schloezer served as Secretary of Legation under Bismarck as Ambassador at St. Petersburg, he committed the outrage of challenging his chief to a duel. Bismarck declined, nor would it, according to diplomatic etiquette, have been possible for him not to decline. Later on, however, Schloezer was placed *en disponibilité*, that is to say, he was politely dismissed. He had to pay a kind of farewell visit to Bismarck, who was then omnipotent. Being asked by Bismarck what he intended to do, and whether he could be of any service to him, Schloezer said very quietly, "Yes, your Excellency, I shall take to writing my Memoirs, and you know that I have seen much in my time which many people will be interested to learn." Bismarck was quiet for a time, looking at some papers, and then remarked quite unconcernedly, "You would not care to go to the United States as Minister?" "I am ready to go to-morrow," replied Schloezer, and having carried his point, having in fact outwitted Bismarck, he started at once for Washington. Bismarck knew that Schloezer could wield a sharp pen, and there was a time when he was sensitive to such pen-pricks. They did not see much of each other afterwards, but, owing to the protection of the Empress, Schloezer was later accredited as Prussian envoy to the Pope, and died too soon for his friends in beautiful Italy.

One of my oldest friends at Paris was a Baron d'Eckstein, a kind of diplomatic agent who knew everybody in Paris, and wrote for the newspapers, French and German. He had, I believe, a pension from the French Government, and was, as a Roman Catholic, strongly allied with the Clerical Party. This did not concern me. What concerned me was his love of Sanskrit and the ancient religion of India. He would sit with me for hours, or take me to dine with him at a restaurant, discussing all the time the Vedas and the Upanishad and the Vedanta philosophy. There are several articles of his written at this time in the *Journal Asiatique*, and I was especially grateful to him, for he gave me plenty of work to do, particularly in the way of copying Sanskrit MSS. for him, and he paid me well and so helped me to keep afloat in Paris. Knowing as he did everybody, he was very anxious to introduce me to his friends, such as George Sand, Lamennais, the Comtesse d'Agoult (Daniel Stern), Lamartine, Victor Hugo, and others; but I much preferred half an hour with him or with Burnouf to paying formal visits. I heard afterwards many unkind things about Baron d'Eckstein's political and clerical opinions, but though in becoming a convert to Roman Catholicism he may have shown weakness, and as a political writer may have been influenced by his near friends and patrons, I never found him otherwise than kind, tolerant, and trustworthy. His life was to have been written by Professor Windischmann, but he too died; and who knows what may have become of the curious memoirs which he left? At the time of the February revolution in 1848, he was in the very midst of it. He knew Lamartine, who was the hero of the day, though of a few days only. He attended meetings with Lamartine, Odilon, Barrot, and others, and he assured me that there would be no revolution, because nobody was prepared for it.

Lamartine who had been asked by his friends, all of them royalists and friends of order, whether he would, in case of necessity, undertake to form a ministry under the Duchesse d'Orléans as regent, scouted such an idea at first, but at last promised to be ready if he were wanted. The time came sooner than he expected, and the Duchesse d'Orléans counted on him when she went to the Chamber and her Regency was proclaimed. Lamartine was then so popular that he might have saved the situation. But the mob broke into the Chamber, shots were fired, and thero was no Lamartine. The Duchesse d'Orléans had to fly, and fortunately escaped under the protection of the Duc de Nemours, the only son of Louis Philippe then in Paris, and the dynasty of the Orléans was lost—never to return. Baron d'Eckstein lost many of his influential friends at that time, possibly his pension also, but he had enough to live upon, and he died at last as a very old man in a Roman Catholic monastery, a most interesting and charming man, whose memoirs would certainly have been very valuable.

But to return to Burnouf, I never can adequately express my debt of gratitude to him. He was of the greatest assistance to me in clearing my thoughts and directing them into one channel. "Either one thing or the other," he said. "Either study Indian philosophy and begin with the Upanishads and Sankara's commentary, or study Indian religion and keep to the Rig-veda, and copy the hymns and Sâyana's commentary, and then you will be our great benefactor." A great benefactor! that was too much for me, a mere dwarf in the presence of giants. But Burnouf's words confirmed me more and more in my desire to give myself up to the Veda.

Burnouf told me not only what Vedic MSS. there were at the Bibliothèque Royale, he also brought me his own MSS. and lent them to me to copy, with the condition, however, that I should not smoke while working at them. He himself did not smoke, and could not bear the smell of smoke, and he showed me several of his MSS. which had become quite useless to him, because they smelt of stale tobacco smoke. I did all I could to guard these sacred treasures against such profanation.

Another and even more useful warning came to me from Burnouf. "Don't publish extracts from the commentary only," he said; "if you do, you will publish what is easy to read, and leave out what is difficult." I certainly thought that extracts would be sufficient, but I soon found out that here also Burnouf was right, though there was always the fear that I should never find a publisher for so immense a work. This fear I confided to Burnouf, but he always maintained his hopeful view. "The commentary must be published, depend upon it, and it will be," he said.

So I stuck to it and went on copying and collating my Sanskrit MSS., always trusting that a publisher would turn up at the proper time. I had, of course, to do all the drudgery for myself, and I soon found out that it was not in human nature, at least not in my nature, to copy Sanskrit from a MS. even for three or four hours without mistakes. To my great disappointment I found mistakes whenever I collated my copy with the original. I found that like the copyists of classical MSS. my eye had wandered from one line to another where the same word occurred, that I had left out a word when the next word ended with the same termination, nay that I had even left out whole lines. Hence I had either to collate my own copy, which was very tedious, or invent some new process. This new process

I discovered by using transparent paper, and thus tracing every letter. I had some excellent *papier végétal* made for me, and, instead of copying, traced the whole Sanskrit MS. This had the great advantage that nothing could be left out, and that when the original was smudged and doubtful I could carefully trace whatever was clear and visible through the transparent paper. At first I confess my work was slow, but soon it went as rapidly as copying, and it was even less fatiguing to the eyes than the constant looking from the MS. to the copy, and from the copy to the MS. But the most important advantage was, that I could thus feel quite certain that nothing was left out, so that even now, after more than fifty years, these tracings are as useful to me as the MS. itself. There was room left between the lines or on the margin to note the various readings of other MSS.; in fact, my materials grew both in extent and in value.

Still there remained the question of a publisher. To print the Rig-veda in six volumes quarto of about a thousand pages each, and to provide the editor with a living wage during the many years he would have to devote to his task, required a large capital. I do not know exactly how much, but what I do know is that, when a second edition of the text of the Veda in four volumes was printed at the expense of the Maharajah of Vizianagram, it cost that generous and patriotic prince four thousand pounds, though I then gave my work gratuitously.

While I was working at the Bibliothèque Ròyale, Humboldt had used his powerful influence with the king of Prussia, Frederick William IV, to help me in publishing my edition of the Rig-veda in Germany. Nothing, however, came of that plan; it proved too costly for any private publisher, even with royal assistance.

Then came a vague offer from St. Petersburg. Boehtlingk, the great Sanskrit scholar, as a member of the Imperial Russian Academy, invited me to come to St. Petersburg and print the Veda there, in collaboration with himself, and at the expense of the Academy. Burnouf and Goldstücker both warned me against accepting this offer, but, hopeless as I was of getting my Veda published elsewhere, I expressed my willingness to go on condition that some provision should be made for me before I decided to migrate to Russia, as I possessed absolutely nothing but what I was able to earn myself. Boehtlingk, I believe, suggested to the Academy that I should be appointed Assistant Keeper of the Oriental Museum at St. Petersburg, but his colleagues did not apparently consider so young a man, and a mere German scholar, a fit candidate for so responsible a post. Boehtlingk wished me to send him all my materials, and he would get the MSS. of the Rig-veda and of Sâyana's commentary from the Library of the East India Company, and Paris. No definite proposition, however, came from the Imperial Academy, but an announcement of Boehtlingk's appeared in the papers in January, 1846, to the effect that he was preparing, in collaboration with Monsieur Max Müller of Paris, a complete edition of the Rig-veda.

All this, I confess, began to frighten me. For me, a poor scholar, to go to St. Petersburg without any official invitation, without any appointment, seemed reckless, and though I have no doubt that Boehtlingk would have done his best for me, yet even he could only suggest private lessons, and that was no cheerful outlook. The Academy would do nothing for me unless I joined Boehtlingk, but at last offered to buy my materials, on which I had spent so much labour and the small fund at my disposal. If the Academy could have got the necessary MSS. from Paris and London, I should have been perfectly helpless. Boehtlingk could have done the whole work himself, in some respects better than I, because he was my senior, and besides, he knew Pânini, the old Indian grammarian who is constantly referred to in Sâyana's Commentary, better than I did. With all these threatening clouds around me, my decision was by no means easy.

It was Burnouf's advice that determined me to remain quietly in Paris. He warned me repeatedly against trusting to Boehtlingk, and promised, if I would only stay in Paris, to give me his support with Guizot, who was then Minister for Foreign Affairs, and very much interested in Oriental studies.

Boehtlingk seems never to have forgiven me, and he and several of his friends were highly displeased at my ultimate success in securing a publisher for the Rig-veda in England. Their language was most unbecoming, and they tried, and actually urged other Sanskrit scholars, to criticize my edition, though I must say to their credit that they afterwards confessed that it was all that could be desired.

Many years later, Boehtlingk published a violent attack on me, entitled *F. Max Müller als Mythendichter*, but I thought it unnecessary to take up the dispute, and preferred to leave my friends to judge for themselves between me and this propounder of accusations, the legitimacy of which he was utterly unable to establish. However, as I discovered later that he accused me of having acted discourteously towards the Imperial Academy of St. Petersburg, with whom I had never had any direct dealings, and stated that he had prevented that illustrious body from ever making me a corresponding member, I thought it right to offer an explanation to the Secretary, and I have in my possession his reply, in which he wrote that there was no foundation whatever for Professor Boehtlingk's statements.

However, the outcome of it was that I did not go to St. Petersburg, but went on with my work at the Library in Paris, till one day I found it necessary to run over to London, to copy and collate certain MSS., and there I found the long-sought-for benefactors, who were to enable me to carry out the work of my life.

Of course, during my stay in Paris there was no idea of my going into society, or of buying tickets for theatres or concerts. I went out to dinner at some small restaurant, but otherwise I remained at home, and viewed Paris life from my high windows, looking out on the Chambre des Députés on one side, the Madeleine close to me on the left, and the Porte St. Martin far away at the end of the Boulevards. Baron d'Eckstein, as I have said, was willing to introduce me into society, but I refused his kind offers. In fact, I was more or less of a bear, and I now regret having missed meeting many interesting characters, and having kept aloof from others, because my interests were absorbed elsewhere. Burnouf asked me sometimes to his house; so did a Monsieur Troyer, who had been in India and published some Sanskrit texts, and whose daughter, the Duchesse de Wagram, made much of me, as she was very fond of music. There were some German families also, some rich, some poor, who showed me great kindness.

I was too much oppressed with cares and anxieties about my life and my literary plans to think much of society and enjoyment. Even of the students and student life I saw but little, though I was actually attending lectures with them. I must say, however, that the little I did see of student life in Paris gave me a very different idea from what is generally thought of their vagaries and extravagances. A Frenchman, if he once begins to work, can work and does work very hard. I remember seeing several instances of this, but it is possible that I may have seen the pick of the Quartier Latin only. One who was then a young man, preparing for the Church, but already with an eye to higher flights, was Renan. At first he still looked upon all young Germans with suspicion, but this feeling soon disappeared. I remember him chiefly at the Bibliothèque Royale, where he had a very small place in the Oriental Department. Hase, the Greek scholar, Reinaud, the Arabist, and Stanislas Julien, the Sinologue, were librarians then. Hase, a German by birth, was most obliging, but he was greatly afraid of speaking German, and insisted on our always speaking French to him. Often did he call Renan to fetch MSS. for me: "Renan," he would call out very loudly, "allez chercher, pour Monsieur Max Müller, le manuscrit sanscrit, numéro . . . ," and then followed a pause, till he had translated "1637" into French. In later years Renan and I became great friends, but we German scholars were often puzzled at his great popularity, which certainly was owing to his style more even than to his scholarship. Some time later, when I was already established in England, we had a little controversy, and I printed a rather fierce attack on his *Grammaire Sémitique*. But we were intimate enough for me to show him my pamphlet, and when he wrote to me, "Pardonnez-moi, je n'ai pas compris ce que vous vouliez dire," I suppressed the pamphlet, though it was printed, and we remained friends for life. He translated my first article on Comparative Mythology, and I had a number of most interesting letters from him. It was his wife who did the translation, while he revised it. That French pamphlet is very scarce now; my own pamphlet was entirely suppressed; even I myself can find no copy of it among the rubbish of my early writings, and what I regret most, I threw away his letters, not thinking how interesting they would become in time.

With all my work, however, I found time to attend some lectures at the Collège de France, and to make the acquaintance of some distinguished French *savants* of the *Institut*. I went there with Burnouf, or Stanislas Julien, or Reinaud, little dreaming that I should some day belong to the same august body. Many of my young French friends, who afterwards became *Membres de l'Institut*, rose to that dignity much later. I was made not only a corresponding, but a real member of the Académie des Inscriptions et Belles Lettres in 1869, before my friends, such as G. Perrot 1874, Michel Bréal 1875, Gaston Paris 1876, and Jules Oppert 1881, occupied their well-merited academical *fauteuils*. The struggle when I was elected in 1869 was a serious one; it was between Mommsen and myself, between classical and Oriental scholarship, and for once Oriental scholarship carried the day. Mommsen, however, was elected in 1895, and there can be little doubt that his strong and outspoken political antipathies had something to do with the late date of his election.

I am sorry to say that one result of my seeing so little of French life was that my French did not make such progress as I expected. Though I was able to express myself *tant bien que mal*, I have always felt hampered in a long conversation. Of course, the French themselves have always been polite enough to say that they could not have detected that I was a German, but I knew better than that, and never have I, even in later years, gained a perfect conversational command of that difficult language.

CHAPTER VI

ARRIVAL IN ENGLAND

WHILE working in Paris I constantly felt the want of some essential MSS. which were at the Library of the East India Company in London, and my desire to visit England consequently grew stronger and stronger; but I had not the wherewithal to pay for the journey, much less for a stay of even a fortnight in London. At last (June, 1846) I thought that I had scraped together enough to warrant my starting. At that time I had never seen the sea, and I was very desirous of doing so. I well remember my unbounded rapture at my first sight of the silver stream, and like Xenophon's Greeks I could have shouted, *θάλαττα, θάλαττα.* Once on board my rapture soon collapsed and was succeeded by that well-known feeling of misery which I have so frequently experienced since then, and I huddled myself up in a corner of the deck.

There a young fellow-traveller saw the poor bundle of misery, and tried to comfort me, and brought me what he thought was good for me, not, however, without a certain merry twinkle in his eye and a few kindly jokes at my expense. We landed at the docks in London, a real drizzly day, rain and mist, and such a crowd rushing on shore that I missed my cheerful friend and felt quite lost. In addition to all this a porter had run away with my portmanteau, which contained my books and MSS., in fact all my worldly goods. At that moment my young friend reappeared, and seeing the plight I was in, came to my assistance. "You stay here," he said, "and I will arrange everything for you;" and so he did. He fetched a four-wheeler, put my luggage on the top, bundled me inside, and drove with me through a maze of London streets to his rooms in the Temple. Then, still knowing nothing about me, he asked me to spend the night in his rooms, gave me a bed and everything else I wanted for the night. The next morning he took me out to look for lodgings, which we found in Essex Street, a small street leading out of the Strand.

The room which I took was almost entirely filled by an immense four-post bed. I had never seen such a structure before, and during the first night that I slept in it, I was in constant fear that the top of the bed would fall and smother me as in the German *Märchen*. When the landlady came in to see me in the morning, after asking how I had slept, the first thing she said was, "But, sir, don't you want another 'pillar'?" I looked bewildered, and said: "Why, what shall I do with another pillar? and where will you put it?" She then touched the pillows under my head and said, "Well, sir, you shall have another 'pillar' to-morrow." "How shall I ever learn English," I said to myself, "if a 'pillar' means really a soft pillow?"

But to return to my unknown friend, he came every day to show me things which I ought to see in London, and brought me tickets for theatres and concerts, which he said were sent to him. His name was William Howard Russell, endeared to so many, high and low, under the name of "Billy" Russell, the first and most brilliant war-correspondent of *The Times* during the Crimean War. He remained my warm and true friend through life, and even now when we are both cripples, we delight in meeting and talking over very distant days.

I had come over to London expecting to stay about a fortnight, but I had been there working at the Library in Leadenhall Street for nearly a month, and my work was far from done, when I thought that I ought to call and pay my respects to the Prussian Minister, Baron Bunsen. I little thought at the time when I was ushered into his presence that this acquaintance was to become the turning-point of my life. If I owed much to Burnouf, how can I tell what I owed to Bunsen? I was amazed at the kindness with which from the very first he received me. I had no claim whatever on him, and I had as yet done very little as a scholar. It is true that he had known my father in Italy, and that Humboldt, with his usual kindness, had written him a strong letter of recommendation on my behalf, but that was hardly sufficient reason to account for the real friendship with which he at once honoured me.

Baroness Bunsen, in the life of her husband, writes: "The kindred mind, their sympathy of heart, the unity in highest aspirations, a congeniality in principles, a fellowship in the pursuit of favourite objects, which attracted and bound Bunsen to his young friend (i. e. myself), rendered this connexion one of the happiest of his life." I am proud to think it was so.

At first the chief bond between us was that I was engaged on a work which as a young man he had proposed to himself as the work of his life, namely, the *editio princeps* of the Rig-veda. Often has he told me how, at the time when he was prosecuting his studies at Göttingen, the very existence of such a book was unknown as yet in Germany. The name of Veda had no doubt been known, and there was a halo of mystery about it, as the oldest book of the world. But what it was and where it was to be found no one could tell. Mr. Astor, a pupil of Bunsen's at Göttingen, had arranged to taken Bunsen to India to carry on his researches there. But Bunsen waited and waited in Italy, till at last, after maintaining himself by giving private lessons, he went to Rome, was taken up by Brandes and Niebuhr, the Prussian Ambassador there, became the friend of the future Frederick William IV, and thus gradually drifted into diplomacy, giving up all hopes of discovering or rescuing the Rig-veda.

People have hardly any idea now, how, in spite of the East India Company conquering and governing India, India itself remained a *terra incognita*, unapproachable by the students of England and of Europe. That there were literary treasures to be discovered in India, that the Brahmans were the depositaries of ancient wisdom, was known through the labours of some of the most eminent servants of the East India Company. It had been known even before, through the interesting communications of Roman Catholic missionaries in India, that the manuscripts themselves, at least those of the Veda, were not forthcoming. Even as late as the times of Sir W. Jones, Colebrooke, and Professor Wilson, the Brahmans were most unwilling to part with MSS. of the Veda, except the Upanishads. Professor Wilson told me that once, when examining the library of a native Râjah, he came across some MSS. of the Rig-veda, and began turning them over; but "I observed," he said, "the ominous and threatening looks of some of the Brahmans present, and thought it wiser to beat a retreat." Dr. Mill had known of a gentleman who had a very sacred hymn of the Veda, the Gayatri, printed at Calcutta. The Brahmans were furious at this profanation, and when the gentleman died soon after, they looked upon his premature death as the vengeance of the offended gods. Colebrooke, however, was allowed to possess himself of several most valuable Vedic MSS., and he found Brahmans quite ready to read with him, not only the classical texts, but also portions of the Veda. "They do not even," he writes, "conceal from us the most sacred texts of the Veda." His own essays on the Veda appeared in the *Asiatic Researches* as early as 1801. But people went on dreaming about the Veda, instead of reading Colebrooke's essays.

It was curious, however, that at the time when I prepared my edition of the Rig-veda, Vedic scholarship was at a very low ebb in Bengal itself, and there were few Brahmans there who knew the whole of the Rig-veda by heart, as they still did in the South of India. Manuscripts were never considered in India as of very high authority; they were always over-ruled by the oral traditions of certain schools. However, such manuscripts, good and bad, but mostly bad, existed, and after a time some of them reached England, France, and even Germany. Portions of those in Berlin and Paris I had copied and collated, so that I could show Bunsen the very book which he had been in search of in his youth. This opened his heart to me as well as the doors of his house. "I am glad," he said, "to have lived to see the Veda. Whatever you want, let me know; I look upon you as myself grown young again." And he did help me, as only a father can help his son.

Perhaps he expected too much from the Veda, as many other people did at that time, and before the *verba ipsissima* were printed. As the oldest book that ever was composed, the Veda was supposed to give us a picture of what man was in his most primitive state, with his most primitive ideas, and his most primitive language. Everybody interested in the origin and the first development of language, thought, religion, and social institutions, looked forward to the Veda as a new revelation. All such dreams, natural enough before the Veda was known, were dispersed by my laying sacrilegious hands on the Veda itself, and actually publishing it, making it public property, to the dismay of the Brahmans in India, and to the delight of all Sanskrit scholars in Europe. The learned essays of Colebrooke in India, and the extracts published by Rosen, the Oriental librarian of the British Museum, might indeed have taught people that the Veda was not a book without any antecedents, that it would not tell us the secrets of Adam and Eve, or of Deukalion and Pyrrha. I myself had both said and written that the Veda, like an old oak tree, shows hundreds and thousands of circles within circles; and yet I was afterwards held responsible for having excited the wildest hopes among archaeologists, when I had done my best, if not to destroy them, at all events to reduce them to their proper level. Schelling seemed quite disappointed when I showed him some of the translations of the hymns of the Rig-veda; and Bunsen, who was still under Schelling's influence, had evidently expected a great many more of such philosophical hymns as the famous one beginning:

"There was not nought nor was there aught at that time."

To the scholar, no doubt, the Veda remained and always will remain the oldest of real books, that has been preserved to us in an almost miraculous way. By book, however, as I often explained, I mean a book divided into chapters and verses, having a beginning and an end, and handed down to us in an alphabetic form of writing. China may have possessed older books in a half phonetic, half symbolic writing; Egypt certainly possessed older hieroglyphic inscriptions and papyri; Babylon had its cuneiform monuments; and certain portions of the Old Testament may have existed in a written form at the time of Josiah, when Hilkiah, the high priest, found the law book in the sanctuary (2 Kings xxii. 8). But the Veda, with its ten books or *Mandalas*, its 1017 hymns or *Suktas*, with every consonant and vowel and accent plainly written, was a different thing. It may safely be called a book. No doubt it existed for a long time, as it does even at present, in oral tradition, but as it was in tradition, so it was when reduced to writing, and in either form I doubt whether any other real book can rival it in antiquity. More important, however, than the purely chronological antiquity of the book, is the antiquity or primitiveness of the thoughts which it contains. If the people of the Veda did not turn out to be quite such savages as was hoped and expected, they nevertheless disclosed to us a layer of thought which can be explored nowhere else. The Vedic poets were not ashamed of exposing their fear that the sun might tumble down from the sky, and there are no other poets, as far as I know, who still trembled at the same not quite unnatural thought. Nor do I find even savages who still wonder and express their surprise that black cows should produce white milk. Is not that childish enough for any ancient or modern savage? Mere chronology is here of as little avail as with modern savages, whose customs and beliefs, though known as but of yesterday, are represented to us as older than the Veda, older than Babylonian cylinders, older than anything written. When certain modern savages recognize the relationship of paternity, maternity, and consanguinity, this is called very ancient. If they admit traditional restrictions as to marriage, food, the treatment of the dead, nay, even a life to come, this too, no doubt, may be very old; but it may be of yesterday also. There are even quite new gods, whose genesis has been watched by living missionaries. The great difficulty in all such researches is to distinguish between what is common to human nature, and what is really inherited or traditional. All such questions have only as yet been touched upon, and they must wait for their answer till real scholars will take up the study of the language of living savages, in the same scholarlike spirit in which they have taken up the study of Vedic and Babylonian savages. But we must have patience and learn to wait. It has been a favourite idea among anthropologists that the savage races inhabiting parts of India give us a correct idea of what the Aryans of India were before they were civilized. It may safely be said of this as of other mere ideas, that it may be true, but that there is no evidence to show that it is true. At all events it takes much for granted, and neglects, as it would seem, the very lessons which the theory of evolution has taught us. It is the nature of evolution to be continuous, and not to proceed *per saltum.* Therein lies the beauty of genealogical evolution that we can recognize the fibres which connect the upper strata with the lower, till we strike the lowest, or at least that which contains what seem to be the seeds and germs of early thoughts, words, and acts. We can trace the most modern forms of language back to Sanskrit, or rather to that postulated linguistic stratum of which Sanskrit formed the most prominent representative, just as we can trace the French *Dieu* back to Latin *Deus* and Sanskrit *Devas,* the brilliant beings behind the phenomena of nature; and again behind them, *Dyaus,* the brilliant sky, the Greek *Zeus,* the Roman *Iovis* and *Iuppiter,* the most natural of all the Aryan gods of nature. This is real evolution, a real causal nexus between the present and the past. It used to be called history or pragmatic history, whether we take history in the sense of the description of evolution, or in that of evolution itself. History has generally to begin with the present, to go back to the past, and to point out the palpable steps by which the past became again and again the present. Evolution, on the contrary, prefers to begin with the distant past, to postulate formations, even if they have left no traces, and to speak of those almost imperceptible changes by which the postulated past became the perceptible present, as not only necessary, but as real. Perhaps the difference is of no importance, but the historical method seems certainly the more accurate, and the more satisfactory from a purely scientific point of view.

In all such evolutionary researches language has always been the most useful instrument, and the study of the science of language may truly be said to have been the first science which was treated according to evolutionary or historical principles. Here, too, no doubt, intermediate links which must have existed, are sometimes lost beyond recovery, and when we arrive at the very roots of language, we feel that there may have been whole aeons before that radical period. Here science must recognize her inevitable horizons, but here again no surviving literary monument could carry us so far as the Veda. Hence its supreme importance for Aryan philology—for the philology of the most important languages of historical mankind. Other languages, whether Babylonian or Accadian, whether Hottentot or Maori, may be, for all we know, much more ancient or much more primitive; but, as scientific explorers, we can only speak of what we know, and we must renounce all conjectures that go beyond facts.

In all these researches no one took a livelier interest and encouraged me more than Bunsen. When some of my translations of the Vedic hymns seemed fairly satisfactory, I used to take them to him, and he was always delighted at seeing a little more of that ancient Aryan torso, though at the time he was more specially interested in Egyptian chronology and archaeology. Often when I was alone with him did we discuss the chronological and psychological dates of Egyptian and Aryan antiquity. Kind-hearted as he was, Bunsen could get very excited, nay, quite violent in arguing, and though these fits soon passed off, yet it made discussions between His Excellency the Prussian Minister and a young German scholar somewhat difficult. At that time much less was known of the earliest Egyptian chronology than is now. But I was never much impressed by mere dates. If a king was supposed to have lived 5,000 years before our era, "What is that to us?" I used to say, "He sits on his throne *in vacuo*, and there is nothing to fix him by, nothing contemporary which alone gives interest to history. In India we have no dates; but whatever dates and names of kings and accounts of battles the Egyptian inscriptions may give us, as a book there is nothing so old in Egypt as the Veda in India. Besides, we have in the Veda thoughts; and in the chronology of thought the Veda seems to me older than even the Book of the Dead."

As to the actual date of the Veda, I readily granted that chronologically it was not so old as the pyramids, but supposing it had been, would that in any way have increased its value for our studies? If we were to place it at 5000 B. C., I doubt whether anybody could refute such a date, while if we go back beyond the Veda, and come to measure the time required for the formation of Sanskrit and of the Proto-Aryan language I doubt very much whether even 5,000 years would suffice for that. There is an unfathomable depth in language, layer following after layer, long before we arrive at roots, and what a time and what an effort must have been required for their elaboration, and for the elaboration of the ideas expressed in them.

Our battles waxed sometimes very fierce, but we generally ended by arriving at an understanding. As a young man, Bunsen had clearly perceived the importance of the Veda for an historical study of mankind and the growth of the human mind, but he was not discouraged when he saw that it gave us less than had been expected. "It is a fortress," he used to say, "that must be besieged and taken, it cannot be left in our rear." But he little knew how much time it would take to approach it, to surround it, and at last to take it. It has not been surrendered even now, and will not be in my time. It is true there are several translations of the whole of the Rig-veda, and their authors deserve the highest credit for what they have done. People have wondered why I have not given one of them in my Sacred Books of the East. I thought it was more honest to give, in co-operation with Oldenburg, specimens only in vols. xxxii and xlvi of that series, and let it be seen in the notes how much uncertainty there still is, and how much more of hard work is required, before we can call ourselves masters of the old Vedic fortress.

Bunsen's interest in my work, however, took a more practical turn than mere encouragement. It was no good encouraging me to copy and collate Sanskrit MSS. if they were not to be published. He saw that the East India Company were the proper body to undertake that work. Bunsen's name was a power in England, and his patronage was the very best introduction that I could have had. It was no easy task to persuade the Board of Directors—all strictly practical and commercial men—to authorize so considerable an expenditure, merely to edit and print an old book that none of them could understand, and many of them had perhaps never even heard of. Bunsen pointed out what a disgrace it would be to them, if some other country than England published this edition of the Sacred Books of the Brahmans.

Professor Wilson, Librarian of the Company, also gave my project his support, and at last, not quite a year after my arrival in England, after a long struggle and many fears of failure, it was settled that the East India Company were to bear the cost of printing the Veda, and were meanwhile to enable me to stay in London, and prepare my work for press.

I had already been working five years copying and collating, and my first volume of the Rig-veda was progressing, but it was only when all was settled that I realized how much there was still to do, and that I should have very hard work indeed before the printing could begin. I must enter into some details to show the real difficulties I had to face.

I felt convinced that the first thing to do was to publish a correct text of the Rig-veda. That was not so difficult, though it brought me the greatest kudos. The MSS. were very correct, and the text could easily be restored by comparing the Pada and Sanhitâ texts, i. e. the text in which every word was separated, and the text in which the words were united according to the rules of Sandhi. Anybody might have done that, yet this, as I said, was the part of my work for which I have received the greatest praise.

When my edition of the Rig-veda containing text and commentary was nearly finished, another scholar, who had assisted me in my work, and who had always had the use of my MSS., my Indices, in fact of the whole of my *apparatus criticus*, published a transcript of the text in Latin letters, and thus anticipated part of the last volume of my edition. His friends, who were perhaps not mine, seemed delighted to call him the first editor of the Rig-veda, though they ceased to do so when they discovered misprints or mistakes of my own edition repeated in his. He himself was far above such tactics. He knew, and they knew perfectly well that, whatever the *vulgus profanum* may think, my real work was the critical edition of Sâyana's commentary on the Rig-veda. I had determined that this also should be edited according to the strictest rules of criticism. I knew what an amount of labour that would involve, but I refused to yield to the pressure of my colleagues to proceed more quickly but less critically.

Sâyana quotes a number of Sanskrit works which, at the time when I began my edition, had not yet been edited. Such were the Nirukta, the glossary of the Rig-veda; the Aitareya-brâhmana, a very old explanation of the Vedic sacrifice; the Âsvalâyana Sûtras, on the ceremonial; and sundry works of the same character. Sâyana generally alludes very briefly only to these works and presupposes that they are known to us, so that a short reference would suffice for his purposes. To find such references and to understand them required, however, not only that I should copy these works, which I did, but that I should make indices and thus be able to find the place of the passages to which he alluded. This I did also, but over and over again was I stopped by some short enigmatical reference to Pânini's grammar or Yaska's glossary, which I could not identify. All these references are now added to my edition, and those who will look them up in the originals, will see what kind of work it was which I had to do before a single line of my edition could be printed. How often was I in perfect despair, because there was some allusion in Sâyana which I could not make out, and which no other Sanskrit scholar, not even Burnouf or Wilson, could help me to clear up. It often took me whole days, nay, weeks, before I saw light. A good deal of the commentary was easy enough. It was like marching on the high road, when suddenly there rises a fortress that has to be taken before any further advance is to be thought of. In the purely mechanical part other men could and did help me. But whenever any real difficulty arose, I had to face it by myself, though after a time I gladly acknowledged that here, too, their advice was often valuable to me. In fact I found, and all my assistants seemed to have found out the same, that if they were useful to me, the work they did for me was useful to them, and I am proud to say that nearly all of them have afterwards risen to great prominence in Sanskrit scholarship. From time to time I also worked at interpreting and translating some of the Vedic hymns, though I had always hoped that this part of the work would be taken up by other scholars.

Bunsen was also my social sponsor in London, and my first peeps into English society were at the Prussian Legation. He often invited me to his breakfast and dinner parties, and when I saw for the first time the magnificent rooms crowded with ministers, and dukes, and bishops, and with ladies in their grandest dresses, I was as in a dream, and felt as if I had been lifted into another world. Men were pointed out to me such as Sir Robert Peel, the Duke of Wellington, Van der Weyer, the Belgian Minister, Thirlwall, Bishop of St. David's and author of the *History of Greece*, Archdeacon Hare, Frederick Maurice, and many more whom I did not know then, though I came to know several of them afterwards. Anybody who had anything of his own to produce was welcome in Bunsen's house, and among the men whom I remember meeting at his breakfast parties, were Rawlinson, Layard, Hodgson, Birch, and many more. Those breakfast parties were then quite a new institution to me, and it is curious how entirely they have gone out of fashion, though Sir Harry Inglis, Member for Oxford, Gladstone, Member for Oxford, Monckton Milnes (afterwards Lord Houghton), kept them up to the last, while in Oxford they survived perhaps longer than anywhere else. They had one great advantage, people came to them quite fresh in the morning; but they broke too much into the day, particularly when, as at Oxford, they ended with beer, champagne, and cigars, as was sometimes the case in undergraduates' rooms.

How I was able to swim in that new stream, I can hardly understand even now. I had been quite unaccustomed to this kind of society, and was ignorant of its simplest rules. Bunsen, however, was never put out by my gaucheries, but gave me friendly hints in feeling my way through what seemed to me a perfect labyrinth. He told me that I had offended people by not returning their calls, or not leaving a card after having dined with them, paying the so-called digestion-visit to them. How should I know? Nobody had ever told me, and I thought it obtrusive to call. Nor did I know that in England to touch fish with a knife, or to help yourself to potatoes with a fork, was as fatal as to drop or put in an *h*. Nor did I ever understand why to cut crisp pastry on your plate with a knife was worse manners than to divide it with a fork, often scattering it over your plate and possibly over the table-cloth. I must confess also that fish-knives always seemed to me more civilized than forks in dividing fish, but fish-knives did not exist when I first came to England. The really interesting side of all this is to watch how customs change—come in and go out—and by what a slow and imperceptible process they are discarded. Let us hope it is by the survival of the fittest. When I first went to Oxford everybody took wine with his neighbours, now it is only at such conservative colleges as my own—All Souls—that the old custom still survives. But then we have not even given up wax candles yet, and we look upon gas as a most objectionable innovation.

Another great difficulty I had was in writing letters and addressing my friends properly as Sir, or Mr. Smith, or Smith. I was told that the rule was very simple and that you addressed everybody exactly as they addressed you. What was the consequence? When I received an invitation to dine with the Bishop of Oxford who addressed me as "My dear Sir," I wrote back "My dear Sir," and said that I should be very happy. How Samuel Wilberforce must have chuckled when he read my epistle. But how is any stranger to know all the intricacies of social literature, particularly if he is wrongly informed by the highest authorities. I must confess that even later in life I have often been puzzled as to the right way of addressing my friends. There is no difficulty about intimate friends, but as one grows older one knows so many people more or less intimately, and according to their different characters and stations in life, one often does not know whether one offends by too great or too little familiarity. I was once writing to a very eminent man in London who had been exceedingly friendly to me at Oxford, and I addressed him as "My dear Professor H." At the end of his answer he wrote, "Don't call me Professor." All depends on the tone in which such words are said. I imagined that living in fashionable society in London, he did not like the somewhat scholastic title of Professor which, in London particularly, has always a by-taste of diluted omniscience and conceit. I accordingly addressed him in my next letter as "My dear Sir," and this, I am sorry to say, produced quite a coldness and stiffness, as my friend evidently imagined that I declined to be on more intimate terms with him, the fact being that through life I have always been one of his most devoted admirers. I did my best to conform to all the British institutions, as well as I could, though in the beginning I must no doubt have made fearful blunders, and possibly given offence to the truly insular Briton. Bunsen seemed to delight in asking me whenever he had Princes or other grandees to lunch or dine with him.

One day he took me with him to stay at Hurstmonceux with Archdeacon Hare, and a delightful time it was. There were books in every room, on the staircase, and in every corner of the house, and the Archdeacon knew every one of them, and as soon as a book was mentioned, he went and fetched it. He generally knew the very place at which the passage that was being discussed, occurred, and excelled even the famous dog, which at one of these literary breakfast parties—I believe in Hallam's house—was ordered on the spur of the moment to fetch the fifth volume of Gibbon's *History*, and at once climbed up the ladder and brought down from the shelf the very volume in which the disputed passage occurred. He had been taught this one trick of fetching a certain volume from the shelves of the library, and the conversation was turned and turned till it was brought round to a passage in that very volume. The guests were, no doubt, amazed, but as it was before the days of Darwin and Lubbock, it led to no more than a good laugh. I was surprised and delighted at the honesty with which the Archdeacon admitted the weak points of the Anglican system, and the dangers which threatened not only the Church, but the religion of England. The real danger, he evidently thought, came from the clergy, and their hankering after Rome. "They have forgotten their history," he said, "and the sufferings which the sway of a Roman priesthood has inflicted for centuries on their country." I think it was he who told me the story of a young Romanizing curate, who declared that he could never see what was the use of the laity.

One day when I called on Bunsen with my books, and I frequently called when I had something new to show him, he said: "You must come with me to Oxford to the meeting of the British Association." This was in 1847. Of course I did not know what sort of thing this British Association was, but Bunsen said he would explain it all to me, only I must at once sit down and write a paper. He, Bunsen, was to read a paper on the "Results of the recent Egyptian Researches in reference to Asiatic and African Ethnology and the Classification of Languages," and he wanted Dr. Karl Meyer and myself to support him, the former with a paper on Celtic Philology, and myself with a paper on the Aryan and Aboriginal Languages of India. I assured him that this was quite beyond me. I had hardly been a year in England, and even if I could write, I knew but too well that I could not read a paper before a large audience. However, Bunsen would take no refusal. "We must show them what we have done in Germany for the history and philosophy of language," he said, "and I reckon on your help." There was no escape, and to Oxford I had to go. I was fearfully nervous, for, as Prince Albert was to be present, ever so many distinguished people had flocked to the meeting, and likewise some not very friendly ethnologists, such as Dr. Latham, and Mr. Crawford, known by the name of the Objector General. Our section was presided over by the famous Dr. Prichard, the author of that classical work, *Researches into the Physical History of Mankind*, in five volumes, and it was he who protected me most chivalrously against the somewhat frivolous objections of certain members, who were not over friendly towards Prince Albert, Chevalier Bunsen, and all that was called German in scholarship. All, however, went off well. Bunsen's speech was most successful, and it is a pity that it should be buried in the *Transactions of the British Association for* 1847. At that time it was considered a great honour that his speech should appear there *in extenso.* When Bunsen declared that he would not give it, unless Dr. Meyer's paper and my own were published in the *Transactions* at the same time, there was renewed opposition. I was so little proud of my own essay, that I should much rather have kept it back for further improvement, but printed it was in the *Transactions*, and much canvassed at the time in different journals.

I have always been doubtful about the advantages of these public meetings, so far as any scientific results are concerned. Everybody who pays a guinea may become a member and make himself heard, whether he knows anything on the subject or not. The most ignorant men often occupy the largest amount of time. Some people look upon these congresses simply as a means of advertising themselves, and I have actually seen quoted among a man's titles to fame the fact that he had been a member of certain congresses. Another drawback is that no one, not even the best of scholars, is quite himself before a mixed audience. Whereas in a private conversation a man is glad to receive any new information, no one likes to be told in public that he ought to have known this or that, or that every schoolboy knows it. Then follows generally a squabble, and the best pleader is sure to have the laughter on his side, however ignorant he may be of the subject that is being discussed. But Dr. Prichard was an excellent president and moderator, and though he had unruly spirits to deal with, he succeeded in keeping up a certain decorum among them. Dr. Prichard's authority stood very high, and justly so, and his *Researches into the Physical History of Mankind* still remain unparalleled in ethnology. His careful weighing of facts and difficulties went out of fashion when the theory of evolution became popular, and every change from a flea to an elephant was explained by imperceptible degrees. He dealt chiefly with what was perceptible, with well-observed facts, and many of the facts which he marshalled so well, require even now, in these post-Darwinian days I should venture to say, renewed consideration. Like all great men, he was wonderfully humble, and allowed me to contradict him, who ought to have been proud to listen and to learn from him.

But though I cannot say that the result of these meetings and wranglings was very great or valuable, I spent a few most delightful days at Oxford, and I could not imagine a more perfect state of existence than to be an undergraduate, a fellow, or a professor there. A kind of silent love sprang up in my heart, though I hardly confessed it to myself, much less to the object of my affections. I knew I had to go back to be a University tutor or even a master in a public school in Germany, and that was a hard life compared with the freedom of Oxford. To be independent and free to work as I liked, that was everything to me, but how I ever succeeded in realizing my ideal, I hardly know. At that time I saw nothing but a life of drudgery and severe struggle before me, but I did not allow myself to dwell on it; I simply worked on, without looking either right or left, behind or before.

While at Oxford on this my first flying visit, I had a room in University College, the very college in which my son was hereafter to be an undergraduate. My host was Dr. Plumptre, the Master of the College, a tall, stiff, and to my mind, very imposing person. He was then Vice-Chancellor, and I believe I never saw him except in his cap and gown and with two bedels walking before him, the one with a gold, the other with a silver poker in his hands. We have no Esquire bedels any longer! All the professors, too, and even the undergraduates, dressed in their mediaeval academic costume, looked to me very grand, and so different from the German students at Leipzig or still more at Jena, walking about the streets in pink cotton trousers and dressing-gowns. It seemed to me quite a different world, and I made new discoveries every day. Being with Bunsen I was invited to all the official dinners during the meeting of the British Association, and here, too, the Vice-Chancellor acted his part with becoming dignity. He never unbent; he never indulged in a joke or joined in the laughter of his neighbours. When I remarked on his immovable features, I was told that he slept in starched sheets—and I believed it. At one of these dinners, Prince Louis Lucien Bonaparte caused a titter during a speech about the freedom which people enjoyed in England. "In France," he said, "with all the declamations about *Liberté*, *Égalité*, *Fraternité*, there is very little freedom, and, with all the trees of *liberté* which are being planted along the boulevards, there is very little of real liberty to be found there!" "But you in England," he finished, "you have your old tree of liberty, which is always flowering and showering *peas* on the whole world." He wanted to say peace. We tried to look solemn but failed, and a suppressed laugh went round till it reached the Vice-Chancellor. There it stopped. He was far too well bred to allow a single muscle of his face to move. "He throws a cold blanket on everything," my neighbour said; and my knowledge of English was still so imperfect that I accepted many of these metaphorical remarks in their literal sense, and became more and more puzzled about my host. It was evidently a pleasure to my friends to see how easily I was taken in. On the walls of the houses at Oxford I saw the letters F. P. about ten feet from the ground. Of course it was meant for Fire Plug, but I was told that it marked the height of the Vice-Chancellor, whose name was Frederick Plumptre.

My visit to Oxford was over all too soon, and I returned to London to toil away at my Sanskrit MSS. in the little room that had been assigned to me in the Old East India House in Leadenhall Street. That building, too, in which the reins of the mighty Empire of India were held, mostly by the hands of merchants, has vanished, and the place of it knoweth it no more. However, I thought little of India, I only thought of the library at the East India House, a real Eldorado for an eager Sanskrit student, who had never seen such treasures before. I saw little else there, I only remember seeing Tippoo Sahib's tiger which held an English soldier in his claws, and was regularly wound up for the benefit of visitors, and then uttered a loud squeak, enough to disturb even the most absorbed of students. I felt quite dazed by all the books and manuscripts placed at my disposal. and revelled in them every day till it became dark, and I had to walk home through Ludgate Hill, Cheapside, and the Strand, generally carrying ever so many books and papers under my arms. I knew nobody in the city, and no one knew me; and what did I care for the world, as long as I had my beloved manuscripts?

In March, 1848, I had to go over to Paris to finish up some work there, and just came in for the revolution. From my windows I had a fine view of all that was going on. I well remember the pandemonium in the streets, the aspect of the savage mob, the wanton firing of shots at quiet spectators, the hoisting of Louis Philippe's nankeen trousers on the flag-staff of the Tuileries. When bullets began to come through my windows, I thought it time to be off while it was still possible. Then came the question how to get my box full of precious manuscripts, &c., belonging to the East India Company, to the train. The only railway open was the line to Havre, which had been broken up close to the station, but further on was intact, and in order to get there we had to climb three barricades. I offered my *concierge* five francs to carry my box, but his wife would not hear of his risking his life in the streets; ten francs—the same result; but at the sight of a louis d'or she changed her mind, and with an "Allez, mon ami, allez toujours," dispatched her husband on his perilous expedition. Arrived in London I went straight to the Prussian Legation, and was the first to give Bunsen the news of Louis

Philippe's flight from Paris. Bunsen took me off to see Lord Palmerston, and I was able to show him a bullet that I had picked up in my room as evidence of the bloody scenes that had been enacted in Paris. So even a poor scholar had to play his small part in the events that go to make up history.

CHAPTER VII

EARLY DAYS AT OXFORD

It had been settled that my edition of the Rig-veda should be printed at the Oxford University Press, and I found that I had often to go there to superintend the printing. Not that the printers required much supervision, as I must say that the printing at the University Press was, and is, excellent—far better than anything I had known in Germany. In providing copy for a work of six volumes, each of about 1000 pages, it was but natural that *lapsus calami* should occur from time to time. What surprised me was that several of these were corrected in the proof-sheets sent to me. At last I asked whether there was any Sanskrit scholar at Oxford who revised my proof-sheets before they were returned. I was told there was not, but that the queries were made by the printer himself. That printer was an extraordinary man. His right arm was slightly paralysed, and he had therefore been put on difficult slow work, such as Sanskrit. There are more than 300 types which a printer must know in composing Sanskrit. Many of the letters in Sanskrit are incompatible, i. e. they cannot follow each other, or if they do, they have to be modified.

Every *d*, for instance, if followed by a *t*, is changed to *t*; every *dh* loses its aspiration, becomes likewise *t*, or changes the next *t* into *dh*. Thus from *budh* + *ta*, we have *Buddha*, i.e. awakened. In writing I had sometimes neglected these modifications, but in the proof-sheets these cases were always either queried or corrected. When I asked the printer, who did not of course know a word of Sanskrit, how he came to make these corrections, he said: "Well, sir, my arm gets into a regular swing from one compartment of types to another, and there are certain movements that never occur. So if I suddenly have to take up types which entail a new movement, I feel it, and I put a query." An English printer might possibly be startled in the same way if in English he had to take up an *s* immediately following an *h*. But it was certainly extraordinary that an unusual movement of the muscles of the paralysed arm should have led to the discovery of a mistake in writing Sanskrit. In spite of the extreme accuracy of my printer, however, I saw, that after all it would be better for myself, and for the Veda, if I were on the spot, and I decided to migrate from London to Oxford.

My first visit had filled me with enthusiasm for the beautiful old town, which I regarded as an ideal home for a student. Besides, I found that I was getting too gay in London, and in order to be able to devote my evenings to society, I had to get up and begin work soon after five. May, therefore, saw me established for the first time in Oxford, in a small room in Walton Street. The moving of my books and papers from London did not take long. At that time my library could still be accommodated in my portmanteau, it had not yet risen to 12,000 volumes, threatening to drive me out of my house. A happy time it was when I possessed no books which I had not read, and no one sent books to me which I did not want, and yet had to find a place for in my rooms, and to thank the author for his kindness.

I at once found that my work went on more rapidly at Oxford than in London, though if I had expected to escape from all hospitality I certainly was not allowed to do that. Accustomed as I was to the Spartan diet of a German *convictorium*, or a dinner at the Palais Royal *à deux francs*, the dinners to which I was invited by some of the Fellows in Hall, or in Common Room, surprised me not a little. The old plate, the old furniture, and the whole style of living, impressed me deeply, particularly the after-dinner railway, an ingenious invention for lightening the trouble of the guests who took wine in Common Room. There was a small railway fixed before the fire-place, and on it a wagon containing the bottles went backwards and forwards, halting before every guest till he had helped himself. That railway, I am afraid, is gone now; and what is more serious, the pleasant, chatty evenings spent in Common Room are likewise a thing of the past. Married Fellows, if they dine in Hall, return home after dinner, and junior Fellows go to their books or pupils. In my early Oxford days, a married Fellow would have sounded like a solecism. The story goes that married Fellows were not entirely unknown, and that you could hold even a fellowship, if you could hold your tongue. Young people, however, who did not possess that gift of silence, had often to wait till they were fifty, before a college living fell vacant, and the quinquagenarian Fellow became a young husband and a young vicar.

What impressed me, however, even more than the great hospitality of Oxford, was the real friendliness shown to an unknown German scholar. After all, I had done very little as yet, but the kind words which Bunsen and Dr. Prichard had spoken about me at the meeting of the British Association, had evidently produced an impression in my favour far beyond what I deserved. I must have seemed a very strange bird, such as had never before built his nest at Oxford. I was very young, but I looked even younger than I was, and my knowledge of the manners of society, particularly of English society, was really nil. Few people knew what I was working at. Some had a kind of vague impression that I had discovered a very old religion, older than the Jewish and the Christian, which contained the key to many of the mysteries that had puzzled the ancient, nay, even the modern world. Frequently, when I was walking through the streets of Oxford, I observed how people stared at me, and seemed to whisper some information about me. Tradespeople did not always trust me, though I never owed a penny to anybody; when I wanted money I could always make it by going on faster with printing the Rig-veda, for which I received four pounds a sheet. This seemed to me then a large sum, though many a sheet took me at first more than a week to get ready, copy, collate, understand, and finally print. If I was interested in any other subject, my exchequer suffered accordingly—but I could always retrieve my losses by sitting up late at night. Poor as I was, I never had any cares about money, and when I once began to write in English for English journals, I had really more than I wanted. My first article in the *Edinburgh Review* appeared in October, 1851.

At that time the idea of settling at Oxford, of remaining in this academic paradise, never entered my head. I was here to print my Rig-veda and work at the Bodleian; that I should in a few years be an M.A. of Christ Church, a Fellow of the most exclusive of colleges, nay, a married Fellow—a being not even invented then—and a professor of the University, never entered into my wildest dreams. I could only admire, and admire with all my heart. Everything seemed perfect, the gardens, the walks in the neighbourhood, the colleges, and most of all the inhabitants of the colleges, both Fellows and undergraduates. My ideas were still so purely continental that I could not understand how the University could do such a thing as incorporate a foreign scholar—could, in fact, govern itself without a Minister of Education to appoint professors, without a Royal Commissioner to look after the undergraduates and their moral and political sentiments. And here at Oxford I was told that the Government did not know Oxford, nor Oxford the Government, that the only ruling power consisted in the Statutes of the University, that professors and tutors were perfectly free so long as they conformed to these statutes, and that certainly no minister could ever appoint or dismiss a professor, except the Regius professors. "If we want a thing done," my friends used to explain to me, "we do it ourselves, as long as it does not run counter to the statutes."

But Oxford changes with every generation. It is always growing old, but it is always growing young again. There was an old Oxford four hundred years ago, and there was an old Oxford fifty years ago. To a man who is taking his M.A. degree, Oxford, as it was when he was a freshman, seems quite a thing of the past. By the public at large no place is supposed to be so conservative, so unchanging, nay, so stubborn in resisting new ideas, as Oxford; and yet people who knew it forty or fifty years ago, like myself, find it now so changed that, when they look back they can hardly believe it is the same place. Even architecturally the streets of the University have changed, and here not always for the better.

Architects unfortunately object to mere imitation of the old Oxford style of building; they want to produce something entirely their own, which may be very good by itself, but is not always in harmony with the general tone of the college buildings. I still remember the outcry against the Taylor Institution, the only Palladian building at Oxford, and yet everybody has now grown reconciled to it, and even Ruskin lectured in it, which he would not have done, if he had disapproved of its architecture. He would never lecture in the Indian Institute, and wrote me a letter sadly reproving me for causing Broad Street to be defaced by such a building, when I had had absolutely nothing to do with it. He was very loud in his condemnation of other new buildings. He abused even the New Museum, though he had a great deal to do with it himself. He had hoped that it would be the architecture of the future, but he confessed after a time that he was not satisfied with the result.

In his days we still had the old Magdalen Bridge, the Bodleian unrestored, and no trams. Ruskin was so offended by the new bridge, by the restored Bodleian, and by the tram-cars, that he would go ever so far round to avoid these eyesores, when he had to deliver his lectures; and that was by no means an easy pilgrimage. There was, of course, no use in arguing with him. Most people like the new Magdalen Bridge because it agrees better with the width of High Street; they consider the Bodleian well restored, particularly now that the new stone is gradually toning down to the colour of the old walls, and as to tram-cars, objectionable as they are in many respects, they certainly offend the eye less than the old dirty and rickety omnibuses. The new buildings of Merton, in the style of a London police-station, offended him deeply, and with more justice, particularly as he had to live next door to them when he had rooms at Corpus.

These new buildings could not be helped at Oxford. The stone, with which most of the old colleges were built, was taken from a quarry close to Oxford, and began to peel off and to crumble in a very curious manner. Artists like these chequered walls, and by moonlight they are certainly picturesque, but the colleges had to think of what was safe. My own college, All Souls, has ever so many pinnacles, and we kept an architect on purpose to watch which of them were unsafe and had to be restored or replaced by new ones. Every one of these pinnacles cost us about fifty pounds, and at every one of our meetings we were told that so many pinnacles had been tested, and wanted repairing or replacing. Many years ago, when I was spending the whole Long Vacation at Oxford, I could watch from my windows a man who was supposed to be testing the strength of these pinnacles. He was armed with a large crowbar, which he ran with all his might against the unfortunate pinnacle. I doubt whether the walls of any Roman castellum could have resisted such a ram. I spoke to some of the Fellows, and when the builder made his next report to us, we rather objected to the large number of invalids. He was not to be silenced, however, so easily, but told us with a very grave countenance that he could not take the responsibility, as a pinnacle might fall any day on our Warden when he went to chapel. This, he thought, would settle the matter. But no, it made no impression whatever on the junior Fellows, and the number of annual cripples was certainly very much reduced in consequence.

It is true that Oxford has always loved what is old better than what is new, and has resisted most innovations to the very last. A well-known liberal statesman used to say that when any measure of reform was before Parliament, he always rejoiced to see an Oxford petition against it, for that measure was sure to be carried very soon. It should not be forgotten, however, that there always has been a liberal minority at Oxford. It is still mentioned as something quite antediluvian, that Oxford, that is the Hebdomadal Council, petitioned against the Great Western Railway invading its sacred precincts; but it is equally true that not many years later it petitioned for a branch line to keep the University in touch with the rest of the world.

Many things, of course, have been changed, and are changing every year before our very eyes; but what can never be changed, in spite of some recent atrocities in brick and mortar, is the natural beauty of its gardens, and the historical character of its architecture. Whether Friar Bacon, as far back as the thirteenth century, admired the colleges, chapels, and gardens of Oxford, we do not know; and even if we did, few of them could have been the same as those which we admire to-day. We must not forget that Greene's *Honourable History of Friar Bacon* does not give us a picture of what Oxford was when seen by that famous philosopher, who is sometimes claimed as a Fellow of Brasenose College, probably long before that College existed; but what is said in that play in praise of the University, may at least be taken as a recollection of what Greene saw himself, when he took his degree as Bachelor of Arts in 1578. In his play of the *History of Friar Bacon*, Greene introduces the Emperor of Germany, Henry II, 1212-50, as paying a visit to Henry III of England, 1216-73, and he puts into his mouth the following lines, which, though they cannot compare with Shelley's or Mat Arnold's, are at all events the earliest testimony to the natural attractions of Oxford. Anyhow, Shelley's and Mat Arnold's lines are well known and are always quoted, so that I venture to quote Greene's lines, not for the sake of their beauty, but simply because they are probably known to very few of my readers:

"Trust me, Plantagenet, these Oxford schools
Are richly seated near the river-side:
The mountains full of fat and fallow deer,

**The battling[1] pastures lade with kine and flocks,
The town gorgeous with high built colleges,
And scholars seemly in their grave attire."**

The mountains round Oxford we must accept as a bold poetical licence, whether they were meant for Headington Hill or Wytham Woods. The German traveller, Hentzner, who described Oxford in 1598, is more true to nature when he speaks of the wooded hills that encompass the plain in which Oxford lies.

But while the natural beauty of Oxford has always been admired and praised by strangers, the doctors and professors of the old University have not always fared so well at the hands of English and foreign critics. I shall not quote from Giordano Bruno, who visited England in 1583-5, and calls Oxford "the widow of true science[2]," but Milton surely cannot be suspected of any prejudice against Oxford. Yet he writes in 1656 in a letter to Richard Jones: "There is indeed plenty of amenity and salubrity in the place when you are there. There are books enough for the needs of a University: if only the amenity of the spot contributed so much to the genius of the inhabitants as it does to pleasant living, nothing would seem wanting to the happiness of the place."

These ill-natured remarks about the Oxford Dons seem to go on to the very beginning of our century.

[1] Will it be believed that the battels (bills) in College are connected with this word?

[2] *Opere*, ed. Wagner, i. p. 179.

The buildings and gardens are praised, but by way of contrast, it would seem, or from some kind of jealousy, their inhabitants are always treated with ridicule. Not long ago a book was published, *Memoirs of a Highland Lady.* Though published in 1898, it should be remembered that the memoirs go back as far as 1809. Nor should it be forgotten that at that time the authoress was hardly more than thirteen years of age, and certainly of a very girlish, not to say frivolous, disposition. She stayed some time with the then Master of University, Dr. Griffith, and for him, it must be said, she always shows a certain respect. But no one else at Oxford is spared. She arrived there at the time of Lord Grenville's installation as Chancellor of the University. Though so young, she was taken to the Theatre, and this is her description of what she saw and heard:—"It was a shock to me; I had expected to be charmed with a play, instead of being nearly set to sleep by discourses in Latin from a pulpit. There were some purple, and some gold, some robes and some wigs, a great crowd, and some stir at times, while a deal of humdrum speaking and dumb show was followed by the noisy demonstrations of the students, as they applauded or condemned the honours bestowed; but in the main I tired of the heat and the mob, and the worry of these mornings, and so, depend upon it, did poor Lord Grenville, who sat up in the chair of state among the dignitaries, like the Grand Lama in his temple guarded by his priests." One thing only she was delighted with, that was the singing of Catalani at one of the concerts. Yet even here she cannot repress her remark that she sang "Gott safe the King." She evidently was a flippant young lady or child, and with her sister, who afterwards joined her at Oxford, seems to have found herself quite a fish out of water in the grave society of the University.

The room in the Master's Lodge which appalled her most and seems to have been used as a kind of schoolroom, was the Library, full of Divinity books, but without curtains, carpet, or fireplace. Here they had lessons in music, drawing, arithmetic, history, geography, and French. "And the Master," she adds, "opened to us what had been till then a sealed book, the New Testament, so that this visit to Oxford proved really one of the fortunate chances of my life."

This speaks well for the young lady, who in later life seems to have occupied a most honoured and influential position in Scotch society. But Oxford society evidently found no favour in her eyes.

Her uncle and aunt, as she tells us, were frequently out at dinner with other Heads of Houses, for there was, of course, no other society. These dinners seem to have been very sumptuous, though their own domestic life was certainly very simple. For breakfast they had tea, and butter on their bread, and at dinner a small glass of ale, college home-brewed ale. "How fat we got!" she exclaims.

The Master seems to have been a man of refined taste, fond of drawing, and what was called poker-painting; he was given also to caricaturing, and writing of squibs. The two young ladies were evidently fond of his society, but of the other Oxford society she only mentions the ultra-Tory politics, and the stupidity and frivolity of the Heads of Houses. "The various Heads," she writes, "with their respective wives, were extremely inferior to my uncle and aunt. More than half of the Doctors of Divinity were of humble origin, the sons of small gentry or country clergy, or even of a lower grade. Many of these, constant to the loves of their youth, brought ladies of inferior manners to grace what appeared to them so dignified a station. It was not a good style; there was little talent, and less polish, and no sort of knowledge of the world. And yet the ignorance of this class was less offensive than the assumption of another, when a lady of high degree had fallen in love with her brother's tutor, and got him handsomely provided for in the Church, that she might excuse herself for marrying him. Of the lesser clergy, there were young witty ones—odious; young learned ones—bores; and elderly ones—pompous; all, however, of all grades, kind and hospitable. But the Christian pastor, humble, gentle, considerate, and self-sacrificing, had no representative, as far as I could see, among these dealers in old wines, rich dinners, fine china, and massive plate."

"The religion of Oxford appeared in those days to consist in honouring the King and his Ministers, and in perpetually popping in and out of chapel. Chapel was announced by the strokes of a big hammer, beaten on every staircase half an hour before by a scout. The education was suited to Divinity. A sort of supervision was said to be kept over the young, riotous community, and to a certain extent the Proctors of the University and the Deans of the different colleges did see that no very open scandal was committed. There were rules that had in a general way to be obeyed, and lectures that had to be attended, but as for care to give high aims, provide refining amusements, give a worthy tone to the character of responsible beings, there was none ever even thought of. The very meaning of the word 'education' did not appear to be understood. The college was a fit sequel to the school. The young men herded together; they lived in their rooms, and they lived out of them, in the neighbouring villages, where many had comfortable establishments. . . . All sorts of contrivances were resorted to to enable the dissipated to remain out all night, to shield a culprit, to deceive the dignitaries." This was in 1809, and even later.

And yet with all this, and while we are told that those who attended lectures were laughed at, it seems strange that the best divines, and lawyers, and politicians of the first half of our century, some of whom we may have known ourselves, must have been formed under that system. We can hardly believe that it was as bad as here described, and we must remember that much of the *Memoirs* of this Scotch lady can have been written from memory only, and long after the time when she and her sister lived at University College. Life there, no doubt, may have been very dull, as there were no other young ladies at Oxford, and it cannot have been very amusing for these young girls to dine with sixteen Heads of Houses, all in wide silk cassocks, scarves and bands, one or two in powdered wigs, so that, as we are told, they often went home crying. All intercourse with the young men was strictly forbidden, though it seems to have been not altogether impossible to communicate, from the garden of the Master's Lodge, with the young men bending out of the college windows, or climbing down to the gardens.

One of these young men, who was at University College at the same time, might certainly not have been considered a very desirable companion for these two Scotch girls. It was no other than Shelley. What they say of him does not tell us much that is new, yet it deserves to be repeated. "Mr. Shelley," we read, "afterwards so celebrated, was half crazy. He began his career with every kind of wild prank at Eton. At University he was very insubordinate, always infringing some rule, the breaking of which he knew could not be overlooked. He was slovenly in his dress, and when spoken to about these and other irregularities, he was in the habit of making such extraordinary gestures, expressive of his humility under reproof, as to overset first the gravity and then the temper of the lecturing tutor. When he proceeded so far as to paste up atheistical squibs on the chapel doors, it was considered necessary to expel him privately, out of regard to Sir Timothy Shelley, the father, who came up at once. He and his son left Oxford together."

No one would recognize in this picture the University of Oxford, as it is at present. *Nous avons changé tout cela* might be said with great truth by the Heads of Houses, the Professors, and Fellows of the present day. And yet what the Highland lady, or rather the Highland girl, describes, refers to times not so long ago but that some of the men we have known might have lived through it. How this change came about I cannot tell, though I can bear testimony to a few survivals of the old state of things.

The Oxford of 1848 was still the Oxford of the Heads of Houses and of the Hebdomadal Board. That board consisted almost entirely of Heads of Houses, and a most important board it was, considering that the whole administration of the University was really in its hands. The colleges, on the other hand, were very jealous of their independence; and even the authority of the Proctors, who represented the University as such, was often contested within the gates of a college. It is wonderful that this old system of governing the University through the Heads of Houses should have gone on so long and so smoothly. Having been trusted by the Fellows of his own society with considerable power in the administration of his own college, it was supposed that the Head would prove equally useful in the administration of the University. A Head of a House became at once a member of the Council. And, on the whole, they managed to drive the coach and horses very well. But often when I had to take foreigners to hear the University Sermon, and they saw a most extraordinary set of old gentlemen walking into St. Mary's in procession, with a most startling combination of colours, black and red, scarlet and pink, on their heavy gowns and sleeves, I found it difficult to explain who they were. "Are they your professors?" I was asked. "Oh, no," I said, "the professors don't wear red gowns, only Doctors of Divinity and of Civil Law, and as every Head of a House must have something to wear in public, he is invariably made a Doctor." I remember one exception only, and at a much later time, namely, the Master of Balliol, who, like Canning at the Congress of Vienna, considered it among his most valued distinctions never to have worn the gown of a D.C.L. or D.D. It is well known that when Marshal Blücher was made a Doctor at Oxford he asked, in the innocence of his heart, that General

Gneisenau, his right-hand man, might at least be made a chemist. He certainly had mixed a most effective powder for the French army under Napoléon.

"But," my friend would ask, "have you no *Senatus Academicus*, have you no faculties of professors such as there are in all other Christian universities?" "Yes and no," I said. "We have professors, but they are not divided into faculties, and they certainly do not form the *Senatus Academicus*, or the highest authority in the University."

It seems very strange, but it is nevertheless a fact, that as soon as a good tutor is made a professor, he is considered of no good for the real teaching work of the colleges. His lectures are generally deserted; and I could quote the names of certain professors who afterwards rose to great eminence, but who at Oxford were simply ignored and their lecture-rooms deserted. The real teaching or coaching or cramming for examination is left to the tutors and Fellows of each college, and the examinations also are chiefly in their hands. Many undergraduates never see a professor, and, as far as the teaching work of the University is concerned, the professorships might safely be abolished. And yet, as I could honestly assure my foreign friends, the best men who take honour degrees at Oxford are quite the equals of the best men at Paris or Berlin. The professors may not be so distinguished, but that is due to a certain extent to the small salaries attached to some of the chairs. England has produced great names both in science and philosophy and scholarship, but these have generally drifted to some more attractive or lucrative centres. When I first came to Oxford one professor received £40 a year, another £1,500, and no one complained about these inequalities. A certain amount of land had been left by a king or bishop for endowing a certain chair, and every holder of the chair received whatever the endowment yielded. The mode of appointing professors was very curious at that time. Often the elections resembled parliamentary elections, far more regard being paid to political or theological partisanship than to scientific qualifications. Every M.A. had a vote, and these voters were scattered all over the country. Canvassing was carried on quite openly. Travelling expenses were freely paid, and lists were kept in each college of the men who could be depended on to vote for the liberal or the conservative candidate. Imagine a professor of medicine or of Greek being elected because he was a liberal! Some appointments rested with the Prime Minister, or, as it was called, the Crown; and it was quoted to the honour of the Duke of Wellington, that he, when Chancellor of the University, once insisted that the electors should elect the best man, and they had to yield, though there were electors who would declare their own candidate the best man, whatever the opinion of really qualified judges might be. All this election machinery is much im proved now, though an infallible system of electing the best men has not yet been discovered. One single elector, who is not troubled by too tender a conscience, may even now vitiate a whole election; to say nothing of the painful position in which an elector is placed, if he has to vote against a personal friend or a member of his own college, particularly when the feeling that it is dishonourable to disclose the vote of each elector is no longer strong enough to protect the best interests of the University.

It took me some time before I could gain an insight into all this. The old system passed away before my very eyes, not without evident friction between my different friends, and then came the difficulty of learning to understand the working of the new machinery which had been devised and sanctioned by Parliament. Reformers arose even among the Heads of Houses, as, for instance, Dr. Jeune, the Master of Pembroke College, who was credited with having *rajeuni l'ancienne université*. But he was by no means the only, or even the chief actor in University reform. Many of my personal friends, such as Dr. Tait, afterwards Archbishop of Canterbury, the Rev. H. G. Liddell, afterwards Dean of Christ Church, Professor Baden-Powell, and the Rev. G. H. S. Johnson, afterwards Dean of Wells, with Stanley and Goldwin Smith as Secretaries, did honest service in the various Royal and Parliamentary Commissions, and spent much of their valuable time in serving the University and the country. I could do no more than answer the questions addressed to me by the Commissioners and by my friends, and this is really all the share I had at that time in the reform of the University, or what was called Germanizing the English Universities. At one time such was the unpopularity of these reformers in the University itself that one of them asked one of the junior professors to invite him to dinner, because the Heads of Houses would no longer admit him to their hospitable boards.

Certainly to have been a member of the much abused Hebdomadal Board, and a Head of a College in those pre-reform days must have been a delightful life. Before the days of agricultural distress the income of the colleges was abundant; the authority of the Heads was unquestioned in their own colleges; not only undergraduates, but Fellows also had to be submissive. No junior Fellow would then have dared to oppose his Head at college meetings. If there was by chance an obstreperous junior, he was easily silenced or requested to retire. The days had not yet come when a Master of Trinity ventured to remark that even a junior Fellow might possibly be mistaken. Colleges seemed to be the property of the Heads, and in some of them the Fellows were really chosen by them, and the rest of the Fellows after some kind of examination. The management of University affairs was likewise entirely in the hands of the Heads of Colleges, and it was on rare occasions only that a theological question stirred the interest of non-resident M.A.s, and brought them to Oxford to record their vote for or against the constituted authorities. Men like the Dean of Christ Church, Dr. Gaisford, the Warden of Wadham, Dr. Parsons, and the Provost of Oriel, Dr. Hawkins, were in their dominions supreme, till the rebellious spirit began to show itself in such men as Dr. Jeune, Professor Baden-Powell, A. P. Stanley, Goldwin Smith and others.

Nor were there many very flagrant abuses under the old régime. It was rather the want of life that was complained of. It began to be felt that Oxford should take its place as an equal by the side of foreign Universities, not only as a high school, but as a home of what then was called for the first time "original research." There can be no question that as a teaching body, as a high school at the head of all the public schools in England, Oxford did its duty nobly. A man who at that time could take a Double First was indeed a strong man, well fitted for any work in after life. He would not necessarily turn out an original thinker, a scholar, or a discoverer in physical science, but he would know what it was to know anything thoroughly. To take honours at the same time in classics and mathematics required strength and grasp, and the effort was certainly considerable, as I found out when occasionally I read a Greek or Latin author with a young undergraduate friend. What struck me most was the accurate knowledge a candidate acquired of special authors and special books, but also the want of that familiarity with the language, Greek or Latin, which would enable him to read any new author with comparative ease. The young men whom I knew at the time they went in for their final examination, were certainly well grounded in classics, and what they knew they knew thoroughly.

The personal relations existing between undergraduates and their tutors were very intimate. A tutor took a pride in his pupils, and often became their friend for life. The teaching was almost private teaching, and the idea of reading a written lecture to a class in college did not exist as yet. It was real teaching with questions and answers; while lectures, written and read out, were looked down upon as good enough for professors, but entirely useless for the schools. The social tone of the University was excellent. Many of the tutors and of the undergraduates came of good families, and the struggle for life, or for a college living, or college office, was not, as yet, so fierce as it became afterwards. College tutors toiled on for life, and certainly did their work to the last most conscientiously. There was perhaps little ambition, little scheming or pushing, but the work of the University, such as the country would have it, was well done. If the Honour-Lists were small, the number of utter failures also was not very large.

For a young scholar, like myself, who came to live at Oxford in those distant days, the peace and serenity of life were most congenial, though several of my friends were among the first who began to fret, and wished for more work to be done and for better use to be made of the wealth and the opportunities of the University. My impression at that time was the same as it has been ever since, that a reform of the Universities was impossible till the public schools had been thoroughly reformed. The Universities must take what the schools send them. There is every year a limited number of boys from the best schools who would do credit to any University. But a large number of the young men who are sent up to matriculate at Oxford are not up to an academic standard. Unless the colleges agree to stand empty for a year or two, they cannot help themselves, but have to keep the standard of the matriculation examination low, and in fact do, to a great extent, the work that ought to have been done at school. Think of boys being sent up to Oxford, who, after having spent on an average six years at a public school, are yet unable to read a line of Greek or Latin which they have not seen before. Yet so it was, and so it is, unless I am very much misinformed. It is easy for some colleges who keep up a high standard of matriculation to turn out first-class men; the real burden falls on the colleges and tutors who have to work hard to bring their pupils up to the standard of a pass degree, and few people have any idea how little a pass degree may mean. Those tutors have indeed hard work to do and get little credit for it, though their devotion to their college and their pupils is highly creditable. Fifty years ago even a pass degree was more difficult than it is now, because candidates were not allowed to pass in different subjects at different times, but the whole examination had to be done all at once, or not at all.

I had naturally made it a rule at Oxford to stand aloof from the conflict of parties, whether academical, theological, or political. I had my own work to do, and it did not seem to me good taste to obtrude my opinions, which naturally were different from those prevalent at Oxford. Most people like to wash their dirty linen among themselves; and though I gladly talked over such matters with my friends who often consulted me, I did not feel called upon to join in the fray. I lived through several severe crises at Oxford, and though I had some intimate friends on either side, I remained throughout a looker on.

Seldom has a University passed through such a complete change as Oxford has since the year 1854. And yet the change was never violent, and the University has passed through its ordeal really rejuvenated and reinvigorated. It has been said that our constitution has now become too democratic, and that a University should be ruled by a Senatus rather than by a Juventus. This is true to a certain extent. There has been too much unrest, too constant changes, and a lack of continuity in the studies and in the government of the University. Every three years a new wave of young masters came in, carried a reform in the system of teaching and examining, and then left to make room for a new wave which brought new ideas, before the old ones had a fair trial. Senior members of the University, heads of houses and professors, have no more voting power than the young men who have just taken their degrees, nay, have in reality less influence than these young Masters, who always meet together and form a kind of compact phalanx when votes are to be taken. There was even a Non-placet club, ready to throw out any measure that seemed to emanate from the reforming party, or threatened to change any established customs, whether beneficial or otherwise to the University. The University, as such, was far less considered than the colleges, and money drawn from the colleges for University purposes was looked upon as robbery, though of course the colleges profited by the improvement of the University, and the interests of the two ought never to have been divided, as little as the interests of an army can be divided from the interests of each regiment.

When I came to Oxford there was still practically no society except that of the Heads of Houses, and there were no young ladies to grace their dinners. Each head took his turn in succession, and had twice or three times during term to feed his colleagues.

These dinners were sumptuous repasts, though they often took place as early as five. To be invited to them was considered a great distinction, and, though a very young man, I was allowed now and then to be present, and I highly appreciated the honour. The company consisted almost entirely of Heads of Houses, Canons, and Professors; sometimes there was a sprinkling of distinguished persons from London, and even of ladies of various ages and degrees. I confess I often sat among them, as we say in German, *verrathen und verkauft.* After dinner I saw a number of young men streaming in, and thought the evening would now become more lively. But far from it. These young men with white ties and in evening dress stood in their scanty gowns huddled together on one side of the room. They received a cup of tea, but no one noticed them or spoke to them, and they hardly dared to speak among themselves. This, as I was told, was called "doing the perpendicular," and they must have felt much relieved when towards ten o'clock they were allowed to depart, and exchange the perpendicular for a more comfortable position, indulging in songs and pleasant talk, which I sometimes was invited to join.

At that time I remember only very few houses outside the circle of Heads of Houses, where there was a lady and a certain amount of social life—the houses of Dr. Acland, Dr. Greenhill, Professor Baden-Powell, Professor Donkin, and Mr. Greswell.

In their houses there was less of the strict academical etiquette, and as they were fond of music, particularly the Donkins, I spent some really delightful evenings with them. Nay, as I played on the pianoforte, even the Heads of Houses began to patronize music at their evening parties, though no gentleman at that time would have played at Oxford. I being a German, and Professor Donkin being a confirmed invalid, we were allowed to play, and we certainly had an appreciative, though not always a silent, audience.

In one respect, the old system of Oxford Fellowships was still very perceptible in the society of the University. No Fellows were allowed to marry, and the natural consequence was that most of them waited for a college living, a professorship or librarianship, which generally came to them when they were no longer young men. Headships of colleges also had so long to be waited for that most of them were generally filled by very senior and mostly unmarried men. Besides, headships were but seldom given for excellence in scholarship, science, or even divinity, but for the sake of personal popularity, and for business habits. Some of the Fellows gave pleasant and, as I thought, very Lucullic dinners in college; and I still remember my surprise when I was asked to the first dinner in Common Room at Jesus College. My host was Mr. Ffoulkes, who afterwards became a Roman Catholic, and then an Anglican clergyman again. The carpets, the curtains, the whole furniture and the plate quite confounded me, and I became still more confounded when I was suddenly called upon to make a speech at a time when I could hardly put two words together in English.

The City society was completely separated from the University society, so that even rich bankers and other gentlemen would never have ventured to ask members of the University to dine.

Considering the position then held by the Heads of Houses, I feel I ought to devote some pages to describing some of the most prominent of them. At my age I may well hold to the maxim *seniores priores*, and will therefore begin with Dr. Routh, the centenarian President of Magdalen, as, though the headship of a house seems to be an excellent prescription for longevity, there was no one to dispute the venerable doctor's claim to precedence in this respect. He was then nearly a hundred years old, and he died in his hundredth year, and obtained his wish to have the *C*, *anno centesimo*, on his gravestone, for, though tired of life, he often declared, so I was told, that he would not be outdone in this respect by another very old man, who was a dissenter; he never liked to see the Church beaten. I might have made his personal acquaintance, some friends of the old President offering to present me to him. But I did not avail myself of their offer, because I knew the old man did not like to be shown as a curiosity. When I saw him sitting at his window he always wore a wig, and few had seen him without his wig and without his academic gown. He was certainly an exceptional man, and I believe he stood alone in the whole history of literature, as having published books at an interval of seventy years. His edition of the *Enthymemes* and *Gorgias of Plato* was published in 1784, his papers on the *Ignatian Epistles* in 1854. His *Reliquia Sacra* first appeared in 1814, and they are a work which at that time would have made the reputation of any scholar and divine. His editions of historical works, such as Burnet's *History of his own Time* and the *History of the reign of King James*, show his considerable acquaintance with English history. I have already mentioned how he used to speak of events long before his time, such as the execution of Charles I, as if he had been present; nor did he hesitate to declare that even Bishop Burnet was a great liar. He certainly had seen many things which connected him with the past. He had seen Samuel Johnson mounting the steps of the Clarendon building in Broad Street, and though he had not himself seen Charles I when he held his Parliament at Oxford, he had known a lady whose mother had seen the king walking round the Parks at Oxford.

However, we must not forget that many stories about the old President were more or less mythical, as indeed many Oxford stories are. I was told hat he actually slept in wig, cap and gown, so that once when an alarm of fire was raised in the quadrangle of his College, he put his head out of window in an incredibly short time, fully equipped as above. Many of these stories or "Common-Roomers" as they were called, still lived in the Common Rooms in my time, when the Fellows of each College assembled regularly after dinner, to take wine and dessert, and to talk on anything but what was called *Shop*, i.e. Greek and Latin. No one inquired about the truth of these stories, as long as they were well told. In a place like Oxford there exists a regular descent, by inheritance, of good stories. I remember stories told of Dr. Jenkins, as Master of Balliol, and afterwards transferred to his successor, Mr. Jowett. Bodleian stories descended in like manner from Dr. Bandinell to Mr. Coxe, and will probably be told of successive librarians till they become quite incongruous. I am old enough to have watched the descent of stories at Oxford, just as one recognizes the same furniture in college rooms occupied by successive generations of undergraduates. To me they sometimes seem threadbare like the old Turkish carpets in the college rooms, but I never spoil them by betraying their age, and, if well told, I can enjoy them as much as if I had never heard them before.

Dr. Hawkins, Provost of Oriel, was quite a representative of Old Oxford, and a well-known character in the University. I had been introduced to him by Baron Bunsen, and he showed me much hospitality. I was warned that I should find him very stiff and forbidding. His own Fellows called him the East-wind. But though he certainly was condescending, he treated me with great urbanity. He had a very peculiar habit; when he had to shake hands with people whom he considered his inferiors, he stretched out two fingers, and if some of them who knew this peculiarity of his, tendered him two fingers in return, the shaking of hands became rather awkward. One of the Fellows of his college told me that, as long as he was only a Fellow, he never received more than two fingers; when, however, he became Head Master of a school, he was rewarded with three fingers, or even with the whole hand, but, as soon as he gave up this place, and returned to live in college, he was at once reduced to the statutable two fingers. I don't recollect exactly how many fingers I was treated to, and I may have shaken them with my whole hand. Anyhow, I am quite conscious now of how many times I must have offended against academic etiquette. How, for instance, is a man to know that people who live at Oxford during term-time never shake hands except once during term? I doubt, in fact, whether that etiquette existed when I first came to Oxford, but it certainly had existed for some time before I discovered it.

Dr. Jenkins, Master of Balliol, was also the hero of many anecdotes. It was of him that it was first told how he once found fault with an undergraduate because, whenever he looked out of window, he invariably saw the young man loitering about in the quad; to which the undergraduate replied: "How very curious, for whenever I cross the quad, I always see you, Sir, looking out of window." He had a quiet humour of his own, and delighted in saying things which made others laugh, but never disturbed a muscle of his own face. One of his undergraduates was called Wyndham, and he had to say a few sharp words to him at "handshaking," that is, at the end of term. After saying all he wanted, he finished in Latin: "Et nunc valeas Wyndhamme,"—the last two syllables being pronounced with great emphasis. The Master's regard for his own dignity was very great. Once, when returning from a solitary walk, he slipped and fell. Two undergraduates seeing the accident ran to assist him, and were just laying hands on him to lift him up, when he descried a Master of Arts coming. "Stop," he cried, "stop, I see a Master of Arts coming down the street." And he dismissed the undergraduates with many thanks, and was helped on to his legs by the M.A.

Accidents, or slips of the tongue, will happen to everybody, even to a Head of a House. One of these old gentlemen, Dr. Symons, of Wadham, when presiding at a missionary meeting, had to introduce Sir Peregrine Maitland, a most distinguished officer, and a thoroughly good man. When dilating on the Christian work which Sir Peregrine had done in India, he called him again and again Sir Peregrine Pickle. The effect was most ludicrous, for everybody was evidently well acquainted with *Roderick Random*, and Sir Peregrine had great difficulty in remaining serious when the Chairman called on Sir Peregrine Pickle once more to address his somewhat perplexed audience.

But whatever may be said about the old Heads of Houses, most of them were certainly gentlemen both by birth and by nature. They are forgotten now, but they did good in their time, and much of their good work remains. If I consider who were the Dean and Canons and Students I met at Christ Church when I first became a member of the House, I should have to give a very different account from that given by the Highland lady in her *Memoirs*. The Dean of Christ Church, who received me, who proposed me for the degree of M.A., and afterwards allowed me to become a member of the House, was Dr. Gaisford, a real scholar, though it may be of the old school. He was considered very rough and rude, but I can only say he showed me more of real courtesy in those days than anybody else at Oxford. He was, I believe, a little shy, and easily put out when he suspected anybody, particularly the young men, of want of consideration. I can quite believe that when an undergraduate, in addressing him, stepped on the hearthrug on which he was standing, he may have said: "Get down from my hearthrug," meaning, "keep at your proper distance."

I can only say that I never found him anything but kind and courteous. It so happened that he had been made a Member of the Bavarian Academy, and I, though very young, had received the same distinction as a reward for my Sanskrit work, and the Dean was rather pleased when he heard it. When I asked him whether he would put my name on the books of the House, he certainly hesitated a little, and asked me at last to come again next day and dine with him. I went, but I confess I was rather afraid that the Dean would raise difficulties. However, he spoke to me very nicely, "I have looked through the books," he said, "and I find two precedents of Germans being members of the House, one of the name of Wernerus, and another of the name of Nitzschius," or some such name. "But," he continued, smiling, "even if I had not found these names, I should not have minded making a precedent of your case." People were amazed at Oxford when they heard of the Dean's courtesy, but I can only repeat that I never found him anything but courteous.

Most of the Heads of Houses asked me to dine with them by sending me an invitation. The Dean alone first came and called on me. I was then living in a small room in Walton Street in which I worked, and dined, and smoked. My bedroom was close by, and I generally got up early, and shaved and finished my toilet at about 11 o'clock. I had just gone into my bedroom to shave, my face was half covered with lather, when my landlady rushed in and told me the Dean had called, and my dogs were pulling him about. The fact was I had a Scotch terrier with a litter of puppies in a basket, and when the Dean entered in full academical dress, the dogs flew at him, pulling the sleeves of his gown and barking furiously. Covered with lather as I was, I had to rush in to quiet the dogs, and in this state I had to receive the Very Rev. the Dean, and explain to him the nature of the work that brought me to Oxford. It was certainly awkward, but in spite of the disorder of my room, in spite also of the tobacco smoke of which the Dean did not approve, all went off well, though, I confess, I felt somewhat ashamed. In the same interview the Dean asked me about an Icelandic Dictionary which had been offered to the press by Cleasby and Dasent. "Surely it is a small barbarous island," he said, "and how can they have any literature?" I tried, as well as I could, to explain to the Dean the extent and the value of Icelandic literature, and soon after the press, which was then the Dean, accepted the Dictionary which was brought out later by Dr. Vigfusson, in a most careful and scholarlike manner. It might indeed safely be called his Dictionary, considering how many dictionaries are called, not after the name of the compiler or compilers, but after that of their editor.

This Dr. Vigfusson was quite a character. He was perfectly pale and bloodless, and had but one wish, that of being left alone. He came to Oxford first to assist Dr. Dasent, to whom Cleasby, when he died, had handed over his collections; but afterwards he stayed, taking it for granted that the University would give him the little he wanted. But even that little was difficult to provide, as there were no funds that could be used for that purpose, however uselessly other funds might seem to be squandered. That led to constant grumbling on his part. Ever so many expedients were tried to satisfy him, but none quite succeeded. At last he fell ill and died, and when he was a patient at the Acland Home, where the nurses did all they could for him, he several times said to me when I sat with him, that he had never been so happy in his life as in that Home. I sometimes blame myself for not having seen more of him at Oxford. But he always seemed to me full of suspicions and very easily offended, and that made any free intercourse with him difficult and far from pleasant. Perhaps it was my fault also. He may have felt that he might have claimed a professorship of Icelandic quite as well as I, and he may have grudged my settled position in Oxford, my independence and my freedom. Whenever we did work together, I always found him pleasant at first, but very soon he would become wayward and sensitive, do what I would, and I had to let him go his own way, as I went mine.

I remember dining with the famous Dr. Bull,

Canon of Christ Church, who certainly managed to produce a dinner that would have done credit to any French chef. He was one of the last pluralists, and many stories were told about him. One story, which however was perfectly true, showed at all events his great sagacity. A well-known banker had been for years the banker of Christ Church. Dr. Bull who was the College Bursar had to transact all the financial business with him. No one suspected the banking house which he represented. Dr. Bull, however, the last time he invited him to dinner, was struck by his very pious and orthodox remarks, and by the change of tone in his conversation, such as might suit a Canon of Christ Church, but not a luxurious banker from London. Without saying a word, Dr. Bull went to London next day, drew out all the money of the college, took all his papers from the bank, and the day after, to the dismay of London, the bank failed, the depositors lost their money, but Christ Church was unhurt.

Another of the Canons of Christ Church at that time had spent half a century in the place, and read the lessons there twice every day. Of course he knew the prayer-book by heart, and as long as he could see to read there was no harm in his reading. But when his eyesight failed him and he had to trust entirely to his memory, he would often go from some word in the evening prayer to the same word in the marriage service, and from there to the burial service, with an occasional slip into baptism. The result of it was that he was no longer allowed to read the service in Chapel except during Long Vacation when the young men were away. I frequently stayed at Oxford during vacation, and thought of course that the evening service would never end, till at last I was asked to name the child, and then I went home.

One Sunday I remember going to chapel, and after prayers had begun the following conversation took place, loud enough to be heard all through the chapel. Enter old Canon preceded by a beadle. He goes straight to his stall, and finding it occupied by a well-known D.D. from London, who is deeply engaged in prayer, he stands and looks at the interloper, and when that produces no effect, he says to the beadle: "Tell that man this is my stall; tell him to get out."

Beadle: "Dr. A.'s compliments, and whether you would kindly occupy another stall."

D.D.: "Very sorry; I shall change immediately."

Old Canon settles in his stall, prayers continue, and after about ten minutes the Canon shouts: "Beadle, tell that man to dine with me at five."

Beadle: "Dr. A.'s compliments, and whether you would give him the pleasure of your company at dinner at five."

D.D.: "Very sorry, I am engaged."

Beadle: "D.D. regrets he is engaged."

Old Canon: "Oh, he won't dine!"

The cathedral was very empty, and fortunately

this conversation was listened to by a small congregation only. I can, however, vouch for it, as I was sitting close by and heard it myself.

Bodley's Library, too, was full of good stories, though many of them do not bear repeating. When I first began to work there, Dr. Bandinell was Bodleian Librarian. Working in the Bodleian was then like working in one's private library. One could have as many books and MSS. as one desired, and the six hours during which the Library was open were a very fair allowance for such tiring work as copying and collating Sanskrit MSS. I well remember my delight when I first sat down at my table near one of the windows looking into the garden of Exeter. It seemed a perfect paradise for a student. I must confess that I slightly altered my opinion when I had to sit there every day during a severe winter without any fire, shivering and shaking, and almost unable to hold my pen, till kind Mr. Coxe, the sub-librarian, took compassion on me and brought me a splendid fur that had been sent him as a present by a Russian scholar, who had witnessed the misery of the Librarian in this Siberian Library. Now all this is changed. The Library is so full of students, both male and female, that one has difficulty in finding a place, certainly in finding a quiet place; and all sorts of regulations have been introduced which have no doubt become necessary on account of the large number of readers, but which have completely changed, or as some would say, improved the character of the place. As to one improvement, however, there can be no two opinions. The Library and the reading-room, the so-called Camera, are now comfortably warmed, and students may in the latter place read for twelve hours uninterruptedly, and not be turned out as we were by a warning bell at four o'clock. And woe to you if you failed to obey the warning. One day an unfortunate reader was so absorbed in his book that he did not hear the bell, and was locked in. He tried in vain to attract attention from the windows, for it was no pleasant prospect to pass a night among so many ghosts. At last he saw a solitary woman, and shouted to her that he was locked in. "No," she said, "you are not. The Library is closed at four." Whether he spent the night among the books is not known. Let us hope that he met with a less logical person to release him from his cold prison.

Dr. Bandinell ruled supreme in his library, and even the Curators trembled before him when he told them what had been the invariable custom of the Library for years, and could not be altered. And, curiously enough, he had always funds at his disposal, which is not the case now, and whenever there was a collection of valuable MSS. in the market he often prided himself on having secured it long before any other library had the money ready. Now and then, it is true, he allowed himself to be persuaded by a plausible seller of rare books or MSS., but generally he was very wary. He was not always very courteous to visitors, and still less so to his under-librarians. The Oriental under-librarian Professor Reay, in particular, who was old and somewhat infirm, had much to suffer from him, and the language in which he was ordered about was such as would not now be addressed to any menial. And yet Professor Reay belonged to a very good family, though Dr. Bandinell would insist on calling him Ray, and declared that he had no right to the e in his name. In revenge some people would give him an additional i and call him Dr. Bandinelli, which made him very angry, because, as he would say to me, "he had never been one of those dirty foreigners." Silence was enjoined in the library, but the librarian's voice broke through all rules of silence. I remember once, when Professor Reay had been looking for ever so long to find his spectacles without which he could not read the Arabic MSS., and had asked everybody whether they had seen them, a voice came at last thundering through the library: "You left your spectacles on my chair, you old ——, and I sat on them!" There was an end of spectacles and Arabic MSS. after that. There were two men only of whom Dr. Bandinell and H. O. Coxe also were afraid, Dr. Pusey, who was one of the Curators, and later on, Jowett, the Master of Balliol.

There was a vacancy in the Oriental sub-librarianship, and a very distinguished young Hebrew scholar, William Wright, afterwards Professor at Cambridge, was certainly by far the best candidate. But as ill-luck—I mean ill-luck for the Library—would have it, he had given offence by a lecture at Dublin, in which he declared that the people of Canaan were Semitic, and not, as stated in Genesis, the children of Ham. No one doubts this now, and every new inscription has confirmed it. Still a strong effort was made to represent Dr. Wright as a most dangerous young man, and thus to prevent his appointment at Oxford. The appointment was really in the hands of Dr. Bandinell; and after I had frankly explained to him the motives of this mischievous agitation against Dr. Wright, and assured him that he was a scholar and by no means given to what was then called "free-handling of the Old Testament," he promised me that he would appoint him and no one else. However, poor man, he was urged and threatened and frightened, and to my great surprise the appointment was given to some one else, who at that time had given hardly any proofs of independent work as a Semitic scholar, though he afterwards rendered very good and honest service. I did not disguise my opinion of what had happened; and for more than a year Dr. Bandinell never spoke to me nor I to him, though we met almost daily at the library. At last the old man, evidently feeling that he had been wrong, came to tell me that he was sorry for what had happened, but that it was not his fault: after this, of course, all was forgotten. Dr. Wright had a much more brilliant career opened to him, first at the British Museum, and then as professor at Cambridge, than he could possibly have had as sub-librarian at Oxford. He always remained a scholar, and never dabbled in theology.

Some very heated correspondence passed at the time, and I remember keeping the letters for a long while. They were curious as showing the then state of theological opinion at Oxford; but I have evidently put the correspondence away so carefully that nowhere can I find it now. Let it be forgotten and forgiven.

Many, if not all, of the stories that I have written down in this chapter may be legendary, and they naturally lose or gain as told by different people. Who has not heard different versions of the story of a well-known Canon of Christ Church in my early days, who, when rowing on the river, saw a drowning man laying hold of his boat and nearly upsetting it. "Providentially," he explained, "I had brought my umbrella, and I had presence of mind enough to hit him over the knuckles. He let go, sank, and never rose again." Nobody, I imagine, would have vouched for the truth of this story, but it was so often repeated that it provided the old gentleman with a nickname, that stuck to him always.

I could add more Oxford stories, but it seems almost ill-natured to do so, and I could only say in most cases *relata refero.* When I first came here Oxford and Oxford society were to me so strange that I probably accepted many similar stories as gospel truth. My young friends hardly treated me quite fairly in this respect. I had many questions to ask, and my friends evidently thought it great fun to chaff me and to tell me stories which I naturally believed, for there were many things which seemed to me very strange, and yet they were true and I had to believe them. The existence of Fellows who received from £300 to £800 a year, as a mere sinecure for life, provided they did not marry, seemed to me at first perfectly incredible. In Germany education at Public Schools and Universities was so cheap that even the poorest could manage to get what was wanted for the highest employments, particularly if they could gain an exhibition or scholarship. But after a man had passed his examinations, the country or the government had nothing more to do with him. "Swim or drown" was the maxim followed everywhere; and it was but natural that the first years of professional life, whether as lawyers, medical men, or clergymen, were years of great self-denial. But they were also years of intense struggle, and the years of hunger are said to have accounted for a great deal of excellent work in order to force the doors to better employment. To imagine that after the country had done its duty by providing schools and universities, it would provide crutches for men who ought to learn to walk by themselves, was beyond my comprehension, particularly when I was told how large a sum was yearly spent by the colleges in paying these fellowships without requiring any *quid pro quo*.

Having once come to believe that, and several cther to me unintelligible things at Oxford, I was ready to believe almost anything my friends told me. There are some famous stone images, for instance, round the Theatre and the Ashmolean Museum. They are hideous, for the sandstone of which they are made has crumbled away again and again, but even when they were restored, the same brittle stone was used. They are in the form of Hermae, and were planned by no less an architect than Sir Christopher Wren. When I asked what they were meant for, I was assured quite seriously that they were images of former Heads of Houses. I believed it, though I expressed my surprise that the stonemason who made new heads, when the old showed hardly more than two eyes and a nose, and a very wide mouth, should carefully copy the crumbling faces, because, as I was informed, he had been told to copy the former gentlemen.

It was certainly a very common amusement of my young undergraduate friends to make fun of the Heads of Houses. They did not seem to feel that shiver of unspeakable awe for them of which Bishop Thorold speaks; nay, they were anything but respectful in speaking of the Doctors of Divinity in their red gowns with black velvet sleeves. If it is difficult for old men always to understand young men, it is certainly even more difficult for young men to understand old men. There is a very old saying, "Young men think that old men are fools, but old men know that young men are." Though very young myself, I came to know several of the old Heads of Houses, and though they certainly had their peculiarities, they did by no means all belong to the age of the Dodo. They were enjoying their *otium cum dignitate*, as befits gentlemen, scholars, and divines, and they certainly deserved greater respect from the undergraduates than they received.

At the annual *Encaenia*, a great deal of licence was allowed to the young men; and I know of several strangers, especially foreigners, who have been scandalized at the riotous behaviour of the undergraduates in the Theatre, the Oxford *Aula*, when the Vice-Chancellor stood up to address the assembled audience. My first experience of this was with Dr. Plumptre, who, as I have said, was very tall and stately; when his first words were not quite distinct, the undergraduates shouted, "Speak up, old stick." When the Warden of Wadham, the Rev. Dr. Symons, was showing some pretty young ladies to their seats in the Theatre, he was threatened by the young men, who yelled at the top of their voices, "I'll tell Lydia, you wicked old man." Now Lydia was his most excellent spouse. At first the remarks of the undergraduates at the *Encaenia*, or rather *Saturnalia*, were mostly good-natured and at least witty; but they at last became so rude that distinguished men, whom the University wished to honour by conferring on them honorary degrees, felt deeply offended. Sir Arthur Helps declared that he came to receive an honour, and received an insult. Well do I remember the Rev. Dr. Salmon, who was asked where he had left his lobster sauce; Dr. Wendell Holmes was shouted at, whether he had come across the Atlantic in his "One Hoss Shay"; the Right Hon. W. H. Smith, First Lord of the Admiralty, was presented with a Pinafore, and Lord Wolseley with a Black Watch. There was a certain amount of wit in these allusions, and the best way to take the academic row and riot was Tennyson's, who told me on coming out that "he felt all the time as if standing on the shingle of the sea shore, the storm howling, and the spray covering him right and left." After a time, however, these *Saturnalia* had to be stopped, and they were stopped in a curious way, by giving ladies seats among the undergraduates. It speaks well for them that their regard for the ladies restrained them, and made them behave like gentlemen.

The reign of the Heads of Houses, which was in full force when I first settled in Oxford, began to wane when it was least expected. There had, however, been grumblings among the Fellows and Tutors at Oxford, who felt themselves aggrieved by the self-willed interference of the Heads of Colleges in their tutorial work, and, it may be, resented the airs assumed by men who, after all, were their equals, and in no sense their betters, in the University.

Society distinctly profited when Fellows and Tutors were allowed to marry, and when several of the newly-elected of the Heads of Houses, having wives and daughters, opened their houses, and had interesting people to dine with them from the neighbourhood and from London.

The Deanery of Christ Church was not only made architecturally into a new house, but under Dr. Liddell, with his charming wife and daughters, became a social centre not easily rivalled anywhere else. There one met not only royalty, the young Prince of Wales, but many eminent writers, artists, and political men from London, Gladstone, Disraeli, Richmond, Ruskin, and many others. Another bright house of the new era was that of the Principal of Brasenose, Dr. Cradock, and his cheerful and most amusing wife. There one often met such men as Lord Russell, Sir George C. Lewis, young Harcourt, and many more. She was the true Dresden china marquise, with her amusing sallies, which no doubt often gave offence to grave Heads of Houses and sedate Professors. No one knew her age, she was so young; and yet she had been maid of honour to some Queen, as I told her once, to Queen Anne. Having been maid of honour, she never concealed her own peculiar feelings about people who had not been presented. When she wanted to be left alone, she would look out of window, and tell visitors who came to call, "Very sorry, but I am not at home to-day." Queen's College also, under Dr. Thomson, the future Archbishop of York, was a most hospitable house. Mrs. Thomson presided over it with her peculiar grace and genuine kindness, and many a pleasant evening I spent there with musical performances. But here, too, the old leaven of Oxford burst forth sometimes. Of course, we generally performed the music of Handel and other classical authors; Mendelssohn's compositions were still considered as mere twaddle by some of the old school. At one of these evenings, the old organist of New College, with his wooden leg, after sitting through a rehearsal of Mendelssohn's *Hymn of Praise*, which I was conducting at the pianoforte, walked up to me, as I thought, to thank me; but no, he burst out in a torrent of real and somewhat coarse abuse of me, for venturing to introduce such flimsy music at Oxford. I did not feel very guilty, and fortunately I remained silent, whether from actual bewilderment or from a better cause, I can hardly tell.

Long before Commissions came down on Oxford a new life seemed to be springing up there, and what was formerly the exception became more and more the rule among the young Fellows and Tutors. They saw what a splendid opportunity was theirs,

Walker & Cockerell, ph. sc.

F. Max Müller
Aged 30.

having the very flower of England to educate, having the future of English society to form. They certainly made the best of it, helped, I believe, by the so-called Oxford Movement, which, whatever came of it afterwards, was certainly in the beginning thoroughly genuine and conscientious. The Tutors saw a good deal of the young men confided to their care, and the result was that even what was called the "fast set" thought it a fine thing to take a good class. I could mention a number of young noblemen and wealthy undergraduates who, in my early years, read for a first class and took it; and my experience has certainly been that those who took a first class came out in later life as eminent and useful members of society. Not that eminence in political, clerical, literary, and scientific life was restricted to first classes, far from it. But first-class men rarely failed to appear again on the surface in later life. It may be true that a first class did not always mean a first-class man, but it always seemed to mean a man who had learned how to work honestly, whether he became Prime Minister or Archbishop, or spent his days in one of the public offices, or even in a counting-house or newspaper office.

I felt it was an excellent mixture if a young man, after taking a good degree at Oxford, spent a year or two at a German University. He generally came back with fresh ideas, knew what kind of work still had to be done in the different branches of study, and did it with a perseverance that soon produced most excellent results. Of course there was always the difficulty that young men wished to make their way in life, that is to make a living. The Church, the bar, and the hospital, absorbed many of those who in Germany would have looked forward to a University career. In my own subject more particularly, my very best pupils did not see their way to gaining even an independence, unless they gave their time to first securing a curacy, or a mastership at school; and they usually found that, in order to do their work conscientiously, they had to give up their favourite studies in which they would certainly have done excellent work, if there had been no *dira necessitas.* I often tried to persuade my friends at Oxford to make the fellowships really useful by concentrating them and giving studious men a chance of devoting themselves at the University to non-lucrative studies. But the feeling of the majority was always against what was called derisively Original Research, and the fellowship-funds continued to be frittered away, payment by results being considered a totally mistaken principle, so that often, as in the case of the new septennial fellowships, there remained the payment only, but no results.

Still all this became clear to me at a much later time only. My first years at Oxford were spent in a perfect bewilderment of joy and admiration. No one can see that University for the first time, particularly in spring or autumn, without being enchanted with it. To me it seemed a perfect paradise, and I could have wished for myself no better lot than that which the kindness of my friends later secured for me there.

CHAPTER VIII

EARLY FRIENDS AT OXFORD

I WAS still very young when I came to settle at Oxford, only twenty-four in fact; and, though occasionally honoured by invitations from Heads of Houses and Professors, I naturally lived chiefly with undergraduates and junior Fellows, such as Grant, Sellar, Palgrave, Morier, and others. Grant, afterwards Sir Alexander Grant and Principal of the University of Edinburgh, was a delightful companion. He had always something new in his mind, and discussed with many flashes of wit and satire. He possessed an aristocratic contempt for anything commonplace, or self-evident, so that one had to be careful in conversing with him. But he was generous, and his laugh reconciled one to some of his sharp sallies. How little one anticipates the future greatness of one's friends. They all seem to us no better than ourselves, when suddenly they emerge. Grant had shown what he could do by his edition of Aristotle's *Ethics*. He became one of the Professors at the new University at Bombay and contributed much to the first starting of that University, so warmly patronized by Sir Charles Trevelyan. On returning to this country he was chosen to fill the distinguished place of Principal of the Edinburgh University. More was expected of him when he enjoyed this *otium cum dignitate*, but his health seemed to have suffered in the enervating climate of India, and, though he enjoyed his return to his friends most fully and spending his life as a friend among friends, he died comparatively young, and perhaps without fulfilling all the hopes that were entertained of him. But he was a thoroughly genial man, and his handshake and the twinkle of his eye when meeting an old friend will not easily be forgotten.

Sellar was another Scotchman whom I knew as an undergraduate at Balliol. When I first came to know him he was full of anxieties about his health, and greatly occupied with the usual doubts about religion, particularly the presence of evil or of anything imperfect in this world. He was an honest fellow, warmly attached to his friends; and no one could wish to have a better friend to stand up for him on all occasions and against all odds. He afterwards became happily married and a useful Professor of Latin at Edinburgh. I stayed with him later in life in Scotland and found him always the same, really enjoying his friends' society and a talk over old days. He had begun to ail when I saw him last, but the old boy was always there, even when he was miserable about his chiefly imaginary miseries. Soon after I had left him I received his last message and farewell from his death-bed. We are told that all this is very natural and what we must be prepared for—but what cold gaps it leaves. My thoughts often return to him, as if he were still among the living, and then one feels one's own loneliness and friendlessness again and again.

Palgrave roused great expectations among undergraduates at Oxford, but he kept us waiting for some time. He took early to office life in the Educational Department, and this seems to have ground him down and unfitted him for other work. He had a wonderful gift of admiring, his great hero being Tennyson, and he was more than disappointed if others did not join in his unqualified panegyrics of the great poet. At last, somewhat late in life, he was elected Professor of Poetry at Oxford, and gave some most learned and instructive lectures. His knowledge of English Literature, particularly poetry, was quite astounding. I certainly never went to him to ask him a question that he did not answer at once and with exhaustive fullness. Some of his friends complained of his great command of language, and even Tennyson, I am told, found it sometimes too much. All I can say is that to me it was a pleasure to listen to him. I owe him particular thanks for having, in the kindest manner, revised my first English compositions. He was always ready and indefatigable, and I certainly owed a good deal to his corrections and his unstinted advice. His *Golden Treasury* has become a national possession, and certainly speaks well both for his extensive knowledge and for his good taste.

Lastly there was Morier, of whom certainly no one expected when he was at Balliol that he would rise to be British Ambassador at St. Petersburg. His early education had been somewhat neglected, but when he came to Balliol he worked hard to pass a creditable examination. He was a giant in size, very good-looking, and his manners, when he liked, most charming and attractive. Being the son of a diplomatist there was something both English and foreign in his manner, and he certainly was a general favourite at Oxford. His great desire was to enter the diplomatic service, but when that was impossible, he found employment for a time in the Education Office. But society in London was too much for him, he was made for society, and society was delighted to receive him. But it was difficult for him at the same time to fulfil his duties at the Education Office, and the result was that he had to give up his place. Things began to look serious, when fortunately Lord Aberdeen, a great friend of his father, found him some diplomatic employment; and that once found, Morier was in his element. He was often almost reckless; but while several of his friends came altogether to grief, he managed always to fall on his feet and keep afloat while others went down. As an undergraduate he came to me to read Greek with me, and I confess that with such mistakes in his Greek papers as *οἱ πάθοι* instead of *τὰ πάθη*, I trembled for his examinations. However, he did well in the schools, knowing how to hide his weak points and how to make the best of his strong ones. I travelled with him in Germany, and when the Schleswig-Holstein question arose, he wrote a pamphlet which certainly might have cost him his diplomatic career. He asked me to allow it to be understood that the pamphlet, which did full justice to the claims of Holstein and of Germany, had been written by me. I received many compliments, which I tried to parry as well as I could. Fortunately Lord John Russell stood by Morier, and his prophecies did certainly turn out true. "Don't let the Germans awake from their slumbers and find a work ready made for them on which they all agree." But the signatories of the treaty of London did the very thing against which Morier had raised his warning voice, as the friend of Germany as it was, though perhaps not of the Germany that was to be. Schleswig-Holstein *meer-umschlungen* became the match, (the Schwefel-hölzchen), that was to light the fire of German unity, a unity which for a time may not have been exactly what England could have wished for, but which in the future will become, we hope, the safety of Europe and the support of England.

Morier's later advance in his diplomatic career was certainly most successful. He possessed the very important art of gaining the confidence of the crowned heads and ministers he had to deal with. Bismarck, it is true, could not bear him, and tried several times to trip him up. Even while Morier was at Berlin, as a Secretary of Legation, Bismarck asked for his removal, but Lord Granville simply declined to remove a young diplomatist who gave him information on all parties in Germany, and to do so had to mix with people whom Bismarck did not approve of. Besides, Morier was always a *persona grata* with the Crown Prince and the Crown Princess, and that was enough to make Bismarck dislike him. Later in life Bismarck accused him of having conveyed private information of the military position of the Germans to the French Guards, such information being derived from the English Court. The charge was ridiculous. Morier was throughout the war a sympathizer with Germany as against France. The English Court had no military information to convey or to communicate to Morier, and Morier was too much of a diplomatist and a gentleman, if by accident he had possessed any such information, to betray such a secret to an enemy in the field. Bismarck was completely routed, though his son seemed inclined to fasten a duel on the English diplomatist. Morier rose higher and higher, and at last became Ambassador at St. Petersburg. When I laughed and congratulated him he said, "He must be a great fool who does not reach the top of the diplomatic tree." That was too much modesty, and yet modesty was not exactly his fault; but he agreed with me as to *quam parva sapientia regitur mundus.*

Nothing could seem more prosperous than my friend Morier's career; but few people knew how utterly miserable he really was. He had one son, in many respects the very image of his father, a giant in stature, very handsome, and most attractive. In spite of all we said to him he would not send his son to a public school in England, but kept him with him at the different embassies, where his only companions were the young attachés and secretaries. He had a private tutor, and when that tutor declared that young Morier was fit for the University, his father managed to get him into Balliol, recommending him to the special care of the Master. He actually lived in the Master's house for a time, but enjoyed the greatest liberty that an undergraduate at Oxford may enjoy. His father was wrapped up in his boy, but at the same time tried to frighten him into hard work, or at least into getting through the examinations. All was in vain; young Morier was so nervous that he could never pass an examination. What might be expected followed, and the father had at last to remove him to begin work as an honorary attaché at his own embassy. I liked the young man very much, but my own impression is that his nervousness quite unfitted him for serious work. The end was beyond description sad. He went to South Africa in the police force, distinguished himself very much, came back to England, and then on his second voyage to the Cape died suddenly on board the steamer. I have seldom seen such utter misery as his father's. He loved his son and the son loved his father passionately, but the father expected more than it was physically and mentally possible for the son to do. Hence arose misunderstandings, and yet beneath the surface there was this passionate love, like the love of lovers. When I saw my old friend last, he cried and sobbed like a child: his heart was really broken. He went on for a few years more, suffering much from ill health, but really killed at last by his utter misery. I knew him in the bright morning of his life, at the meridian of his great success, and last in the dark night when light and life seems gone, when the moon and all the stars are extinguished, and nothing remains but patient suffering and the hope of a brighter morn to come.

How little one dreamt of all this when we were young, and when an ambassador, nay, even a professor, seemed to us far beyond the reach of our ambition. I could go on mentioning many more names of men with whom I lived at Oxford in the most delightful intimacy, and who afterwards turned up as bishops, archbishops, judges, ministers, and all the rest. True, it is quite natural that it should be so with a man who, as I did, began his English life almost as an undergraduate among undergraduates. Nearly all Englishmen who receive a liberal education must pass either through Oxford or through Cambridge, and I was no doubt lucky in making thus early the acquaintance of a number of men who later in life became deservedly eminent. The only drawback was that, knowing my friends very intimately, I did not perhaps later preserve on all occasions that deference which the dignity of an ambassador or of an archbishop has a right to demand.

Thomson was a dear friend of mine when he was still a fellow of Queen's College. We worked together, as may be seen by my contributions to his *Laws of Thought*, and the translation of a Vedic hymn which he helped me to make. I think he had a kind of anticipation of what was in store for him. Though for a time he had to be satisfied, even when he was married, with a very small London living, he soon rose in the Church, at a time when clergymen of a liberal way of thinking had not much chance of Crown preferment. But having gone at the head of a deputation to Lord Palmerston, to inform him that Gladstone's next election as member for Oxford was becoming doubtful, owing to all the bishoprics being given to the Low Church party—the party of Lord Shaftesbury—Palmerston remembered his stately and courteous bearing, and when the see of Gloucester fell vacant, gave him that bishopric to silence Gladstone's supporters. This was a very unexpected preferment at Oxford, but Thomson made such good use of his opportunity that, when the Archbishopric of York became vacant, and Palmerston found it difficult to make his own or Lord Shaftesbury's nominee acceptable to the Queen, he suggested that any one of the lately elected bishops approved of by the Crown might go to York, and some one else fill the see thus vacated. It so happened that Thomson's name was the first to be mentioned, and he was made Archbishop, probably one of the youngest Archbishops England has ever known. He certainly fulfilled all expectations and proved himself the people's Archbishop, for he was himself the son of a small tradesman, a fact of which he was never ashamed, though his enemies did not fail to cast it in his teeth. I confess I felt at first a little awkward with my old friend who formerly had discussed every possible religious and philosophical problem quite freely with me, and was now His Grace the Lord Archbishop, with a palace to inhabit and an income of about £10,000 a year. However, though as a German and as a friend of Bunsen I was looked upon as a kind of heretic, I never made the Archbishop blush for his old friend, and I always found him the same to the end of his life, kind, courteous, and ready to help, though it is but fair to remember that an Archbishop of York is one of the first subjects of the Queen, and cannot do or say everything that he might like to do or to say. When I had to ask him to do something for a friend of mine, who as a clergyman had given great offence by his very liberal opinions, he did all he could do, though he might have incurred great obloquy by so doing.

But when I think of these men, friends and acquaintances of mine, whom I remember as young men, very able and hard working no doubt, yet not so entirely different from others who through life remained unknown, it is as if I had slept through a number of years and dreamt, and had then suddenly awoke to a new life. Some of my friends, I am glad to say, I always found the same, whether in ermine or in lawn sleeves; others, however, I am sorry to say, had *become* something, the old boy in them had vanished, and nothing was to be seen except the bishop, the judge, or the minister.

It was not for me to remind them of their former self, and to make them doubt their own identity, but I often felt the truth of Matthew Arnold's speeches, who, in social position, never rose beyond that of inspector of schools, and who often laughed when at great dinners he found himself surrounded by their Graces, their Excellencies, and my Lords, recognizing faces that sat below him at school and whose names in the class lists did not occupy so high a place as his own. Not that Matthew Arnold was dissatisfied; he knew his worth, but, as he himself asked for nothing, it is strange that his friends should never have asked for something for him, which would have shown to the world at large that he had not been left behind in the race. It strikes one that while he was at Oxford, few people only detected in Arnold the poet or the man of remarkable genius. I had many letters from him, but I never kept them, and I often blame myself now that in his, as in other cases, I should have thrown away letters as of no importance. Then suddenly came the time when he returned to Oxford as the poet, as the Professor of poetry, nay, afterwards as the philosopher also, placed high by public opinion among the living worthies of England. What was sometimes against him was his want of seriousness. A laugh from his hearers or readers seemed to be more valued by him than their serious opposition, or their convinced assent. He trusted, like others, to *persiflage*, and the result was that when he tried to be serious, people could not forget that he might at any time turn round and smile, and decline to be taken *au grand sérieux*. People do not know what a dangerous game this French *persiflage* is, particularly in England, and how difficult it becomes to exchange it afterwards for real seriousness.

Those early Oxford days were bright days for me, and now, when those young and old faces, whether undergraduates or archbishops, rise up again before me, I being almost the only one left of that happy company, I ask again, "Did they also belong to a mere dreamland, they who gave life to my life, and made England my real home?" When I first saw them at Oxford, I was really an undergraduate, though I had taken my Doctor's degree at Leipzig. I lived, in fact, my happy university life over again, and it would be difficult to say which academical years I enjoyed more, those at Leipzig and Berlin, or those at Oxford. There were intermediate years in Paris, but during my stay there I saw but little of students and student life. I was too much oppressed with cares and anxieties about my present and future to think much of society and enjoyment. At Oxford, these cares had become far less, and I could by hard work earn as much money as I wanted, and cared to spend. In Paris, I was already something of a scholar and writer; at Oxford I became once more the undergraduate.

This young society into which I was received was certainly most attractive, though that it contained the germs of future greatness never struck me at the time. What struck me was the general tone of the conversation. Of course, as Lord Palmerston said of himself when he was no longer very young, "boys will be boys," but there never was anything rude or vulgar in their conversation, and I hardly ever heard an offensive remark among them. Most of my friends came from Balliol, and were serious-minded men, many of them occupied and troubled by religious, philosophical, and social problems.

What puzzled me most was the entire absence of duels. Occasionally there were squabbles and high words, which among German students could have had one result only—a duel. But at Oxford, either a man apologized at once or the next morning, and the matter was forgotten, or, if a man proved himself a cad or a snob, he was simply dropped. I do not mean to condemn the students' duels in Germany altogether. Considering how mixed the society of German universities is, and the perfect equality that reigns among them—they all called each other "thou" in my time—the son of a gentleman required some kind of protection against the son of a butcher or of a day-labourer. Boxing and fisticuffs were entirely forbidden among students, so that there remained nothing to a young student who wanted to escape from the insults of a young ruffian, but to call him out. As soon as a challenge was given, all abuse ceased at once, and such was the power of public opinion at the universities that not another word of insult would be uttered. In this way much mischief is prevented. Besides, every precaution is taken to guard against fatal accident, and I believe there are fewer serious accidents on the *mensura* than in the hunting-field in England. When I was at Leipzig, where we had at least four hundred duels during the year, only two fatal accidents happened, and they were, indeed, accidents, such as will happen even at football. Of course duels can never be defended, but for keeping up good manners, also for bringing out a man's character, these academic duels seem useful. However small the danger is, it frightens the coward and restrains the poltroon. For all that, what has taken place in England may in time take place in

Germany also, and men will cease to think that it is impossible to defend their honour without a piece of steel or a pistol. The last thing that a German student desires to do in a duel is to kill his adversary. Hence pistol duels, which are generally preferred by theological students, because they cannot easily get a living if their face is scarred all over, are generally the most harmless, except perhaps for the seconds.

Before closing this chapter, I should like to say a few words on the impressions which the theological atmosphere of Oxford in 1848 produced or me, and which even now fills me with wonder and amazement.

When I came to Oxford, I was strongly recommended to Stanley on one side, and to Manuel Johnson on the other,—a curious mixture. Johnson, the Observer, was extremely kind and hospitable to me. He was a genial man, full of love, possibly a little weak, but thoroughly honest, nay, transparently so. I met at his house nearly all the leaders of the High Church movement, though I never met Newman himself, who had then already gone to reside at his retreat at Littlemore. On the other hand, Stanley received me with open arms as a friend of Bunsen, Frederick Maurice, and Julius Hare, and as I came straight from the February revolution in 1848, he was full of interest and curiosity to know from me what I had seen in Paris.

At first I knew nothing, and understood nothing

of the movement, call it ecclesiastical or theological, that was going on at Oxford at that time. I dined almost every Sunday at Johnson's house, and at his dinners and Sunday afternoon garden parties I met men such as Church, Mozley, Buckle, Palgrave, Pollen, Rigaud, Burgon, and Chrétian, who inspired me with great respect, both for their learning and for what I could catch of their character. Stanley, on the other hand, Froude, and Jowett, proved themselves true friends to me in making me feel at home, and initiating me into the secrets of the place. There was, however, a curious reticence on both sides, and it was by sudden glimpses only that I came to understand that these two sets were quite divided, nay, opposed, and had very different ideals before them.

I had been at a German university, and the historical study of Christianity was to me as familiar as the study of Roman history. Professors whom I had looked up to as great authorities, implicitly to be trusted, such as Lotze and Weisse at Leipzig, Schelling and Michelet at Berlin, had, after causing in me a certain surprise at first, left me with the firm conviction that the Old and New Testament were historical books, and to be treated according to the same critical principles as any other ancient book, particularly the sacred books of the East of which so little was then known, and of which I too knew very little as yet; enough, however, to see that they contained nothing but what under the circumstances they could contain, traditions of extreme antiquity collected by men who gathered all they thought would be useful for the education of the people. Anything like revelation in the old sense of the word, a belief that these books had been verbally communicated by the Deity, or that what seemed miraculous in them was to be accepted as historically real, simply because it was recorded in these sacred books, was to me a standpoint long left behind. To me the questions that occupied my thoughts were to what date these books, such as we have them, could be assigned, what portions of them were of importance to us, what were the simple truths they contained, and what had been added to them by later collectors. Well do I remember when, before going to Oxford, I spoke to Bunsen of the preface to my Rig-veda, and used the expression, "the great revelations of the world," he, perfectly understanding what I meant, warned me in his loud and warm voice, "Don't say that at Oxford." I could see no harm, nor Bunsen either, nor his son who was an Oxford man and a clergyman of the Church of England; but I was told that I should be misunderstood. I knew far too little to imagine that I had a right to speak of what was fermenting and growing within me. During my stay at Leipzig and Berlin, and afterwards in my intercourse with Renan and Burnouf, the principles of the historical school had become quite familiar to me, but the application of these principles to the early history of religion was a different matter. How far the Old and the New Testament would stand the critical tests enunciated by Niebuhr was a frequent subject of controversy, during the time I spent at Paris, between young Renan and myself. Though I did not go with him in his reconstruction of the history of the Jews and the Jewish religion, and of the early Christians and the Christian religion, I agreed with him in principle, objecting only to his too free and too idyllic reconstruction of these great religious movements. Besides, before all things, I was at that time given to philosophical studies, chiefly to an inquiry into the limits of our knowledge in the Kantian sense of the word, the origin of thought and language, the first faltering and half-mythological steps of language in the search for causes or divine agents. All this occupied me far more than the age of the Fourth Gospel and its position by the side of the Synoptic Gospels. I had talked with Schelling and Schopenhauer, and little as I appreciated or understood all their teachings, there were certain aspirations left in my mind which led me far away beyond the historical foundations of Christianity. What can we know? was the question which I often opposed to Renan at the very beginning of our conversations and controversies. That there were great truths in the teaching and preaching of Christ, Renan was always ready to admit, but while it interested me how the truths proclaimed by Christ could have sprung up in His mind and at that time in the history of the human race, Renan's eyes were always directed to the evidence, and to what we could still know of the early history of Christianity and its Founder. I could not deny that, historically speaking, we knew very little of the life, the work, and the teachings of Christ; but for that very reason I doubted our being justified in giving our interpretation and reconstruction to the fragments left to us of the real history of the life and teaching of Christ. To this opinion I remained true through life. I claimed for each man the liberty of believing in his own Christ, but I objected to Renan's idyllic Christ as I objected to Niebuhr's filling the canvas of ancient Roman history with the figures of his own imagination.

Naturally, when I came to Oxford, I thought these things were familiar to all, however much they might admit of careful correction. Nor have I any doubt that to some of my friends who were great theologians, they were better known than to a young Oriental scholar like myself. But unless engaged in conversation on these subjects, and this was chiefly the case with my friends of the Stanley party, I did not feel called upon to preach what, as I thought, every serious student knew quite as well and probably much better than myself, though he might for some reason or other prefer to keep silence thereon.

What was my surprise when I found that most of

these excellent and really learned men were much more deeply interested in purely ecclesiastical questions, in the validity of Anglican orders, in the wearing of either gowns or surplices in the pulpit, in the question of candlesticks and genuflections. "What has all this to do with true religion?" I once said to dear Johnson. He laughed with his genial laugh, and blowing the smoke of his cigar away, said, "Oh, you don't understand!" But I did understand, and a great deal more than he expected. Truly religious men, I thought, might please themselves with incense and candlesticks, provided they gave no offence to their neighbours. It seemed to me quite natural also that men like Johnson, with a taste for art, should prefer the Roman ritual to the simple and sometimes rather bare service of the Anglican Church, but that things such as incense and censers, surplice and gown, should be taken as they are, as paraphernalia, the work of human beings, the outcome of personal and local influences, as church-service, no doubt, but not as service of God. God has to be served by very different things, and there is the danger of the formal prevailing over the essential, the danger of idolatry of symbols as realities, whenever too much importance is attributed to the external forms of worship and divine service.

The validity of Anglican orders was often discussed at the Observatory, and I no doubt gave great offence by openly declaring in my imperfect

English that I considered Luther a better channel for the transmission of the Holy Ghost than a Caesar Borgia or even a Wolsey. Anyhow I could not bring myself to see the importance of such questions, if only the heart was right and if the whole of our life was in fact a real and constant life with God and in God. That is what I called a truly religious and truly Christian life. What struck me particularly, both on the Newman side, and among those whom I met at Jowett's and Froude's, was a curious want of openness and manliness in discussing these simple questions, simple, if not complicated by ecclesiastical theories. When Newman at Iffley was spoken of, it was in hushed tones, and when rumours of his going over to Rome reached his friends at Oxford, their consternation seemed to be like that of people watching the deathbed of a friend. I am sorry I saw nothing of Newman at that time; when I sat with him afterwards in his study at Birmingham, he was evidently tired of controversy, and unwilling to reopen questions which to him were settled once for all, or if not settled, at all events closed and relinquished. I could never form a clear idea of the man, much as I admired his sermons; his brother and his own friends gave such different accounts of him. That even at Littlemore he was still faithful to his own national Church, anxious only to bring it nearer to its ancient possibly Roman type, can hardly be doubted. When he wrote from Littlemore to his friend De Lisle, he had no reason to economize the truth. De Lisle hoped that Newman would soon openly join the Church of Rome, but Newman answered: "You must allow me to be honest with you in adding one thing. A distressing feeling arises in my mind that such marks of kindness as these on your part are caused by a belief that I am ever likely to join your communion . . . I must assure you then with great sincerity that I have not the shadow of an internal movement known to myself towards such a step. While God is with me where I am, I will not seek Him elsewhere. I might almost say in the words of Scripture, 'We have found the Messias!' . . ."

How true this is, and yet the same Newman went over to the unreformed Church, because the Archbishop of Canterbury had sanctioned Bunsen's proposal of an Anglo-German bishopric of Jerusalem, quite forgetful of the fact that Synesius also had been bishop of Ptolemais. Again I say, What have such matters to do with true religion, such as we read of in the New Testament, as an ideal to be realized in our life on earth? And it so happened that at the same time I knew of families rendered miserable through Newman's influence, of young girls, daughters of narrow-minded Anglicans, hurried over to Rome, of young men at Oxford with their troubled consciences which under Newman's direct or indirect guidance could end only in Rome. Newman's influence must have been extraordinary;

the tone in which people who wished to free themselves from him, who had actually left him, spoke of him, seemed tremulous with awe. I would give anything to have known him at that time, when I knew him through his disciples only. They were caught in various ways. I knew of one, a brilliant writer, who had been entrusted by Newman with writing some of the *Lives of the Saints.* He did it with great industry, but in the course of his researches he arrived at the conviction that there was hardly anything truly historical about his Saints and that the miracles ascribed to them were insipid, and might be the inventions of their friends; such legends, he felt, would take no root on English soil, at all events not in the present generation. In consequence he informed Newman that he could not keep his promise, or that, if he did so, he must speak the truth, tell people what they might believe about these Saints, and what was purely fanciful in the accounts of their lives. And what was Newman's answer? He did not respect the young man's scruples, but encouraged him to go on, because, as he said, people would never believe more than half of these Lives, and that therefore some of these unsupported legends also might prove useful, if only as a kind of ballast.

"I rejoice to hear of your success," he writes, August 21, 1843. "As to St. Grimball, of course we must expect such deficiencies; where matter is found, it is all gain, and there are plenty of Lives to put together, as you will see, when you see the whole list.

"I am rather for *inserting* (of course discreetly and in way of selection) the miracles for which you have not good evidence. (1) They are beautiful, you say, and will tell in the narrative. (2) Next you can say that the evidence is weak, and this will be bringing credit for the others where you say the evidence is strong. People will never go *so far* as your narrative. Cut it down to what is true, and they will disbelieve a part of *it;* put in these legends and they will compound for the true at the sacrifice of what may be true, but is not well attested."

I confess I cannot quite follow. If a man like Newman believed in these saints and their miracles, his pleading would become intelligible, but it seems from this very letter that he did not, and yet he tried to persuade his young friend to go on and not to gather the tares, "lest haply he might root up the wheat with them. Let both grow together until the harvest." I do not like to judge, but I doubt whether this kind of teaching could have strengthened the healthy moral fibre of a man's conscience and have led him to depend entirely on his sense of truth. And yet this was the man who at one time was supposed to draw the best spirits of Oxford with him to Rome. This was the man to whom some of the best spirits at Oxford confessed all they had to confess, and that could have been very little, and of whom they spoke with a subdued whisper as the apostle who would restore all faith, and bring back the Anglican sheep to the Roman fold.

I saw and heard all that was going on, the hopes deferred, the secret visits to Littlemore, the rumours and more than rumours of Newman's defection. Such was the devotion of some of these disciples that they expected day by day a great catastrophe or a great victory, for after the publication of so many letters written at the time by Wiseman, Manning, De Lisle, and others, there can be little doubt that a great conversion or perversion of England to the Romish Church was fully expected. De Lisle writes: "England is now in full career of a great Religious Revolution, this time back to Catholicism and to the Roman See as its true centre . . . the best friends of Rome in the Anglican Church are obliged still to be guarded." Such words admit of one meaning only, and if Newman had been followed by a large number of his Oxford friends, the results for England might really have been most terrible. But here, no doubt, the English national feeling came in. What England had suffered under Roman ecclesiastical rule had not yet been entirely forgotten, and the idea that a foreign potentate and a foreign priesthood should interfere with the highest interests of the nation, was fortunately as distasteful as ever, not only to a large party of the clergy, but to a still larger party of the laity also. It seemed to me very curious that so many of Newman's followers did not see the unpatriotic character of their agitation. Either subjection to Rome or civil war at home was the inevitable outcome of what they discussed very innocently at the Observatory, and little as I understood their schemes for the future, I often felt surprised at what sounded to me like very unpatriotic utterances.

Another thing that struck me as utterly un-English and has often been dwelt on by the historians of this movement, was the curiously secret character of the agitation. What has an Englishman to fear when he openly protests against what he disapproves of in Church or State? But Newman's friends at Oxford behaved really, as has been often said, like so many naughty schoolboys, or like conspirators, yet they were neither. A very similar charge, however, was brought against the liberal party. They also seemed to think that they were out of bounds, and were doing in secret what they did not dare to do openly. It is well known that one friend of Newman's, who afterwards became a Roman Catholic, had a small chapel set up in his bedroom in college, with pictures and candles and instruments of flagellation. No one was allowed to see this room, till one evening when the flagellant had retired after dinner and fallen asleep, the servants found him lying before the altar. Nothing remained to him then but to exchange his comfortable college rooms for the less comfortable cell of a Roman monastery, and little was done by his new friends to make the evening of his life serene and free from anxiety. These things were known and talked about in Oxford, and generally with anything but the seriousness that the subject seemed to me to require. Again at the Observatory a point was made of having games in the garden such as *boccia* on a Sunday afternoon, thus evading the strict observance of the Sabbath, without openly trying to restore to it the character which it had in Roman Catholic countries.

German theology was talked about as a kind of forbidden fruit, as if it was not right for them to look at it, to taste it, or to examine it. Even years later people were afraid to meet Professor Ewald, Bishop Colenso, and other so-called heretics at my house. They even fell on poor Ewald at an evening party. Ewald was staying with me and working hard at some Hebrew MSS. at the Bodleian. He was then already an old man, but in his appearance a powerful and venerable champion. He is the only man I remember who, after copying Hebrew MSS. for twelve hours at the Bodleian with nothing but a sandwich to sustain him, complained of the short time allowed there for work. He came home for dinner very tired, and when the conversation or rather the disputation began between him and some of our young liberal theologians, he spoke in short pithy sentences only He considered himself perfectly orthodox, nay, one of the pillars of religion in Germany, and laid down the law with unhesitating conviction. As far as I can remember, he was answering a number of questions about St. Paul, and what he thought of Christ, of the Kingdom of Christ, and the Life to come, and being pestered and driven into a corner by his various questioners, and asked at last how he knew St. Paul's secret thoughts, he not knowing how to express himself in fluent English, exclaimed in a loud voice, "I know it by the Holy Ghost." Here the conversation naturally stopped, and poor Ewald was allowed to finish his dinner in peace. He had been Professor at Bonn, when Pusey came there as a young man to study Hebrew after he had been appointed Canon of Christ Church and Professor of Hebrew, and he expressed to me a wish to see Dr. Pusey. I told him it would not be easy to arrange a meeting, considering how strongly opposed Dr. Pusey was to Ewald's opinions. Personally I always found Pusey tolerant, and his kindness to me was a surprise to all my young friends. But the fact was, we moved on different planes, and though he knew my religious opinions well, they only excited a smile, and he often said with a sigh, "I know you are a German." His own idea was that he was placed at Oxford in order to save the younger generation from seeing the abyss into which he himself had looked with terror. He had read more heresy, he used to say, than anybody, and he wished no one to pass through the trials and agonies through which he had passed, chiefly, I should think, during his stay at a German university. The historical element was wanting in him, nay, like Hegel, he sometimes seemed to lay stress on the unhistorical character of Christianity. My idea, on the contrary, was that Christianity was a true historical event, prepared by many events that had gone before and alone made it possible and real. Even the abyss, if there were such an abyss, was, as it seemed to me, meant to be there on our passage through life, and was to be faced with a brave heart.

But to return to my first experiences of the theological atmosphere of Oxford, I confess I felt puzzled to see men, whose learning and character I sincerely admired, absorbed in subjects which to my mind seemed simply childish. I expected I should hear from them some new views on the date of the gospels, the meaning of revelation, the historical value of revelation, or the early history of the Church. No, of all this not a word. Nothing but discussions on vestments, on private confession, on candles on the altar, whether they were wanted or not, on the altar being made of stone or of wood, of consecrated wine being mixed with water, of the priest turning his back on the congregation, &c. I could not understand how these men, so high above the ordinary level of men in all other respects, could put aside the fundamental questions of Christianity and give their whole mind to what seemed to me rightly called in the newspapers "mere millinery." I sought information from Stanley, but he shrugged his shoulders and advised me to keep aloof and say nothing. This I was most willing to do; I cared for none of these things. My mind was occupied with far more serious problems, such as I had heard explained by men of profound learning and honest purpose in the great universities of Germany; these troubles arose from questions which seemed to me to have no connexion with true religion at all. Even the differences between the reformed and unreformed churches were to me mere questions of history, mere questions of human expediency. I did not consider Roman Catholics as heretics—I had known too many of them of unblemished character in Germany. I might have regretted the abuses which called for reform, the excrescences which had disfigured Christianity like many other religions, but which might be tolerated as long as they did not lead to toleration for intolerance. Luther might no longer appear to me in the light of a perfect saint, but that he was right in suppressing the time-honoured abuses of the Roman Church admitted with me of no doubt whatsoever. Large numbers always had that effect on me, and when I saw how many good and excellent men were satisfied with the unreformed teaching of the Roman Church, I felt convinced that they must attach a different meaning to certain doctrines and ecclesiastical practices from what we did. I had learned to discover what was good and true in all religions, and I could fully agree with Macaulay when he said, "If people had lived in a country where very sensible people worshipped the cow, they would not fall out with people who worship saints."

I know that many of my friends on both sides looked upon me as a latitudinarian, but my conviction has always been that we could not be broad enough. They looked upon me as wishing to keep on good terms with high and low and broad, and I made no secret of it, that I thought I could understand Pusey as well as Stanley, and assign to each his proper place. Stanley was of course more after my own heart than Pusey, but Pusey too was a man who interested me very much. I saw that he might become a great power whether for good or for evil in England. He was, in fact, a historical character, and these were always the men who interested me. He was fully aware of his importance in England, and the great influence which his name exercised. That influence was not always exercised in the right way, so at least it seemed to me, particularly when it was directed against such friends of mine as Kingsley, Froude, or Jowett. Once, I remember, when he had come to my house, I ventured to tell him that he could not have meant what he had said in declaring that the God worshipped by Frederic Maurice was not the same as his God. Curious to say, he relented, and admitted that he had used too strong language. To me everything that was said of God seemed imperfect, and never to apply to God Himself but only to the idea which the human mind had formed of Him. To me even the Hindu, if he spoke of Brahman or Krishna, seemed to have aimed at the true God, in spite of the idolatrous epithets which he used; then how could a man like Frederic Maurice be said to have worshipped a different God, considering that we all can but feel after Him in the dark, not being able to do more than exclude all that seems to us unworthy of Deity?

A very important element in the ecclesiastical views of some of my friends was, no doubt, the artistic. If Johnson leant towards Rome, it was the more ornate and beautiful service that touched and attracted him. I sat near to him in St. Giles' Church; he told me what to do and what not to do during service. In spite of the Prayer-book, it is by no means so easy as people imagine to do exactly the right thing in church, and I had of course to learn a number of prayers and responses by heart. To me the service, as it was in my parish church, seemed already too ornate, accustomed as I had been to the somewhat bare and cold service in the Lutheran Church at Dessau. But Johnson constantly complained about the monotonous and mechanical performances of the clergy. He had a strong feeling for all that was beautiful and impressive in art, and he wanted to see the service of God in church full both of reverence and beauty.

Johnson's private collection of artistic treasures

was very considerable, and I learnt much from the Italian engravings and Dutch etchings which he possessed and delighted in showing. I often spent happy hours with him examining his portfolios, and wondered how he could afford to buy such treasures. But he knew when and where to buy, and I believe when his collection was sold after his death, it brought a good deal more than it had cost him. Another collection of art was that of Dr. Wellesley, the Principal of New Inn Hall, who was a friend of Johnson's and had collected most valuable antiquities during his long stay in Italy. He was the son of the Marquis of Wellesley, a handsome man, with all the refinement and courtesy of the old English gentleman. Though not perhaps very useful in the work of the University, he was most pleasant to live with, and full of information in his own line of study, the history of art, chiefly of Italian art.

The beautiful services of the Roman Church abroad, and particularly at Rome, certainly exercised a kind of magic attraction on many of the friends of Wiseman and Newman, though one wonders that the sunny grandeur of St. Peter's at Rome should ever have seemed more impressive than the sombre sublimity and serene magnificence of Westminster Abbey. Unfortunately, the introduction of a more ornate service, even of harmless candlesticks and the often very useful incense, had always a secret meaning. They were used as symbols of something of which the people had no conception, whereas in the early Church they had been really natural and useful.

In the midst of all this commotion, and chiefly secret commotion, I felt a perfect stranger; I saw the bright and dark sides, but I confess I saw little of what I called religion. Though my own religious struggles lay behind me, still there were many questions which pressed for a solution, but for which my friends at Oxford seemed either indifferent or unprepared. My practical religion was what I had learnt from my mother; that remained unshaken in all storms, and in its extreme simplicity and childishness answered all the purposes for which religion is meant. Then followed, in the Universities of Leipzig and Berlin, the purely historical and scientific treatment of religion, which, while it explained many things and destroyed many things, never interfered with my early ideas of right and wrong, never disturbed my life with God and in God, and seemed to satisfy all my religious wants. I never was frightened or shaken by the critical writings of Strauss or Ewald, of Renan or Colenso. If what they said had an honest ring, I was delighted, for I felt quite certain that they could never deprive me of the little I really wanted. That little could never be little enough; it was like a stronghold with no fortifications, no trenches, and no walls around it. Suppose it was proved to me that, on geological evidence, the earth or the world could not have been created in six days, what was that to me? Suppose it was proved to me that Christ could never have given leave to the unclean spirits to enter into the swine, what was that to me? Let Colenso and Bishop Wilberforce, let Huxley and Gladstone fight about such matters; their turbulent waves could never disturb me, could never even reach me in my safe harbour. I had little to carry, no learned impedimenta to safeguard my faith. If a man possesses this one pearl of great price, he may save himself and his treasure, but neither the tinselled vestments of a Cardinal, nor the triple tiara that crowns the Head of the Church, will serve as life-belts in the gales of doubt and controversy. My friends at Oxford did not know that, though with my one jewel I seemed outwardly poor, I was really richer and safer than many a Cardinal and many a Doctor of Divinity. A confession of faith, like a prayer, may be very long, but the prayer of the Publican may have been more efficient than that of the Pharisee.

After a time I made an even more painful discovery: I found men, who were considered quite orthodox, but who really were without any belief. They spoke to me very freely, because they imagined that as a German I would think as they did, and that I should not be surprised if they looked on me as not quite sincere. It was not only honest doubt that disturbed them. They had done with honest doubt, and they were satisfied with a kind of Voltairian philosophy, which at last ended in pure agnosticism. But even that, even professed agnosticism, I could understand, because it often meant no more than a confession of ignorance with regard to God, which we all confess, and need not necessarily amount to the denial of the existence of Deity. But that Voltairian levity which scoffs at everything connected with religion was certainly something I did not expect to meet with at Oxford, and which even now perplexes me. Of course, I should never think of mentioning names, but it seemed to me necessary to mention the fact, to complete the curious mosaic of theological and religious thought that existed at Oxford at the time of my arrival.

CHAPTER IX

A CONFESSION

One confession I have to make, and one for which I can hardly hope for absolution, whether from my friends or from my enemies. I have never done anything; I have never been a doer, a canvasser, a wirepuller, a manager, in the ordinary sense of these words. I have also shrunk from agitation, from clubs and from cliques, even from most respectable associations and societies. Many people would call me an idle, useless, and indolent man, and though I have not wasted many hours of my life, I cannot deny the charge that I have neither fought battles, nor helped to conquer new countries, nor joined any syndicate to roll up a fortune. I have been a scholar, a *Stubengelehrter*, and *voilà tout!*

Much as I admired Ruskin when I saw him with his spade and wheelbarrow, encouraging and helping his undergraduate friends to make a new road from one village to another, I never myself took to digging, and shovelling, and carting. Nor could I quite agree with him, happy as I always felt in listening to him, when he said: "What we think, or what we know, or what we believe, is in the end of little consequence. The only thing of consequence is what we do." My view of life has always been the very opposite! What we do, or what we build up, has always seemed to me of little consequence. Even Nineveh is now a mere desert of sand, and Ruskin's new road also has long since been worn away. The only thing of consequence, to my mind, is what we think, what we know, what we believe! To Ruskin's ears such a sentiment was downright heresy, and I know quite well that it would be condemned as extremely dangerous, if not downright wicked, by most people, particularly in England. My friend, Charles Kingsley, preached muscular Christianity, that is, he was always up and doing. Another old friend of mine, Carlyle, preached all his life that "it was no use talking, if one would not do." There is an old proverb in German, too,

> "Die nicht mit thaten,
> Die nicht mit rathen";

actually denying the right of giving advice to those who had not taken a part in the fight.

However, though I have not been a doer, a *faiseur*, as the French would say, I do not wish to represent myself as a mere idle drone during the long years of my quiet life. Nor did I stand quite alone in looking on a scholar's life—even when I was living in a garret *au cinquième*—as a paradise on earth. Did not Emerson write, "The scholar is the man of the age"? Did not even Mazzini, who certainly was constantly up and trying to do, did not even he confess that men must die, but that the amount of truth they have discovered does not die with them? And Carlyle? Did he ever try to get into Parliament? Did he ever accept directorates? Did he join either the Chartists or the Special Constables in Trafalgar Square? As in a concert you want listeners as well as performers, so in public life, those who look on are quite as essential as those who shout and deal heavy blows.

Nature has not endowed everybody with the requisite muscle to be a muscular Christian. But it may be said, that even if Carlyle and Ruskin were absolved from doing muscular work in Trafalgar Square, what excuse could they plead for not walking in procession to Hyde Park, climbing up one of the platforms and haranguing the men and women and children? I suppose they had the feeling which the razor has when it is used for cutting stones: they would feel that it was not exactly their *métier*. Arguing when reason meets reason is most delightful, whether we win or lose; but arguing against unreason, against anything that is by nature thick, dense, impenetrable, irrational, has always seemed to me the most disheartening occupation. Majorities, mere numerical majorities, by which the world is governed now, strike me as mere brute force, though to argue against them is no doubt as foolish as arguing against a railway train that is going to crush you. Gladstone could harangue multitudes; so could Disraeli; all honour to them for it. But think of Carlyle or Ruskin doing so! Stroking the shell of a tortoise, or the cupola of St. Paul's, would have been no more attractive to them than addressing the discontented, when in their hundreds and their thousands they descended into the streets. All I claim is that there must be a division of labour, and as little as Wayland Smith was useless in his smithy, when he hardened the iron in the fire for making swords or horse-shoes, was Carlyle a man that could be spared, while he sat in his study preparing thoughts that would not bend or break.

But I cannot even claim to have been a man of action in the sense in which Carlyle was in England, or Emerson in America. They were men who in their books were constantly teaching and preaching. "Do this!" they said; "Do not do that!" The Jewish prophets did much the same, and they are not considered to have been useless men, though they did not make bricks, or fight battles like Jehu. But the poor *Stubengelehrte* has not even that comfort. Only now and then he gets some unexpected recognition, as when Lord Derby, then Secretary of State for India, declared that the scholars who had discovered and proved the close relationship between Sanskrit and English, had rendered more valuable service to the Government of India than many a regiment. This may be called a mere assertion, and it is true that it cannot be proved mathematically, but what could have induced a man like Lord Derby to make such a statement, except the sense of its truth produced on his mind by long experience?

However, I can only speak for myself, and of my idea of work. I felt satisfied when my work led me to a new discovery, whether it was the discovery of a new continent of thought, or of the smallest desert island in the vast ocean of truth. I would gladly go so far as to try to convince my friends by a simple statement of facts. Let them follow the same course and see whether I was right or wrong. But to make propaganda, to attempt to persuade by bringing pressure to bear, to canvass and to organize, to found societies, to start new journals, to call meetings and have them reported in the papers, has always been to me very much against the grain. If we know some truth, what does it matter whether a few millions, more or less, see the truth as we see it? Truth is truth, whether it is accepted now or in millions of years. Truth is in no hurry, at least it always seemed to me so. When face to face with a man, or a body of men, who would not be convinced, I never felt inclined to run my head against a stone wall, or to become an advocate and use the tricks of a lawyer. I have often been blamed for it, I have sometimes even regretted my indolence or my quiet happiness, when I felt that truth was on my side and by my side. I suppose there is no harm in personal canvassing, but as much as I disliked being canvassed, did I feel it degrading to canvass others. I know quite well how often it happened at a meeting when either a measure or a candidate was to be carried, that the voters had evidently been spoken to privately beforehand, had in the conscience of their heart promised their votes. The facts and arguments at the meeting itself might all be on one side, but the majority was in favour of the other. Men whose time was of little value had been round from house to house, a majority had been compacted into an inert unreasoning mass; and who would feel inclined to use his spade of reason against so much unreason? Some people, more honest than the rest, after the mischief was done, would say, "Why did you not call? why did you not write letters?" I may be quite wrong, but I can only say that it seemed to me like taking an unfair advantage, unfair to our opponents, and almost insulting to our friends. Still, from a worldly point of view, I was no doubt wrong, and it is certainly true that I was often left in a minority. My friends have told me again and again that if a good measure or a good man is to be carried, good men must do some dirty work. If they cannot do that, they are of no use, and I doubt not that I have often been considered a very useless man by my political and academic friends, because I trusted to reason where there was no reason to trust to. I was asked to write letters, to address and post letters, to promise travelling expenses or even convivial entertainments at Oxford, to get leaders and leaderettes inserted in newspapers. I simply loathed it, and at last declined to do it. If a measure is carried by promise, not by argument, if an election is carried by personal influence, not by reason, what happens is very often the same as what happens when fruit is pulled off a tree before it is ripe. It is expected to ripen by itself, but it never becomes sweet, and often it rots. A premature measure may be carried through the House by a minister with a powerful majority, but it does not acquire vitality and maturity by being carried; it often remains on the Statute-book a dead letter, till in the end it has to be abolished with other rubbish.

However, I have learnt to admire the indefatigable assiduity of men who have slowly and partially secured their converts and their recruits, and thus have carried in the end what they thought right and reasonable. I have seen it particularly at Oxford, where undergraduates were indoctrinated by their tutors, till they had taken their degree and could vote with their betters. I take all the blame and shame upon myself as a useless member of Congregation and Convocation, and of society at large. I was wrong in supposing that the walls of Jericho would fall before the blast of reason, and wrong in abstaining from joining in the braying of rams' horns and the shouts of the people. I was fortunate, however, in counting among my most intimate friends some of the most active and influential reformers in University, Church, and State, and it is quite possible that I may often have influenced them in the hours of sweet converse; nay, that standing in the second rank, I may have helped to load the guns which they fired off with much effect afterwards. I felt that my open partnership might even injure them more than it could help them; for was it not always open to my opponents to say that I was a German, and therefore could not possibly understand purely English questions? Besides, there is another peculiarity which I have often observed in England. People like to do what has to be done by themselves. It seemed to me sometimes as if I had offended my friends if I did anything by myself, and without consulting them. Besides, my position, even after I had been in England for so many years, was always peculiar; for though I had spent nearly a whole life in the service of my adopted country, though my political allegiance was due and was gladly given to England, still I was, and have always remained, a German.

And next to Germany, which was young and full of ideals when I was young, there came India, and Indian thought which exercised their quieting influence on me. From a very early time I became conscious of the narrow horizon of this life on earth, and the purely phenomenal character of the world in which for a few years we have to live and move and have our being. As students of classical and other Oriental history we come to admire the great empires with their palaces and pyramids and temples and capitols. What could have seemed more real, more grand, more likely to impress the young mind than Babylon and Nineveh, Thebes and Alexandria, Jerusalem, Athens, and Rome? And now where are they? The very names of their great rulers and heroes are known to few people only and have to be learnt by heart, without telling us much of those who wore them. Many things for which thousands of human beings were willing to lay down their lives, and actually did lay them down, are to us mere words and dreams, myths, fables, and legends. If ever there was a doer, it was Hercules, and now we are told that he was a mere myth!

If one reads the description of Babylonian and Egyptian campaigns, as recorded on cuneiform cylinders and on the walls of ancient Egyptian temples, the number of people slaughtered seems immense, the issues overwhelming; and yet what has become of it all? The inroads of the Huns, the expeditions of Genghis Khan and Timur, so fully described by historians, shook the whole world to its foundations, and now the sand of the desert disturbed by their armies lies as smooth as ever.

What India teaches us is that in a state advancing towards civilization, there must be always two castes or two classes of men, a caste of Brahmans or of thinkers, and a caste of Kshatriyas, who are to fight; possibly other castes also of those who are to work and of those who are to serve. Great wars went on in India, but they were left to be fought by the warriors by profession. The peasants in their villages remained quiet, accepting the consequences, whatever they might be, and the Brahmans lived on, thinking and dreaming in their forests, satisfied to rule after the battle was over.

And what applies to military struggles seems to me to apply to all struggles—political, religious, social, commercial, and even literary. Let those who love to fight, fight; but let others who are fond of quiet work go on undisturbed in their own special callings. That was, as far as we can see, the old Indian idea, or at all events the ideal which the Brahmans wished to see realized. I do not stand up for utter idleness or sloth, not even for drones, though nature does not seem to condemn even *hoc genus* altogether. All I plead for, as a scholar and a thinker, is freedom from canvassing, from letter-reading and letter-writing, from committees, deputations, meetings, public dinners, and all the rest. That will sound very selfish to the ears of practical men, and I understand why they should look upon men like myself as hardly worth their salt. But what would they say to one of the greatest fighters in the history of the world? What would they say to Julius Caesar, when he declares that the triumphs and the laurel wreaths of Cicero are as far nobler than those of warriors as it is a greater achievement to extend the boundaries of the Roman intellect than the domains of the Roman people?

INDEX